About the author

Hugh Westacott was born in 1932 of parents who were enthusiastic walkers. In the immediate post-war years he was also a keen cyclist until increasing traffic drove him back to walking. He pursued a successful career as a librarian both here and in the United States until, following the publication of the *Walker's Handbook,* taking early retirement to concentrate on writing books and articles about walking and backpacking in publications such as *The Great Outdoors, Trail* and *Country Walking,* and leading walks at home and abroad specializing in trips for ex-pat Americans living in London.

In 1992, he was recruited by Wilderness Travel, one of America's leading adventure travel companies, to set up and lead walking tours in Britain including Wainwright's Coast to Coast Walk, the Cornish Coast Path and the Pembrokeshire Coast Path.

In the course of a long life of walking and backpacking spanning seven decades, which includes nearly fifty years as a walks guide, he has explored on foot:

Wainwright's Coast to Coast forty-eight times
The Pennine Way six times
The South West Coast Path twice
Most of the national trails and national parks of England and Wales
Backpacked from Land's End to Fort William, and from London to Land's End
Knoydart, the Cuillins, the Cairngorms and other areas of Scotland
The French and Swiss Alps
Provence
The GR20 in Corsica
Cinque Terre and Tuscany in Italy
Crossed Iceland
Big Bend and the Guadaloupe Mountains national parks in Texas, Yosemite, Death Valley, and the Grand Canyon

He is a Life Member of the Ramblers' Association and also a member of the Charles Close Society for the Study of Ordnance Survey Maps, and the Long Distance Walkers' Association.

By the same author

Footpaths and Bridleways in North Buckinghamshire; No. 1 Winslow Area.. Footpath Publications, 1974.

Footpaths and Bridleways in North Buckinghamshire; No. 2 Buckingham Area.. Footpath Publications, 1975.

Walks around Buckingham and Winslow. Footpath Publications, 1976.

A Practical Guide to Walking the Devon South Coast Path. Footpath Publications, 1976.

Walks and Rides on Dartmoor. Footpath Publications, 1977.

A Practical Guide to Walking the Ridgeway Path. Footpath Publications, 4th ed., 1978.

Discovering Walking. Shire Publications, 1979.

A Practical Guide to Walking the Dorset Coast Path. Footpath Publications, 1982.

The Devon South Coast Path (with Mark Richards). Penguin Books, 1982.

The Dorset Coast Path (with Mark Richards). Penguin Books, 1982.

The Ridgeway Path (with Mark Richards). Penguin Books, 1982.

The Brecon Beacons National Park (with Mark Richards). Penguin Books, 1983.

Dartmoor for Walkers and Riders (with Mark Richards). Penguin Books, 1983.

The North Downs Way (with Mark Richards). Penguin Books, 1983.

The Somerset and the Devon North Coast Path (with Mark Richards). Penguin Books, 1983.

The Illustrated Encyclopaedia of Walking & Backpacking; Places, People & Techniques. Oxford Illustrated Press, 1991.

The Walker's Handbook

Everything you need to know about walking in the British Isles

5th edition

by

Hugh Westacott

Footpath Publications

For my beloved son, Austin, who is not only the best sixtieth birthday present that any man could wish for, but is also an engaging and caring companion over mountains, on fieldpaths, and in a tent.

First published in 1978 by Penguin Books
Reprinted 1979
Second edition 1980
Third edition 1989 published by The Oxford Illustrated Press
Fourth edition 1991 published by Pan Books

ISBN 978-0-9503696-8-6

Footpath Publications
www.walkwithwestacott.com

Distributed by Cordee Ltd
www.cordee.co.uk

Printed in England by The Witley Press Ltd, 24-26 Greevegate, Hunstanton, Norfolk PE36 6AD.

Contents

Contents

Contents

Contents

Contents

Contents

Contents

Contents

Contents

List of figures

Acknowledgements

Many people have contributed to the writing of this book. They are too numerous to mention individually and some of them might be surprised to learn that they had helped, but particular mention must be made of

Peter Goddard who read the first draft of the manuscript and made many helpful suggestions which has resulted in a much better book.

Members of the Micronavigation forum (www.micronavigation.com) especially Lyle Brotherton and Captain Paranoia who were particularly helpful in correcting my first attempts to describe the Global Navigation Satellite System (popularly and inaccurately known as the Global Positioning System or GPS).

Members of the OutdoorsMagic forum (www.outdoorsmagic.com) especially Captain Paranoia, Peter Clinch, Paddy Dillon, Huskyman, and Jester.

Sarah Slade of the Country Land and Business Association (CLA) who commented upon and improved the chapter dealing with the etiquette of walking.

The Aylesbury and District Ramblers (www.aylesbury-ramblers.org.uk) for supplying the attractive photo for the cover.

Tom Coady (tomwcoady@gmail.com) for designing the striking cover and drawing the figures from my rough sketches.

The Ordnance Survey for granting permission to reproduce figures 1 and 2.

My clever and much loved son, Dorian, who showed remarkable patience and forbearance in solving problems for his computer-incompetent Papa.

My dear friend Teresa Way who proof-read the manuscript and corrected my spelling and grammar.

My heartfelt thanks to you all!

Nevertheless, despite all the help I have received, I alone am responsible for all errors, inaccuracies and faults.

Introduction

It is an odd fact that, despite the ever-increasing popularity of walking, and the numerous books on hill-walking, the Global Navigation Satellite System, navigation, mountain weather, backpacking, rights of way, tables of heights of mountains and hills etc. that have been published in the last decade, there is not one book that covers all aspects of the subject. As its title, *The Walker's Handbook; Everything You Need to Know about Walking in the British Isles* suggests, this is an attempt to fill that gap.

The Walker's Handbook was originally published in 1978 and proved so popular that it went through four editions by 1991. It is now woefully out of date so this edition has been extensively revised to take into account the numerous changes and developments that have taken place in the world of walking. These include the construction of the Global Navigation Satellite System, which has revolutionized navigation, and the internet that has made a huge amount of information readily available to walkers.

Earlier editions of *The Walker's Handbook* had to include much information about subjects such as long distance paths, national parks, and areas of outstanding natural beauty, but this edition gives basic facts and refers the reader to the relevant website from where the most up-to-date information is available.

Much as I love walking, and especially the countryside of England whose beautiful pastoral landscapes can move me close to tears, I have resisted the temptation to eulogize the subject and have confined myself to sticking to facts and hard information. Those looking for inspirational books will find some listed in Appendix 3.

The Walker's Handbook is intended to be a guide to good practice (but what is described is not necessarily the *only* good practice) for my target audience of inexperienced walkers seeking advice and information. Once you have gained sufficient experience and confidence, you will develop your own way of enjoying the delights of walking. I hope, too, that it may widen the horizons of more experienced walkers.

In the course of researching subjects for the book, I have been dismayed by the amount of misinformation contained in books dealing with navigation for walkers. Many do not cover walking in lowland countryside and seem to assume that the techniques used in hill-walking are equally applicable to lowland walking. There is often an implied assumption that walking in upland areas is more 'normal' than walking in lowland countryside. In fact the opposite is true. There is considerably more lowland countryside in the Great Britain than there are upland areas as is demonstrated by the fact that there are 333 *Explorer* maps with the 5-metre contour interval used in low-land countryside compared to the 70 *Explorers* with the 10-metre contour interval employed in upland areas.

Many proficient *practical* navigators seem not to know much about Ordnance Survey maps. They may be expert map-readers but often have little idea of the principles and concepts underlying the maps that they use. Too many books make elementary errors such as stating that the Ordnance Survey is responsible for mapping the United Kingdom or even the whole of the British Isles!

How to use *The Walker's Handbook*

Few walkers will read it from cover to cover. Those who are new to the pastime are likely to be most interested in the chapters that cover subjects such as clothing, footwear, equipment, maps and navigation; others will use it as a reference book.

Particular attention is paid to the needs of those, probably the majority, who walk in lowland countryside. Most books of instruction concentrate on walking in upland areas, but there is much pleasure and quiet delights to be discovered by walking the secret ways through the fields and woods of pastoral countryside. Navigation in lowland countryside is often more demanding, though without the inherent dangers if you lose your way, than navigating in fine weather in upland areas.

To assist readers to find the subjects that interest them, the book contains a detailed index. Within each chapter, every paragraph is numbered so the index entries refer first to the chapter number and then to the relevant main paragraph(s). Thus 4:25-7 refers to Chapter 4 paragraphs 25 to 27 inclusive. This enables readers to home in on specific topics.

At the end of every chapter there is a selective bibliography of books that cover the subject under discussion. The universal resource locator (URL) of useful websites are mentioned in the text. Remember that your search engine is your friend and is likely to throw up more websites than can be mentioned.

Corrections to *The Walker's Handbook*

I have tried to ensure that the book was factually correct *at the time of publication.* The manuscript has been read by a number experts but it is almost inevitable that some errors will have been overlooked (the faults are mine alone). If you discover an error or out-of-date information, please email me at hughwestacott@gmail.com quoting the chapter and paragraph number. The proposed correction will be investigated and if found to be accurate will be acknowledged by email and posted on my website www.walkwithwestacott.com.

A personal note

I am fortunate in that I had parents who were keen walkers and encouraged me to follow in their footsteps which, inspired by their example, I have done for well over seventy years. So I have seen and experienced many changes to the walking scene. My first boots were ex-army issue as was my waterproof gas cape, and for my first pair of shorts, my mother took in the hip seams of a pair women's ex-Land Army shorts. In 1946, I made my first backpacking trip into the wilds of Surrey with a group of school friends. I had a war-surplus commando rucksack, a single-skin tent hastily manufactured by an entrepreneur from parachute silk and for which my ever-patient and enterprising mother made a flysheet from an old cotton bed sheet which I proofed with Nev.

Walking has been good both for and to me. I have been fortunate to be blessed with glowing good health and also to be in the right place at the right time which enabled me to contribute books and articles to the outdoor press, and to lead commercial walking tours. These activities allowed me to take early retirement from librarianship and concentrate on my outdoor activities.

And so I hope that it will not seem too pretentious to look upon this, the fifth, and probably the last, edition of *The Walker's Handbook* as my legacy to the wonderful world of walking.

The pleasures of walking

Walking is one of the most basic of human activities. The majority of us *can* walk, but the way in which each person enjoys the pastime varies greatly. Some like the companionship of walking with a club or with friends; others prefer to walk alone. Walkers have no rules or regulations to follow other than to observe the laws of the countryside and to act sensibly and safely.

Many people delight in beautiful scenery and one of the best way to enjoy and experience the countryside is to explore it on foot. Those who see the countryside from a car miss so much because roads, unlike paths, rarely follow the most scenic route. Most books about walking concentrate on hill-walking and there is no doubt that mountain scenery is exciting and dramatic, but even hardened hill-walkers will find that there is much beauty and enjoyment to be found in lowland countryside.

Walking combines well with other interests. The naturalist has to walk quietly through the landscape to avoid disturbing wildlife, and even casual walkers are likely to see things they will remember for a long time. Some of my special memories are watching buzzards soaring effortlessly over the Cheviots; seeing a vixen carrying a rabbit back to her cubs; almost stepping on a fox in a ditch early in the morning; and watching three young weasels playing tag round an oak tree. One walk in Yorkshire was made memorable by a botanist friend showing me tiny Alpine flowers growing in the grikes of the limestone pavements.

The landscape itself is a fascinating study. Although the shape of the mountains, hills, streams and valleys predates the arrival of humans, yet it is we who have largely created the landscape of the British Isles by felling the primeval forest, draining the land and enclosing the fields with a complicated pattern of hedges, walls and ditches. In the course of moulding the landscape, our ancestors built towns and villages. Discovering the reasons for siting settlements in particular places makes an interesting detective puzzle for the inquisitive to unravel. The walker has time to admire the natural taste and eye for beauty shown by our forebears in building even the humblest dwellings. You cannot walk through Swaledale and fail to remark on the number of elegant stone barns to be seen in the fields. Evidence of change, decay and renewal are everywhere for the interested walker to discover and interpret.

It can be so rewarding to recognize traces of the past. A piece of rough ground fenced off from a fertile pasture turns out to be remains of a motte and bailey castle built by the Normans; a circular barn on a slight bluff is all that is left of an old windmill; that remarkably broad path with a pronounced crown and with ditches on both sides is obviously an old road which investigation may reveal as prehistoric, Roman, or a drove road. It is fascinating to follow some of the abandoned roads and tracks depicted on Ordnance Survey maps of England and Wales as 'restricted byways'. Those interested in antiquities marked on maps will find that accurate use of a satnav or compass is invaluable in pinpointing the location of sites.

There is now a great deal of interest in industrial archaeology and the walker can often observe traces of past industry. The Pennines and Dartmoor are particularly rich in old mine-workings where lead, tin, copper and silver and other metals and minerals were extracted. Because the workings are often some distance from the nearest settlement, they have frequently remained remarkably intact, and it is possible to come across mine shafts, levels, engine sheds, and bits of rusting machinery. The Industrial Revolution started in the valleys of England and some of these early factories still exist as fine buildings in lovely settings. Disused canals, railways and tramways can be found in many parts of the British Isles and are well worth exploring.

Investigating places associated with writers and their work, such as the Hardy country in Dorset or, as he called it, Wessex, and the Brontë country near Keighley in West Yorkshire, can add an extra dimension to walking. Top Withens, the ruined house generally believed to be the inspiration for *Wuthering Heights* in Emily Brontë's eponymous novel, lies on the Pennine Way. Arthur Ransome set many of his books for children in the Lake District, and at Beatrix Potter's home at Far Sawrey near Windermere you can see the vegetable garden where Mr McGregor chased Peter Rabbit, and the chimney that Tom Kitten explored.

Walking is generally regarded as a non-competitive pastime, but for those who enjoy a challenge there are many opportunities and events in which they can test themselves (see Chapter 21). Walking is an excellent way of keeping fit and unlike most sports, can be continued until late into life. There are many seventy year-olds who regularly go into the mountains and can surprise younger, less experienced walkers with their strength and stamina, and it seems that there is some evidence to suggest that walking stimulates mental alertness especially in older people.

Some of our place names are so musical, exciting, even comical, that they positively invite investigation. Who can resist the delights of Brown Willy, Downhayne Brake, High Cup Nick, Dollywaggon Pike, Glaramara, Pike o' Stickle, Ringing Roger, Thunacar Knott, Wayland's Smithy, Black Sail Pass, Wildboarclough, Toller Porcorum, Nether Wallop and Steeple Bumpstead? The predominately Celtic place names of Wales, Scotland and Ireland are equally fascinating and euphonious. A dictionary of place names is a useful addition to the library of the well-informed walker.

In a predominantly urban world, walking is one of the best ways to connect to our heritage.

Chapter 1 Behaviour in the countryside; the etiquette of walking

1   It is incumbent on all walkers to set a good example and act courteously and responsibly in the countryside because thoughtless behaviour can alienate land-holders. For example, when walking on a public path that runs through a farm-yard, respect the privacy of those living there. Walk through quietly and as inconspicuously as possible and refrain from peering into windows or entering buildings.

2   All land in the British Isles has an owner which may be an individual, a corporate body such as the National Trust, the Forestry Commission, or a company. Central and local government agencies actually own very little land but have certain responsibilities and powers over other landholdings irrespective of their ownership.

3   Whenever you are walking in the countryside you are crossing land that belongs to an individual or body who will have an interest in it. This sometimes leads to a conflict of interests between landholders and those who seek their recreation in the countryside which are not always easy to harmonize. It would help matters if more walkers had some understanding of modern farming methods and the ways of the countryside, and if *all* landholders, bearing in mind that the majority do, paid strict attention to their legal obligations towards rights of way and access.

4   Most landholders are friendly towards individual walkers but can be wary of large groups. It is one of the quirks of human nature that people in groups tend not to behave quite as well as each one of them would individually.

5   Many landholders and their national organizations, such as the National Farmers' Union (NFU) and the Country Land and Business Association (CLA), are concerned about some of the long-term aims of the Ramblers' Association. There are already legal rights of access to much open country in England and Wales, and to virtually the whole of Scotland. Legislation is in place to provide a continuous coastal path around England and Wales for which landholders will receive no compensation. There is even provision for 'spreading room' in those areas subject to erosion which means that if the coastal path falls into the sea, the path will be moved a little way inland. The Ramblers' Association is currently making plans to press for access to river banks, woodland and forest. The

organization seems to have little concern about the cost and inconvenience that these schemes have on landholders.

Damage

6   Farming is capital-intensive and there is often a lot of expensive machinery lying around unattended. This makes some landholders feel vulnerable and they fear that large groups of people crossing their land may damage machinery, gates, stiles, crops, and put stock at risk.

7   A group walking carelessly, four or five abreast, can damage wet pasture. Glance through the pages of any popular walking magazine and you are likely to see pictures of groups walking through fields and straying significantly from the line of the path.

Farm animals

8   Apart from bulls, and cows with newly-born calves, cattle are normally harmless but may be inquisitive. Heifers and bullocks are skittish and may come galloping across the field to investigate strangers, but they will come skidding to a halt a few yards away and will then follow at a safe distance. Very occasionally, horses may kick or bite, pigs are reputed to be able to inflict a savage bite, rams and billy goats can be belligerent, and geese noisy and aggressive, but it is rare for a walker to be attacked by these animals.

9   Bulls are the most dangerous animals to be found on farms. No bull is to be trusted, but the most dangerous are the dairy breeds (see 14:40-1, 16:37), particularly Friesians, Jerseys and Guernseys. The safest thing to do if a bull is encountered is to give it a wide berth and get out of the field without attracting the attention of the animal. All cattle are interested in humans and it does not follow that a bull is threatening merely because it comes towards you, but the wise take no chances! The nervous should take comfort from the fact that in the past twenty years, only a handful of walkers have been killed by a bull.

10   Occasionally, the walker will discover animals in trouble. Unless it is easy to do something for them, like releasing them from a wire fence, it is better to inform the nearest farm. Make a note of the exact position of the animal and of any identification marks so that a clear description can be given to the farmer. If it is not his animal he will know to whom it belongs and will contact the owner. Sometimes lambs appear to be lost and will be found bleating piteously, but do not touch them because the mother is likely to be nearby and if her lamb is moved she may never find it. If a sheep gets onto its back and is unable to get to

its feet, it will die of suffocation if the contents of the rumen spill into its wind-pipe. To right the animal, kneel beside it and seize one front leg and pull it across its chest. This will bring the animal onto its side and it will be able to get to its feet.

Diseases of farm animals

11   All farm animals are subject to disease. The most virulent and feared are

- avian influenza (bird flu)
- blue tongue
- bovine spongiform encephalopathy (BSE)
- bovine tuberculosis
- brucellosis (contagious abortion)
- foot and mouth disease
- Newcastle disease (fowl pest)
- swine vesicular disease

12   Under the Animal Health Act 2002, temporary orders extinguishing rights of way may be made if there is an outbreak of disease. You must avoid areas known to be affected and always respect notices forbidding entry because of disease. Unless there is an outbreak of disease there is little likelihood of walkers spreading infection except by inexcusable behaviour such as leaving gates open. Rational arguments that no order has been made forbidding the use of paths during an outbreak of disease are unlikely to convince farmers desperately worried about losing their stock and livelihood.

Avian influenza (bird flu)

13   Avian influenza is a highly contagious viral disease affecting the respiratory, digestive and nervous system of many species of birds. There is a serious risk that it can be transmitted to humans.

Blue tongue

14   Blue tongue is a disease affecting all ruminants, including sheep, cattle, deer and goats. It is characterized by changes to the mucous linings of the mouth and nose and the coronary band of the foot. Fortunately, blue tongue cannot be transmitted to humans.

Bovine spongiform encephalopathy (BSE)

15   BSE is a neurological disease of cattle. Infected animals show signs that include changes in mental state, posture, movement and sensation. The disease usually lasts for several weeks and is always fatal. In rare instances it can be transmitted to humans as Creutzfeldt-Jakob Disease (CJD).

Bovine tuberculosis

16   Bovine TB is an infectious and contagious disease of cattle which can be transmitted to humans. It is believed that badgers are one of the main reservoirs of the infection.

Brucellosis or contagious abortion

17   This is a disease that affects cattle. It causes cows to abort and may be responsible for undulant fever in humans if the unpasteurized milk of infected cows is drunk. The disease can be carried by dogs, by wild animals, and by boots which have come into contact with an infected foetus or afterbirth.

Foot and mouth disease

18   This is a highly infectious disease of cattle, sheep and pigs. Infected animals become feverish, develop blisters in the mouth and on the feet, readily salivate and become lame. It is a notifiable disease and is controlled by the wholesale slaughter of cattle, sheep and pigs on the premises, whether or not they are infected, and the movement of animals for a very wide area around the infected herd is prohibited. The speed with which the disease can spread is frightening and during the bad outbreak of 2001 millions of beasts were destroyed and their carcasses burned in huge funeral pyres. The virus is tenacious and can be spread by wind, rain and snow. Walkers should be aware that it can be spread by clothing, especially by boots, and paths in infected areas should never be used during an outbreak.

Newcastle disease (fowl pest)

19   This is a disease of poultry spread by a highly infectious virus. Since vaccination against the disease is now widespread, it is less common than it was once. Fowl pest can be spread by clothing and walkers should avoid infected farms and broiler houses.

Swine vesicular disease

20   This is a similar disease to foot and mouth but is particular to pigs. The only way to control an outbreak is to slaughter all the pigs on the premises and to control the movement of the animals. It is considered possible to transmit the disease on clothing, so walkers should avoid infected areas.

Dogs

21   The legislation covering paths does not include any mention of dogs, but in the case of *Regina versus Matthias* in 1861, it was held to be legal to push a pram on a public footpath, providing the path was physically capable of accommodating the pram, on the grounds that a pram was a 'natural accompaniment' of a pedestrian. Presumably, the argument could be extended to include dogs.

22   Dogs can be a menace to stock because they instinctively chase any creature that is nervous of them. Apart from the obvious danger that this will encourage the dog to worry sheep, and perhaps eventually kill, there is a serious risk of dairy cows going dry and of pregnant animals aborting. Even the best-behaved dog must be kept on a leash in the presence of stock.

23   Dog faeces can carry *neospora caninum,* a parasite which, if transmitted to livestock can cause abortion, stillbirths, and even death. Walkers should clear up after their dog, and ensure that it is regularly wormed.

24   There are two pieces of legislation in Great Britain that affect dog-owners in the countryside:

a) The Dogs (Protection of Livestock) Act 1953 makes it an offence for a dog to be at large in a field of sheep, and also makes it an offence for a dog to chase or worry livestock.

b) The Animals Act 1971 gives landholders the right, under certain circumstances, to shoot dogs found worrying animals if that is the only way to prevent it happening.

25   Cattle will sometimes menace a dog that gets too close, especially if there are calves in the field. Should your pet be threatened, let go of the leash because most dogs can run faster than cattle. There have been incidents where walkers have been trampled and killed by cattle when trying to protect their dog.

Trespass

26   In lowland areas of England and Wales, walkers should never stray from the right of way without the express permission of the farmer or landholder unless:

a) You are in a designated access area (see 14:59-68).

b) You are forced to deviate by an obstruction (see 14:30-32) but this does not entitle a walker to trespass on the property of another landholder.

27   Trespassing in England and Wales is not normally an offence punishable at law but is a civil wrong or 'tort', but anyone causing damage in the course of trespassing can be sued. It is also possible for a landholder to obtain an injunction to prevent trespass and sue for damages even if no harm has been done. Landholders have a right to insist that trespassers leave their land, or return to the right of way, and may use any reasonable and necessary force to compel them.

28   Farmers are not likely to object to a small group of walkers picnicking in pasture (but not in a hayfield) near the line of the path, but considerate walkers will leave no trace of their meal behind. Animals may die if they swallow plastic bags and can be severely injured by cans and broken bottles.

29   Should walkers using rights of way in England and Wales be approached by landholders and told that they are trespassing, they should discuss the matter courteously and, if agreement cannot be reached, politely but firmly insist on using the public path. But if the situation gets out of hand, it is probably better to ask for the name and address of the landholder and of the person who actually stops you, and report the matter to the highway authority.

30   In Scotland the situation is different. Under the terms of the Land Reform (Scotland) Act 2003, walkers who act responsibly can go virtually anywhere (see 15:5-6) so the question of trespass does not normally arise.

Wild flowers and fruits

31   Wild flowers must never be picked but, under certain conditions, it is permissible to take wild fruits. Mushrooms etc. which grow on the line of the path may be taken, but you can be sued for damages by the landholder if you take anything from his land that is not on the line of the path. However, it is apparently not stealing to take wild mushrooms and fruits, even if they are not on the path, unless you sell them for gain or reward. In practice, of course, it is customary for blackberries to be picked from hedgerows, sometimes in large quantities, and few landholders would object. Never pick anything cultivated.

Hygiene and sanitation

32   Public conveniences are few and far between in the countryside so the alternative, apart from using the facilities at pubs and tea rooms, is to take advantage of the natural cover provided by woods, hedges and walls.

33 Mankind is one of the few animals that finds its excreta offensive and a number of myths have grown around this fact:

    a) Excretion is natural and enriches the soil in the form of manure. It is not normally dangerous if certain simple precautions are observed. Tons of faeces and countless gallons of urine were deposited every day on railway tracks until the recent introduction of sealed tanks on trains, but there appear to be no reports that this has fouled watercourses or caused an outbreak of disease.

    b) There appears to be no evidence to support the popular myth that there are wild animals in the British Isles that will deliberately dig up human faeces.

34 Places where the disposal of human waste is likely to be a problem, and this is more aesthetic than dangerous, is in the neighbourhood of popular bothies and areas that appeal to those who enjoy camping wild. Bear in mind that:

    a) Urine is normally sterile so it poses no particular problem providing that direct contact with watercourses is avoided.

    b) United Utilities, which manages a catchment area of 57,000 hectares in north west England, advises walkers that faeces should be buried as far away as practicable, and in any case not less than 10 metres distant, from the edge of a watercourse, or the top water-level of a reservoir. Stools should have 15 centimetres of soil cover. Note that it is not unusual to see sheep and cattle grazing close to reservoirs.

    c) Toilet tissue can be burned or buried with the faeces. Both stools and tissue will normally break down and disappear within two or three weeks. Antiseptic wipes will take longer to decompose.

    d) Tampons and sanitary products should be placed in plastic bags and disposed of at the conclusion of the walk.

Litter

35 A considerate walker never knowingly drops, buries or hides litter. Keep a plastic bag for litter in your rucksack to either take home or drop in a litter bin at the end of your walk.

Fires

36 Fires should not be lit in the countryside. Not only do they leave unsightly rings of ash but if they get out of hand they can cause untold damage.

Pubs

37   One of the pleasures of walking is a drink in a country pub. Walkers are likely to arrive travel-stained, wearing muddy boots and perhaps soaking wet. Most landlords welcome walkers but may require large rucksacks and muddy boots, unless covered with plastic supermarket bags, be left outside. Groups of walkers should refrain from excessive noise.

38   A considerable number of country pubs have closed in recent years so it is wise to check (www.yell.com) before relying on the accuracy of the beer mug symbol on Ordnance Survey maps. Some country pubs close on one day each week.

Women in the countryside

39   Some female walkers worry about their physical safety in the countryside. Men rarely fear sexual assault or harassment and, despite the thousands of cases of rape and sexual assault reported every year, often find it difficult to appreciate the apprehension felt by some women when encountering a stranger in a lonely place. Although the chances of a woman being assaulted whilst walking in the countryside are negligible, there have been a handful of cases in the last thirty years. Men should be aware that women can be made apprehensive by thoughtless as well as by improper behaviour.

40   Even though the risk is perceived rather than actual, women who are nervous should consider walking with a companion, or a dog, and carry a personal alarm. Men should play their part in allaying fears by being considerate and not overbearingly friendly.

The Countryside Code for England and Wales

41   The Countryside Code is the official guide to good behaviour for both visitors and landholders in England and Wales. It was compiled by Natural England and the Countryside Council for Wales following discussions with interested parties. (Codes of behaviour for Scotland can be found at 15:5 and for Ireland at 16:5.)

Countryside Code - advice for the public

Be safe - plan ahead and follow any signs.
Even when going out locally, it's best to get the latest information about where and when you can go. For example, your rights to go onto some areas of open land may be restricted while work is carried out, for safety reasons,

or during breeding seasons. Follow advice and local signs, and be prepared for the unexpected.

Refer to up-to-date maps or guidebooks, visit the maps page on this website or contact local information centres.

You're responsible for your own safety and for others in your care, so be prepared for changes in weather and other events. Visit our countryside directory for links to organizations offering specific advice on equipment and safety, or contact visitor information centres and libraries for a list of outdoor recreation groups.

Check weather conditions before you leave, and don't be afraid to turn back.

Part of the appeal of the countryside is that you can get away from it all. You may not see anyone for hours, and there are many places without clear mobile phone signals, so let someone know where you're going and when you expect to return.

Get to know the signs and symbols used in the countryside. Download and print out our Finding Your Way Advice Sheet to take with you. It shows all the up to date signs and symbols.

If you're looking for ideas, explore the Things To Do section.

Leave gates and property as you find them

Please respect the working life of the countryside, as our actions can affect people's livelihoods, our heritage, and the safety and welfare of animals and ourselves.

A farmer will normally leave a gate closed to keep livestock in, but may sometimes leave it open so they can reach food and water. Leave gates as you find them or follow instructions on signs. If walking in a group, make sure the last person knows how to leave the gates.

If you think a sign is illegal or misleading such as a 'Private - No Entry' sign on a public footpath, contact the local authority.

In fields where crops are growing, follow the paths wherever possible.

Use gates, stiles or gaps in field boundaries when provided - climbing over walls, hedges and fences can damage them and increase the risk of farm animals escaping.

Our heritage belongs to all of us -do not disturb ruins and historic sites.

Leave machinery and livestock alone - don't interfere with animals even if you think they're in distress. Try to alert the farmer instead.

Protect plants and animals, and take your litter home

We have a responsibility to protect our countryside now and for future generations, so make sure you don't harm animals, birds, plants or trees.

Litter and leftover food doesn't just spoil the beauty of the countryside, it can be dangerous to wildlife and farm animals and can spread disease - so take your litter home with you. Dropping litter and dumping rubbish are criminal offences.

Discover the beauty of the natural environment and take special care not to damage, destroy or remove features such as rocks, plants and trees. They provide homes and food for wildlife, and add to everybody's enjoyment of the countryside.

Wild animals and farm animals can behave unpredictably if you get too close, especially if they're with their young - so give them plenty of space.

Fires can be as devastating to wildlife and habitats as they are to people and property - so be careful not to drop a match or smouldering cigarette at any time of the year. Sometimes controlled fires are used to manage vegetation, particularly on heaths and moors between October and early April, so please check that a fire is not supervised before calling 999.

Keep dogs under close control

The countryside is a great place to exercise dogs, but it's every owner's duty to make sure their dog is not a danger or nuisance to farm animals, wildlife or other people.

By law, you must control your dog so that it does not disturb or scare farm animals or wildlife. On most areas of open country and common land, known as 'access land', you must keep your dog on a short lead on most areas of open country and common land between 1 March and 31 July, and all year round near farm animals.

You do not have to put your dog on a lead on public paths, as long as it is under close control. But as a general rule, keep your dog on a lead if you cannot rely on its obedience. By law, farmers are entitled to destroy a dog that injures or worries their animals.

If a farm animal chases you and your dog, it is safer to let your dog off the lead – don't risk getting hurt by trying to protect it.

Take particular care that your dog doesn't scare sheep and lambs or wander where it might disturb birds that nest on the ground and other wildlife – eggs and young will soon die without protection from their parents.

Everyone knows how unpleasant dog mess is and it can cause infections – so always clean up after your dog and get rid of the mess responsibly. Also make sure your dog is wormed regularly to protect it, other animals and people.

At certain times, dogs may not be allowed on some areas of access land or may need to be kept on a lead. Please follow any signs. You can also find out more by phoning the Open Access Contact Centre on 0845 100 3298.

Consider other people

Showing consideration and respect for other people makes the countryside a pleasant environment for everyone - at home, at work and at leisure.

Busy traffic on small country roads can be unpleasant and dangerous to local people, visitors and wildlife - so slow down and, where possible, leave your vehicle at home, consider sharing lifts and use alternatives such as public transport or cycling.

Respect the needs of local people - for example, don't block gateways, driveways or other entry points with your vehicle.

Keep out of the way when farm animals are being gathered or moved and follow directions from the farmer.

When riding a bike or driving a vehicle, slow down for horses, walkers and livestock and give them plenty of room. By law, cyclists must give way to walkers and horse-riders on bridleways. Support the rural economy - for example, buy your supplies from local shops.

Countryside Code - advice for land managers

Know your rights, responsibilities and liabilities.

People visiting the countryside provide important income for the local economy. Most like to follow a visible route, prefer using proper access points like gates, and generally want to do the right thing - but they need your help.

Visitors are allowed to access land in different ways. For more guidance on how this affects you and what your rights, responsibilities and liabilities are, contact your local authority or National Park authority, and the Open Access website.

The Ordnance Survey's 1:25,000 maps show public rights of way and designated areas of open land. These maps are generally reliable but not 'definitive' so you will need to check the legal status of rights of way with your local authority. You can find out which areas of access land are mapped under the 'Countryside and Rights of Way Act 2000' on the Open Access website.

By law, you must keep rights of way clear and not obstruct people's entry onto access land - it's a criminal offence to discourage rights of public access with misleading signs.

Trespassing is often unintentional - see for advice on tackling trespass. Request a copy of the Managing Public Access booklet from the Open Access Contact Centre on 0845 100 3298.

Contact your local authority or National Park authority, and look on the Managing public access section of the Open Access website. You can check the legal status of rights of way with your local authority.

Where can people go on your land?

Most people who visit the countryside are keen to act responsibly, and trespassing is often unintentional – download the Managing Public Access Guide on the Open Access website for advice on tackling trespass. Alternatively, request a copy from the Open Access Contact Centre on 0845 100 3298.

There are a number of ways you can help them to be responsible. These include:

Keep paths, boundaries, waymarks, signs, gates and stiles in good order. To find out what help is available, contact your local authority or National Park Authority.

Where public access leads through a boundary feature, such as a fence or hedge, create a gap if you can – or use an accessible gate or, if absolutely necessary, a stile. When installing new gates and stiles, make sure you have the permission of the local authority.

Give clear, polite guidance where it's needed – for example, tell visitors about your land management operations.

Rubbish attracts other rubbish - by getting rid of items such as farm waste properly, you'll discourage fly tipping (dumping rubbish illegally) and encourage others to get rid of their rubbish responsibly.

Identify possible threats to visitors' safety

People come to the countryside simply to enjoy themselves safely. As land managers, it is up to us to help them to do so. In fact we have a duty of care under the Occupiers' Liability Acts of 1957 and 1984 to make sure that they can pass through our land safely.

Here are some useful tips to help them to go home in one piece.

Draw the public's attention to potential man-made and natural hazards on your land..

Avoid using electric fencing, barbed wire and other hazards close to areas that people visit, particularly alongside narrow paths and at the height of a child.

Don't let animals that are likely to attack visitors roam freely where the public has access – you may be liable for any resulting harm.

Chapter 2   Walking techniques

1   Most walkers are content to develop their own style of walking but it may be helpful to bear the following points in mind:

   a)   Many walkers setting out on a walk, especially in the upland areas of British Isles where most walks are likely to commence with a climb out of the valley, find it helpful to start off well within their normal walking pace and gradually work up to their usual speed and stride.

   b)   Many walkers find it fatiguing to walk either significantly faster or more slowly than their normal pace.

   c)   The length of your stride will normally shorten when climbing steeply.

   d)   When descending a moderate gradient your stride will tend to lengthen but is likely to shorten markedly if descending steeply.

   e)   It is often more tiring to descend a steep hill than to climb it, especially with a heavy pack. A long descent puts a strain on the muscles at the front of the thighs which can become tender.

   f)   When walking steeply downhill it is helpful to allow the legs to bend slightly at the knee so that the body is not jarred when each foot is put on the ground.

   g)   When walking off-path, and either climbing or descending steeply, it is often helpful to take a zigzag route. This will make the route longer but easier and you will probably cover the ground faster.

   h)   To reduce the risk of slipping it is helpful to put the whole of the foot down on firm ground and, as far as possible, to avoid toe and heel holds.

   i)   It is risky to jump even from low heights with a heavy pack because the weight can easily unbalance the unwary and can cause compression fractures and spinal injury.

2   Your walk may have constraints as for example
   • when you have to complete a walk by a certain time in order to catch a bus or train
   • the need to complete the walk in daylight
   • undertaking a walk that is longer than those to which you have become accustomed and which may be outside your comfort zone

3 There are techniques and procedures that can assist in keeping to a schedule including:

    a) When using a paper map, keep a record of your progress by marking and numbering every two kilometres on your map.

    b) A handheld satnav (see 9:8-10) will give you instant readings of your
- average speed when moving
- overall average speed
- distance from your destination
- estimated time of arrival at your destination

4 Your average speed can be increased without actually walking faster. For example:

    a) A picnic lunch takes less time to consume than a meal in a pub or a café.

    b) When making a stop, combine as many activities as possible including
- eating
- drinking
- adjusting clothing
- calls of nature
- consulting the map

    c) Practise adjusting your clothing whilst continuing to walk using the following technique
- undo hip belt and loosen rucksack shoulder straps
- swing rucksack to the crook of your elbow leaving one arm free
- undo clothing and pull your free arm from the sleeve
- move rucksack to other arm and pull it from the sleeve
- you may have to pull the garment over your head
- undo rucksack and place garment in it
- fasten rucksack and swing it back onto your shoulders
- a similar process can be employed to don clothing

Path surfaces

5 The soils which form the surface of a path have certain qualities and it is useful to know the characteristics of each type.

Chalk

6 Grass-covered chalk is pleasant to walk on. It provides a good firm surface when dry, but is slippery when wet.

Clay

7   Clay can be unpleasant to walk on. If frozen, or baked hard by the sun, it be-comes rutted. When waterlogged, it is slippery and will cling tenaciously to your boots in great lumps, increasing the weight on the feet several-fold. It is difficult to remove, but the worst can be got off with the aid of a stick and plenty of thick wet grass. It is often helpful to kick an imaginary football as this will loosen the largest lumps.

Grass

8   Short grass provides pleasant walking though it may be slippery on steep slopes when wet. Long grass, when wet, will quickly saturate your boots and socks.

Heather

9   Heather is found throughout the upland areas of British Isles. It is abrasive and tiring to traverse in pathless country, especially when wet. It will not grow in standing water and can provide a firm foothold in boggy areas.

Peat

10   Peat is found mostly in the upland areas of the British Isles. It is formed by decomposing vegetation such as heather and bracken, is a dark chocolate colour and can be several metres deep. Dry peat provides a good surface, pleasantly springy underfoot.

11   Wet peat is slightly slippery, but as it tends to be covered with heather it causes difficulties only when deep and free from vegetation. Peat will absorb vast quantities of water and in wet weather it forms bogs into which walkers can sink to their knees. It is often possible to see firmer footing provided by clumps of reed and heather which will keep you from sinking deeply too into the bog.

12   An ankle-deep bog normally poses no problems to walkers but when the bog reaches a particular consistency, a vacuum can be formed around your foot and you will find yourself trapped. The technique to break the vacuum is to gradu-ally rock your leg backwards and forwards until a squelching noise indicates that the vacuum has been broken and your foot will come free.

Rock

13   Dry rock of all kinds, from sandstone to granite, normally provides a good sur-face on which boots will not slip unless it has become polished by heavy use. Boots grip reasonably well on 'clean' (i.e. lichen and mud-free rock) but when covered with lichen or mud (usually known as 'greasy rock') it can be slippery.

Ice-covered rock is extremely dangerous. A thin coating of ice, known as verglas, can form on rock when the air is saturated.

Sand

14   Sandy soils usually drain well and are pleasant to walk on in all weathers.

Scree

15   Scree consists of loose pieces of rock, about the size of large pebbles, on a steep mountain slope. It is fatiguing to climb because when advancing one step you slip back half a step, rather like climbing steep shingle on a beach. Descending scree, known as scree-running, was once a popular pastime but is now discouraged because of the environmental damage that it can cause.

Path furniture

16   Stiles and footbridges are often slippery when wet or frost-covered and care should be taken when crossing them.

Select bibliography

17   Murphy, Sam, *Get Fit Walking.* A & C Black, 2005.

Chapter 3   Clothing, footwear & equipment

1   Those new to walking may find some of the information in this chapter daunting. And if you examine the shelves of outdoor shops, and read the descriptions of some of the specialized clothing in outdoor magazines and in the catalogues of outdoor stores, you may come to the conclusion that walking is a hi-tech and expensive pastime. But this need not be so if you buy wisely and tailor your purchases to the kind of walking that appeals to you.

2   The comfort and enjoyment of walking can be enhanced by wearing suitable clothing. If you only take five-mile strolls in fine weather in lowland countryside then you will need nothing more than a T-shirt, shorts or jeans, and trainers all of which are probably already in your wardrobe. But once you start to undertake longer walks you will probably find it more comfortable to wear footwear and clothing specifically designed for walking.

3   Nowadays, outdoor leisure gear is both street-fashionable and big business and there is a bewildering array of products readily available at your local outdoor shop. You should be aware that many of the expensive, high performance walking jackets worn in Sloane Square may never see conditions more demanding than winter on Hampstead Heath. Nevertheless, the fashion market contributes to sales and designers and manufacturers of walking gear have to keep an eye on it. This can result in compromises that are not always in the best interests of walkers.

4   The drive for innovation has brought many benefits including the development of waterproof, breathable materials (Gore-Tex, for example, is now a household name), but it has also resulted in a relentless quest for new designs to appear every year. Last season's excellent model is sometimes replaced by a new design which may be inferior - but at least it has the virtue of being new! There are only a few designs that sell steadily year after year because the original concept was so good.

5   It is impossible to recommend best products because what suits one person may not appeal, or even work, for someone else. This is particularly true of waterproofs where the metabolism of the wearer may be such that even the most breathable of fabrics will be unable to cope with the amount of sweat and water vapour excreted. Similarly, nobody can tell you which is the best make of boot,

or even the best model, because feet come in all shapes and sizes and you have to find the one that best suits you.

6   There is now such a huge range of outdoor gear available that retailers are only able to stock a selection. The products of companies with large advertising and marketing budgets, together with the ability to offer bigger discounts, ensures that they are readily available. But popularity does not guarantee quality or suitability and it is easy to overlook the excellent products of smaller companies. For example, many experienced walkers will tell you that Páramo waterproofs (see 3:28-31) are as good as, and some would claim better, than most other brands, but you have to go to the company's website to find stockists.

7   The quality and comfort of clothing designed for walkers can be superb. Every item, except salopettes, that Alan Hinkes wore in his successful attempt to climb the highest mountain in each of the seven continents was available over the counter from outdoor shops. Clothing with such a high specification is expensive and relatively few walkers actually need it.

8   Gear, at long last, is now available in women's sizes, so female walkers no longer have to make do with garments designed for small men. Good quality gear for children is also available.

9   For long day-walks anywhere in the British Isles in the temperate months of the year, and anywhere in the lowland areas at any time of the year, you are likely to require most of the following items of clothing and equipment
      • underwear (known as the base layer)
      • shirt fleece or woollen sweater (known as midwear)
      • trousers or shorts (known as legwear)
      • waterproof jacket
      • waterproof overtrousers (also known as rain pants)
      • gaiters
      • socks
      • boots or walking shoes
      • rucksack (also known as a backpack or daypack)
      • hat and gloves
      • whistle (see 11:59)
      • first aid kit (see 19:10)
      • map (described in Chapters 4 and 5)
      • compass (described in 6:21-6:33)
      • handheld satnav (described in Chapter 9)

Clothing

10 The purpose of wearing clothing is keep you dry and at a comfortable temperature whatever the weather. In the British Isles it is not unusual to experience in a single day
- a temperature range of 20°C
- sunshine
- high winds
- driving rain

Walkers need clothing that can cope with all these conditions

11 Factors that affect the choice of clothing include:

a) The type of terrain in which you will be walking. Lowland walking in England does not require clothing with the same level of specification as those who walk in the Highlands of Scotland.

b) The time of year in which you will be walking. If you confine your walking to the temperate seasons, it is likely that you will need little more than waterproofs and boots of medium quality.

12 To appreciate how modern clothing fabrics work, you must understand that the body's temperature is controlled by the pores of the skin. When the body is hot they open and flood the skin with sweat which then evaporates thus cooling the body. When cold, the pores close to prevent sweating, and unless warm clothes are put on, goose pimples will appear and the body will start to shiver in an attempt to generate warmth. When the body is at a comfortable temperature it will give off water vapour which forms an invisible barrier just above the skin which controls the temperature within fine limits. The purpose of clothing is to keep the body dry and comfortable and in a state of reasonable equilibrium between the extremes of heat and cold so that energy is not wasted in either cooling or warming.

13 An important factor that affects the efficiency of clothing is the 'breathability' of the fabrics used. Breathability depends on the efficiency of the fabrics to pass sweat and body vapour from the skin into the atmosphere and is technically known as moisture vapour transmission (MVT).

14 Breathability is affected by your personal metabolism. Those who sweat a great deal, sometimes described as 'running hot', may find that their clothing cannot always cope with the amount of sweat and vapour excreted so that it remains in the clothing and can leave the walker feeling clammy and damp.

15   You can control the temperature of your body by adding and removing clothing as required. This is known as 'layering' and works on the principle of versatility. For example, it is easier to control your body temperature using two thin layers of clothing rather than one thick layer.

16   Clothing can be divided into three main groups:
   a)   Waterproofs that are designed primarily to keep the wearer dry and include
      • jackets
      • overtrousers
      •gaiters

   b)   Clothes worn under waterproofs that are designed to keep the wearer at a comfortable temperature. This category includes
      • base layer (underwear)
      • midwear (shirts, fleeces etc.)
      • legwear (shorts and trousers)

   c)   Footwear designed to keep your feet dry and comfortable
      • boots
      • shoes
      • socks

Waterproof materials

17   Waterproofs, sometimes referred to as 'hard shells' to distinguish then from 'soft shells' (6:60-1), protect the base layer and mid layers from wind and rain. Nearly all hard shell clothing, except the very cheapest, is 'breathable' to a greater or lesser degree. In order to understand this term you have to appreciate that for maximum dryness and comfort, the heat and water vapour given off by the body has to escape into the atmosphere. If it is unable to do so it will condense on the cooler, inner surface of your waterproof and, in time, you will get wet even though no rain has penetrated.

18   Budget waterproofs generally use inexpensive breathable coatings which are perfectly adequate for lowland walkers but are not so breathable as the more expensive garments. As a rule-of-thumb guide, any waterproof that uses a brand name to describe what makes it breathable should perform satisfactorily. However, anecdotal evidence suggests that a minority of walkers who sweat profusely find that some breathable fabrics cannot cope with the amount of moisture given off by their bodies thus allowing condensation to form on the inner face of the fabric. This can lead to misunderstandings and complaints that the garment is not waterproof.

19   The outer surface of hard shell garments is treated with a durable waterproof repellent (DWR) which makes raindrops form little beads on the outer fabric. This prevents the garment from becoming waterlogged, which will not detract from its waterproof qualities, but will hinder moisture vapour passing through to the outside of the fabric. This is yet another cause of condensation forming on the inner face.

20   The waterproof quality of a fabric is established by using the British Standard *Method of Test for the Resistance of Fabrics to Penetration by Water.* This requires a sample of the fabric to be placed in a sealed clamp. One face of the fabric is then subjected to a steadily increasing pressure of water at a rate of one centimetre per minute. When the water penetrates, the pressure, expressed as a height in a vertical tube, is measured and this is known as the hydrostatic head of that sample of material. The higher the hydrostatic head the more waterproof is the fabric (1500 mm is the minimum). Seams are the weakest part of any garment and it is quite normal for the best hard shell clothing to have lower entry pressures at the seams. Note that this is a test of the waterproof qualities of the *fabric* when new, not the garment. The distinction is important because water can reach the skin of the wearer via ill-fitting neck flaps and cuffs.

21   The breathability of hard shell clothing is also dependant on what is worn *under* the garment. It is important to wear clothing, from underwear outwards, that will efficiently transmit water vapour to the inner surface of the waterproof (see 3:13-14).

22   Notwithstanding what the advertisements tell you, if you walk all day in driving rain you are bound to end up damp. However, if you wear appropriate clothing underneath your waterproofs you should at least be warm and comfortable.

23   The seeming miracle of breathability, technically known as moisture vapour transmission (MVT), is generally achieved in one of two ways:
   a) The use of a membrane or a coating which is full of millions of tiny holes. These are so small that they allow molecules of water vapour to pass through unimpeded but, as molecules of rain water are twenty thousand times larger than those of water vapour, rain will not penetrate.

   b) The use of a membrane or coating with two entirely different yet compatible molecular chains. One chain is hydrophilic (meaning water-loving), and the other is hydrophobic (water-hating). Molecules of water vapour from inside the garment are attracted to the hydrophilic molecules in the coating and pass through to the outside. Rain strikes the hydrophobic molecules on the outside of the fabric and is repelled.

24   All membranes and coatings have to be combined with a tough fabric that is tear and abrasion resistant. Some manufacturers use different weights of fabric which can range from ultra-lightweight for summer use to rugged materials for extreme weather conditions. Some membranes and coatings have been developed specifically for particular manufacturers whilst others, such as Gore-Tex, eVent and Sympatex, are used by many firms.

25   Two fabrics, Páramo (see 3:28-31) and Ventile (see 3:33), achieve breathability by different means.

eVent

26   eVent (www.eventfabrics.com) not only allows perspiration to dissipate and vent before it saturates the inside of the fabric, but the membrane is also oleophobic (oil-hating) which, it is claimed, helps prevent the tiny pores becoming clogged with body oils.

Gore-Tex

27   Gore-Tex (www.gore-tex.co.uk) was the first fabric that used a breathable membrane and is still the best-known and the market leader. Gore-Tex will only sell its fabrics to companies whose designs can match its exacting standards.

Páramo

28   Páramo (www.paramo.co.uk) is a highly breathable fabric that works, like an animal's fur, on the principle of capillary depression whereby small diameter water-repellent tubes push out water better than large diameter tubes. It is the gaps between the filaments and fibres that act as capillary tubes which move moisture away from the body thus keeping you dry. The outer fabric is treated with Nikwax TX10 proofing which repels most of the rain. Any that does penetrate to the lining, which is also treated with Nikwax TX10 is, in effect, pumped away by body heat.

29   Although it repels rain as effectively as any fabric on the market, Páramo is not, strictly speaking, waterproof because it has a low hydrostatic head. Thus, if you sit on wet ground the surface water will quickly penetrate the garment.

30   Páramo garments
     • can be re-proofed at home
     • can be punctured without ill-effect
     • can be repaired with a needle and thread
     • carry a lifetime guarantee

31 Unlike most conventional hard shell materials, Páramo is soft to the touch and does not rustle. The fabric is heavier than other waterproof fabrics so some walkers get uncomfortably warm in summer, but it is an excellent garment for cool conditions.

Sympatex

32 The most rugged Sympatex fabrics (www.sympatex.com) have a hydrostatic head of 25 metres and employ a hydrophylic/hydrophobic membrane (see 3:23). The membrane is non-porous so breathability is unaffected by contamination from body oils. The membrane is bonded to fabrics available in three weights and there is a special material for use in footwear.

Ventile

33 Ventile (www.ventile.co.uk) is a high-quality cotton material. The fibres absorb water and swell, thus forming an efficient waterproof barrier that still allows water vapour to escape. It is exceptionally hard-wearing with excellent wind and waterproof qualities that last the lifetime of the garment. It has a pleasant feel and can be repaired at home with needle and thread. But it is heavy, especially when wet, and it takes a long time to dry.

Design of waterproof clothing

34 The water-repellency of the fabric is not the only factor that makes for a good waterproof; design and fit are just as important. A garment can use the most waterproof fabric available and still let in rain because of design faults. The best designs are usually the simplest. Hard shell garments should have no seams at the shoulders, and all exposed zips (other than waterproof zips) and pockets should be protected by storm flaps. Seams should be welded or taped to make them as waterproof as possible.

35 Most waterproofs, except Páramo and Ventile, rely on taping to seal the seams and prevent the ingress of water. Tape can delaminate from the fabric after extensive use.

Waterproof garments

Jackets

36 When walking in driving rain, it is impossible to make a watertight seal between the skin of the extremities and the jacket. The most likely places for rain to penetrate are the cheeks, neck and throat. Hands and wrists can also be a source of seepage when the forearms are raised upwards to examine a map, wipe spectacles, adjusting the hood, and when using walking poles.

37 Jackets come in a variety of designs that can include the following features:

a) A hood is essential. It should be close-fitting around the cheeks, mouth and throat. Many walkers like a wired hood which allows the wearer to adjust the shape according to the weather conditions.

b) Pockets are useful for keeping to hand small items but, unless well-designed, are vulnerable to leakage. Outside pockets should be protected by generous storm flaps and zips. Items that readily absorb moisture such as handkerchiefs and tissues, together with your wallet, should be kept in small plastic bags.

c) If you sweat profusely you may find underarm zips, sometimes described as 'pit zips', useful for extra ventilation but they may leak after prolonged use.

Overtrousers (also known as rain pants)

38 Some of the features that overtrousers are likely to have include:

a) Long leg gussets that enable the garment to be pulled on whilst wearing boots. You can keep mud from the inside of your overtrousers by covering your boots with plastic bags,

b) Flies (convenient but they may allow the ingress of water).

c) Pockets and/or zipped openings which give access to legwear are also useful but both features may allow the ingress of water.

Capes (also known as ponchos)

39 Capes have never found much favour in the British Isles although they are popular in some European countries perhaps due to the differences in weather.

40 A cape is a simple garment incorporating a hood. It is thrown over the head and backpack and usually comes down to mid-calf so overtrousers are not always required if gaiters are worn. The arms are normally kept inside the cape but some have rudimentary sleeves which allow, a map to be examined.

41 Capes can be unpleasant to wear in strong winds and, in extreme cases, dangerous. They are not normally made from breathable materials so they suffer from condensation.

42 Some capes can be used as temporary shelters and are useful whilst eating in wet weather.

Gaiters

43   These useful garments attach to the boot and extend to the knee thus protecting the lower leg from mud and wet vegetation. Breathable gaiters are not essential and cheap, nylon versions serve very well for everyday use. There are gaiters that cover the entire boot which are designed for use in the snow and when fording rivers.

44   In wet weather, gaiters are often worn *underneath* overtrousers to prevent water running down inside the gaiter and into the boots. When walking through abrasive vegetation such as heather and brambles gaiters worn outside legwear will protect against excessive wear.

45   There are ankle-length gaiters, known as stoptous or anklets, which will give some protection from mud, and keep stones and the seeds of grasses etc. from entering the cuff of your boot.

Umbrellas

46   An umbrella can provide comforting protection from heavy rain providing that there is little wind. They can also provide shelter during lunch stops.

Care of waterproofs with a durable water resistant treatment

47   In the course of normal wear, breathable hard shell garments will gradually lose some of their waterproof qualities. Body oils will clog the tiny pores in the fabric and the durable water repellent coating will wear off resulting in the garment becoming saturated. The remedy is to launder and reproof.

48   It is not widely appreciated, although the facts have been known for many years, that it is almost impossible to remove every trace of detergent by rinsing. Detergents contain surfactants one of whose properties attracts water which is why they clean so efficiently. If any trace of detergent is left in the garment then water will be attracted to it like iron filings to a magnet, and the waterproofing qualities will be compromised.

49   Some of the proprietary products for laundering waterproofs recommend using a washing machine. However, the dispensing tray and feeder tubes may have become encrusted with detergent which must be removed before washing. One method is to scrape off as much detergent as possible and then put 100 grams of Alum BP (aluminium potassium sulphate) which is available from pharmacies, or some citric acid, and run a full cycle, including pre-wash, of the empty machine. These products will effectively neutralize any remaining detergent. Experience indicates that their use has no adverse effects on the machine.

50 Your shell clothing can now be laundered using one of the non-detergent based cleaning and waterproofing products marketed by Nikwax and Grangers.

Garments worn under waterproofs

51 Most garments made specifically for walking are manufactured from synthetic materials or Merino wool which have properties that allow water vapour and sweat to pass through the inside face of the garment to the outside. This is known as 'wicking' (the technical term is 'capillary rise') and is a most desirable attribute because it prevents clothing in contact with the skin from getting soaked with perspiration and becoming cold and clammy.

52 Cotton is very absorbent, traps water and takes a long time to dry; it does not wick and is cold to the touch when wet so it should be avoided.

53 The correct combination of clothing allows perspiration and water vapour to pass through each layer in turn and dry off when it reaches the exterior of the top layer leaving the wearer feeling dry and comfortable.

Base layer

54 Basewear, the technical term for underclothes, should wick to remove sweat from the body surface and provide an increased surface area for evaporation.

55 Several styles and weights of wicking underwear are available. For the upper body there are singlets, T-shirts, long-sleeved crew and roll necks. A long-sleeved crew neck is particularly versatile because it can be worn as a shirt and in hot weather the sleeves can be rolled up. Wicking sports bras are available.

56 For the lower body there are various styles of underwear for both men and women ranging from long johns to briefs. The choice of style is a matter of personal preference.

Midwear

57 Midwear clothing is designed to provide insulation and should be made from materials so open in structure that water vapour can pass through easily. The open structure also provides insulation.

58 Garments include fleeces, Merino wool sweaters and wicking shirts in various styles. Fleeces come in weights from 100 grams per square metre (gsm) to 300 gsm. For most walkers a lightweight fleece or Merino wool shirt is a good choice. If you need more warmth for walking in winter buy another lightweight

fleece or Merino shirt to wear over the first one. This is good practice because two lightweight garments are warmer and more versatile than one heavyweight. Extreme conditions may require down clothing (for the qualities of down see 20:25-8).

59   Many walkers like a wickable shirt with chest pockets in which small items such as a compass can be kept. When worn under a fleece they are suitable for winter wear.

Soft shells

60   There is no clear definition of what constitutes a soft shell but, in general terms, they are understood to be hooded jackets, made of stretch materials that provide good wind and rain resistance without being waterproof.

61   Soft shells are more breathable, warmer and comfortable than most waterproofs and are designed for use in light rain and/or strong winds. In heavy rain they can be worn under a waterproof to provide complete weather protection.

Belay jackets

62   A belay jacket is a light insulating garment, designed to be worn over other layers to prevent cooling when the wearer is stationary for some time.

Layering

63   The combination of wearing base layer, midwear, soft shells and waterproofs is known as 'layering' and is designed to keep the wearer dry and comfortable under all conditions. You just add or remove clothing as required. There are three-layer and four-layer systems.

64   The more popular is the three-layer system. It comprises
  • base layer
  • mid-layer
  • waterproofs

65   The four-layer system is more versatile, but also more expensive, and is more suited to serious hill-walkers. It comprises
  • base layer
  • mid-layer
  • soft shell or belay jacket
  • waterproofs

Legwear

66   Shorts and trousers come in a variety of styles and materials including

- a durable water repellent finish that will keep the garment dry in light rain
- belt loops, a built-in belt, or a drawstring
- hip, side and rear pockets with or without zips
- zipped fly

67   There are trousers with legs that zip off to convert to shorts. Ensure that the exposed zip cannot chafe the skin.

68   Some walkers favour close-fitting legwear made from stretch fabrics. These garments often lack a fly, are short on pockets, and are usually supported by a drawstring.

Footwear

69   The received wisdom used to be that boots were always preferred to shoes. However, shoes sometimes referred to as approach shoes and designed for walking long distances, are now becoming popular.

70   Approach shoes are generally lighter than boots and are favoured by athletic walkers who like to travel fast and cover the ground quickly. They do not offer as much protection from mud and wet vegetation as boots although this disadvantage can be mitigated by wearing gaiters. Most approach shoes are not waterproof so you are likely to end up with wet feet. They are not suitable for the minority of walkers who need, or desire, ankle support.

71   Many walkers find that boots have several advantages over approach shoes. The higher cuff provides some support against turning the ankle and will protect the sensitive ankle bone from painful contact with rocks. They also give more protection from mud and surface water, and the thicker sole dulls the impact of sharp rocks. They are generally heavier than approach shoes.

Boots

72   There has been a revolution in the design of walking boots in the last few years with the almost universal adoption of lighter styles. Gone are the clumsy, old-fashioned clodhoppers that had to be worn for many miles before they became comfortable. There is now a wide choice of well-made boots that feel snug as soon as fitted and require little breaking in. The lighter the boot the less energy you will expend. For every kilogram on your feet you will have to lift approximately one tonne for every kilometre that you walk. Boots can be made from leather or fabric or a combination of both.

Leather

73   Several types of leather are used in boots. All types, except suede, can be injected with substances during the tanning process that increase the leather's waterproofing properties:

  a) Full grain calf is widely used in boots of reasonable quality.

  b) Nubuck is a full-grain leather which has had the outside finely sanded which gives a texturized finish which masks any minor cosmetic blemishes.

  c) Anfibio is an expensive, prime-quality leather that is used in the best quality mountaineering boots.

  d) Suede is made from a heavy leather that has been split and the surface abraded to give a fuzzy texture. It was once popular, especially for women's boots, but is now mainly used on boots at the bottom end of the market. It is lighter and more flexible than other leathers and does not give so much ankle support. The rough finish makes it difficult to clean and as it cannot be dressed satisfactorily with conventional leather preservatives, a silicone spray has to be used.

Fabric

74   Some lightweight boots are made from tough fabrics, such as Cordura, often reinforced with suede, but the amount of stitching required often results in weaker construction. They will keep your feet dry if they have a waterproof membrane, such as Gore-Tex, Sympatex or eVent, but they are not always as suitable as leather for the wet conditions found in the British Isles because they take longer to dry. Fabric boots tend to give less ankle support.

Construction

75   Modern walking boots have a patterned sole made of hard-moulded rubber. The uppers are made of leather or a tough fabric, have a bellows tongue to prevent the ingress of water, and hook-lacing for speed and maximum adjustment.

76   Leather is not waterproof although it can be made water-resistant if properly dressed. However, mud and vegetation, especially heather, which is particularly abrasive, will soon remove even the most tenacious dressing.

77   Boots with Gore-Tex, eVent or Sympatex linings are completely waterproof, and breathable unless water washes over the top of the cuff. It is also possible to buy waterproof socks which are worn over conventional socks and are, in effect, detachable boot liners. Some walkers report that waterproof, breathable linings make their feet uncomfortably hot.

78   Some boot manufacturers fit Sorbothane footbeds to their more expensive ranges. Sorbothane absorbs shock and disperses the energy slowly so that the footbed cushions the heel without springing back immediately. Sorbothane foot-beds are sold in outdoor shops to replace the footbed that comes with your boots. Some walkers find that they make their feet too hot.

Choosing and fitting

79   Boots come in a bewildering range of styles and descriptions. Unfortunately, there is no generally accepted grading or category to indicate the use for which they have been designed. Some manufacturers grade their boots by seasonal use, but this is rarely helpful because they don't define which season. Other bootmakers use confusing terms such as 'trekking boots'.

80   A helpful way of selecting a suitable boot is to consider the kind of terrain in which you are likely to walk:

     a)   Lightweight boots are particularly suitable for walking on paths in lowland areas. Their construction is not so robust as heavier boots and they are likely to be less water-resistant unless they have a waterproof membrane. Weights are typically less than 1000 grams per pair for a man's size 9.

     b)   Mid-weight boots are suitable for most terrains and conditions found in the British Isles except in winter in upland areas. They can be worn when back-packing, and some will take a crampon for occasional use (see 3:81). Weights are between 1000 and 1500 grams per pair for a man's size 9.

     c)   Mountain boots are heavy, rugged and have a stiff sole and are most suited to winter conditions in upland areas.

     d)   The majority of walkers probably make do with one pair of serviceable boots so it makes sense to purchase a pair that will satisfy most of your needs.

81   If you plan to walk in conditions that require crampons to be worn, it is impor-tant to select a boot that will accept them because boots that flex too much can

cause a crampon to become dislodged. The following universal rating system ensures boot and crampon compatibility:

Boot rating	Crampon rating
B0	None
B1	C1
B2	C1 & C2
B3	C1 & C2 & C3

A statement of crampon compatibility will normally appear on the care instructions supplied with new boots. Similarly, when purchasing crampons there will be information about the rating.

82 Boots are probably the most difficult item of gear to choose for fit. There is no such thing as a best make of boot that will suit everyone. Subtle differences between manufacturers' lasts means that Brand X will sometimes suit those with narrow feet, but will cripple anyone with wide feet. You have to take time to discover what is your perfect fit, and if the boot performs well, it is a good plan to buy replacement boots of the same brand. Seek out a reputable and experienced retailer who is prepared to ensure that you buy boots that not only fit well but are suitable for your kind of walking. The best retailers encourage customers to wear their new boots indoors for a limited period and if they prove not to be comfortable they will exchange them for a more suitable pair. A good outdoor shop should have an inclined plane that you can walk up and down simulating the action of ascending and descending hills.

83 Some companies have made the retrograde step of starting men's sizes at 7 and dispensing with half sizes. Even when a particular brand is available in both smaller and half sizes, some retailers are reluctant to stock them because sales are low. If you need either a small size or a half size it is worth checking the websites of the major brands where the sizes available are usually listed. With some brands, there seems to be little difference between small sizes for men and larger sizes for women, so men with small feet should check what is available in women's sizes.

84 A few brands allow a choice of width within each size. However, there is no standardization of widths between manufacturers but some use a broader or narrower last than others. Also, the lacing system often allows some adjustment. Those with narrow feet should lace their boots more tightly to reduce the width and provide a good fit. Volume adjusters which fit under the insole can help those with narrow feet. They can either be purchased, or you can make your own from a piece of cardboard using the upturned insole as a template. If you have broad feet, either lace the first few hooks loosely or even start threading the laces halfway up the boot. It is also possible to relieve pressure by lacing tightly at one point and loosely at another by doubling the lace back on itself.

85   Some retailers have invested in a machine that will make custom insoles for your feet. The customer stands on a gel-like substance that moulds itself or your foot from which a matching footbed can be made.

86   When buying boots:

a)   Wear your normal walking socks.

b)   Remove the footbed from the boot you are considering buying and stand on it in your stockinged feet. If you can see the edge of the footbed around the whole of your foot this indicates that there are unlikely to be any pressure points on your foot.

c)   Try on and lace the boots. There should be just enough room to poke your forefinger down the back of the heel.

d)   When you lift your foot behind you and tap the toe smartly on the floor, your toes should not touch the front of the boot. This will allow sufficient room for your feet to swell when they are hot so that when you descend a steep hill you will not bruise your toes.

e)   Walk around the store and try to establish that the boots are comfortable.

87   If you have serious foot problems or find it difficult to find boots that fit properly, it may be worth considering investing in a pair of custom-made boots. Altberg (www.altberg.co.uk), based in Richmond, North Yorkshire, is the only British company that manufactures custom-made boots. The company offers a choice of boots

• made in half sizes and five widths on standard lasts and then tweaked to cope with a particular problem

• made to measure boots where a last is made from measurements taken from the customer's foot

Care of boots

88   New leather boots should be dressed sparingly with a leather preservative. Some manufacturers insist on customers using a particular brand in order keep the guarantee valid. Penetration of the leather can be improved by warming the boots for a few minutes in an oven heated to 50°C, or with a hair drier. The dressing can then be worked into the leather with your fingers.

89   Clean leather boots after every walk by gently washing away the mud with plenty of cold water and a washing-up brush. Stuff them with newspaper and

leave for a few hours in a warm room well away from direct heat. If the dressing has leached apply another coat.

90 Fabric boots should be cleaned in the same way as leather boots, and when dry sprayed with a silicone waterproofing compound.

Socks

91 The best socks are manufactured using techniques that hide the seams and have thicker padding at the heels and toes. Some walkers like to wear a thin pair of socks under their regular walking socks as this assists in keeping the feet cool and sweat-free and, it is claimed, reduces the risk of blisters.

Hats

92 Hats can be used for protection from rain, sun, wind and cold. Experts inform us that up to 10 per cent of body heat is lost through the head if the body is adequately insulated (it seems that the frequently quoted figure of 30-40 per cent is incorrect).

93 In cold weather, it is wise to wear a hat, made from a warm material such as Thinsulate, that will cover your ears. If you get too warm then the hat can be rolled up.

94 A broad-rimmed hat will protect you from the sun. It can also be used to keep your head dry during showers instead of using the hood of your rain jacket.

Gloves

95 Gloves made from wool or Thinsulate will keep you warm but need protection in wet conditions. Gore-Tex over-mitts can be worn to keep your gloves dry, providing that the cuffs are tucked under the sleeves of your jacket. However, wearing mitts means that there is a loss of dexterity when map-reading and adjusting clothing etc.

Equipment

96 Not all walkers will require all the items described below. Note that compasses and satnavs are described in Chapters 6 and 9.

Rucksacks

97 The term rucksack is derived from the German 'rucken' meaning 'back' and 'sack' (alternative names are backpack, daypack and daysack). It is an essential item of equipment for carrying waterproofs, a spare fleece, food and drink etc. The capacity of rucksacks is measured in litres and the size is often incorporated into the model's name as in 'Venom 25' (most daypacks are in the range 25-35 litres). Rucksacks are rarely waterproof and the contents need protection from rain. Bear in mind Westacott's law which states that rucksacks are always filled to capacity!

98 Even small daypacks come in a bewildering array of designs. All packs should have wide, well-padded shoulder straps. Other features are a matter of individual preference and include
- pockets (both exterior and interior)
- loops on the shoulder straps from to which small items such as a compass, camera, handheld satnav etc. can be attached by tiny karabiners
- elasticated nylon netting on the front of the sack for secreting maps etc.
- elasticated nylon netting pockets for water bottles and small items
- hydration bladder and a tube that can be fed onto the shoulder straps to supply water on demand (see 3:108-10)
- chest strap (also known as a sternum strap) to prevent the shoulder straps slipping, and to assist in stability
- waist strap to help stabilize the rucksack and also for attaching small pockets to contain cameras, handheld satnav etc. Some walkers tuck maps into the waist strap
- fastenings for securing ice-axes and walking poles
- waterproof rain cover (a plastic bag inside the pack is cheaper and less fiddly)

Bum bags

99 Bum bags (known a fanny packs in North America) are packs with an integral belt that is secured around the waist rather than suspended from the shoulders like a rucksack. Small bum bags can be used for items such as keys and wallets that are normally kept in trouser pockets. They can be worn with the zippered pouch facing the front, over the hip or, less elegantly, over the buttocks.

100 Some bum bags that are large enough to contain lightweight waterproofs, a fleece and two water bottles. Some models have a diagonal strap that goes over one shoulder to aid stability. Large bum bags are mostly favoured by those who want to walk fast.

Poles

101 Walking poles (sometimes called trekking poles) have become popular in recent years because they
   - reduce the strain on ankles and knees when descending steep slopes
   - provide additional upthrust when climbing steep slopes
   - help maintain balance in awkward situations such as when crossing stepping stones and fording rivers
   - can probe for firm ground in boggy areas
   - can be used as tent poles by backpackers wishing to reduce the weight of their pack (providing that they have a tent of suitable design)
   - help improve upper body strength and general fitness

102 Poles are usually made in three sections which can slide and lock inside each other so that the length of the pole can be adjusted. When not in use the poles can be shortened to about 70 centimetres allowing them to be attached to a backpack.

103 All poles have a rubber or cork grip with an adjustable strap through which the hands are passed. The more sophisticated versions have a spring-loaded mechanism which allow the poles to retract slightly when going downhill thus reducing the amount of shock transmitted to the hands and wrists. The mechanism can be locked to provide the maximum thrust when going uphill.

104 Poles have a hardened spike for use on rocky terrain over which can be fitted baskets to spread the load on snow and soft ground. When the poles are not in use the spike should be protected with a rubber cap to avoid injuring fellow walkers.

How to use poles

105 The generally accepted technique for using most poles is described below but should be modified in the light of experience so that you find a method that suits you:
   a) One pole is good, two poles are more versatile.

   b) The standard advice is to adjust the length of the pole so that, when holding the handle, your upper arm is vertical and lines up with your hip, and your

elbow forms a right-angle with your forearm. Should this not prove comfortable, you can lengthen or shorten the poles as appropriate
  • when walking uphill, *shorten* the poles
  • when walking downhill, *lengthen* the poles

c) Lengthen the strap on the handle and push your hand *under* and through the loop. Grasp the handle of the pole so that the strap lies under your thumb and palm. Adjust the strap just sufficiently so that it is neither slack nor tight over the wrist.

d) When using poles, the weight is taken on the wrist strap and the hands hold the handles loosely and are used only to direct the pole to the next position. Using poles will become second nature after a little practice.

Care of poles

106 Poles require some attention to keep them in good working order:

a) Every so often, pull the sections apart and thoroughly dry and clean them and ensure that the locking mechanism is working satisfactorily.

b) Poles that have been stored for some time may become corroded. Slide the sections rapidly in and out until any oxide dust is removed, then spray lightly with furniture polish.

c) The locking mechanisms will have to be replaced after extended use. Outdoor shops usually stock replacement items for the more popular brands.

Drawbacks to using poles

107 Some walkers have found that excessive reliance on walking poles can lead to a reduction in their sense of balance. Also, it is difficult to use your hands for anything else. During the course of a day's walk you are likely to
  • open and close gates
  • climb stiles
  • take photographs
  • use binoculars
  • consult your map
  • take compass bearings
  • obey calls of nature
  • eat and drink
  • remove, don and adjust clothing
  • use a handheld satnav

a) Poles get in the way of performing these activities conveniently. They are usually propped against a tree, building or fence, laid on the ground, or allowed to dangle from your wrists. When not in use they should be secured to your rucksack.

b) A solution to some of these problems is to tuck the handles under the chest strap of your rucksack or to suspend the poles from a loop of shockcord attached to the shoulder harness of your rucksack. If the poles are clear of the ground it is possible to walk a few yards unencumbered which is helpful when taking photographs etc. (poles that have a screw thread to which a camera can be attached can serve as a unipod). For information on how to attach a map to a pole see 6:17.

Hydration systems

108 In recent years the role of the traditional water bottle has been challenged by sophisticated hydration systems. Water is sucked from a container in the rucksack via a tube that runs down one of the shoulder straps. A valve incorporating a mouthpiece is fitted to the end of the tube which allows the walker to drink whilst moving.

109 Hydration systems make it easier to sip small quantities of water frequently rather than drinking a large amount occasionally which, experts assure us, is healthier. Some rucksacks now incorporate an integral hydration system and others have a pocket into which one of the stand-alone proprietary products will fit. Hydration systems need to be cleaned regularly to prevent the build-up of bacteria.

110 Hydration systems are expensive but you can make your own for less than 50 pence, plus the cost of a proprietary mouthpiece available from outdoor shops, as follows:

a) Obtain a metre of plastic tubing.

b) Drill a hole the same size as the diameter of the tube through the screw cap of a soft drinks bottle.

c) Insert the tube through the cap of the bottle.

d) Attach the mouthpiece to the other end of the tubing.

e) Place the unit in a side pocket of your rucksack and feed the tube through the hauling loop on the top of the rucksack and down one of the shoulder straps (you may have to sew a couple of D-rings onto the shoulder strap to accommodate the tube or, alternatively, if your rucksack has attachment loops you can fit a couple of miniature karabiners).

Feminine hygiene

111 A device called a SheWee (www.sheewee.com) makes it possible for women to urinate whilst standing. It comprises a body-hugging plastic funnel with a tube that directs the stream away from your feet. Unzip your fly, pull your underwear to one side and place the SheWee into position. There are underclothes specially designed for use with the SheWee.

112 The MoonCup (www.mooncup.co.uk) is a product, available from many high street pharmacies, that dispenses with the need for tampons during menstruation. It is like an inverted diaphragm and is worn internally to collect the fluid which is discarded when the MoonCup is removed. This device is especially useful when backpacking.

Purchasing clothing and equipment

113 The most expensive and important items of gear are likely to be
   • rucksack
   • waterproofs
   • boots

114 The following tips will help you to make wise purchases:
   a) Get an experienced walker to recommend and, if possible, accompany you to a knowledgeable and helpful retailer (a good source for advice is your local rambling club).

   b) Make your purchases during school hours because this is normally a slack period when the staff will have more time to assist you. Casual staff employed during busy periods may lack the requisite experience.

   c) Don't hesitate to admit ignorance, request advice and to ask questions.

   d) Check the company's policies on returned goods.

   e) If the goods do not meet your requirements, go elsewhere.

   f) It may be better to avoid purchases by mail order and the internet until you are experienced.

Sources of inexpensive kit and equipment

115 It has already been mentioned that many walkers buy unnecessarily expensive and over-specified clothing and equipment. Few walkers require jackets designed to withstand the rigours of the Himalayas, so those who only walk and

backpack in temperate climes can buy cheaper, but satisfactory, gear by avoiding the upmarket brands. Here are some suggestions for reducing costs:

a) Millets, and its sister company Blacks, the well-known high street stores, market reasonably-priced kit and equipment of acceptable quality including breathable waterproofs, boots, rucksacks and backpacking tents under their own-brand names of Peter Storm, Eurohike and Blacks.

b) Less expensive gear is marketed under brand names such of Wynnster, Regatta, Hi-Tec and Gelert.

c) Many retailers offer discounts to members of organizations such as the Ramblers and the Youth Hostels Association. Shops may give a discount, if asked, in order to clinch a sale. Paying by cash rather than with a credit card can also help.

d) Retailers have sales to dispose of overstocked items and the previous season's gear.

e) In some popular walking areas such as Keswick and Ambleside in the Lake District, every other shop seems to sell outdoor gear so the competition is fierce which results in heavy discounting.

f) Some supermarkets, such as Lidl, Aldi and Tesco, occasionally sell inexpensive gear but the goods require careful examination to assess the quality.

g) TKMaxx and outlet malls sell outdoor gear at very cheap prices but there is no guarantee that what you are looking for will be stocked.

h) Many of the outdoor forums have links to sources of discounted gear. Members of some outdoor forums sometimes offer second-hand goods for sale.

Gear tests

116 Most outdoor magazines devote many pages in every issue to gear test reports because they earn more income from advertisers than they do from the cover price. A knowledgeable gear tester can provide helpful information about materials, weight etc. but there is such an enormous amount of gear on the market that most testers have little time properly to appraise the product under review. Gear is rarely tested for durability.

117 It is perfectly feasible for many different items of kit (e.g. jacket, fleece, socks and boots) to be tested at the same time, but be wary of a review of several jackets by a single gear tester.

118 Clothing, and particularly footwear, are such personal items that it is almost impossible for a tester to recommend authoritatively a 'best buy' that will suit everyone.

Select bibliography

The following outdoor books contain general information about upmarket clothing and equipment that is likely to be overspecified for lowland walkers.

119 British Mountaineering Council, *Safety on Mountains.* British Mountaineering Council, 2010.

120 Langmuir, Eric, *Mountaincraft and Leadership* 4th ed., Mountain Leader Training Board, 2013.

121 Long, Steve, *Hillwalking; the Official Handbook of the Mountain Leader and the Walking Group Leader Schemes.* Mountain Leader Training UK, 2003.

122 Townsend, Chris, *The Backpacker's Handbook* 4th ed. Ragged Mountain Press, 2011. This book by the well-known British outdoor writer is written for an American audience and is available in the United Kingdom. It contains an excellent description of the properties of the fabrics used in clothing for walkers.

123 Much helpful advice and technical information is available on the internet both from outdoor forums, individual gear manufacturers, and also from some of the bigger chain stores such as
   • www.blacks.co.uk
   • www.cotswoldoutdoor.com
   • www.fieldandtrek.com
   • www.ellis-brigham.com
   • www.gooutdoors.co.uk
Advice from retailers is restricted to lines that they sell. You will look in vain for information about products that the company does not stock.

124 Good sources of news of the latest developments in clothing are magazines such as *The Great Outdoors (tgo), Trail* and *Country Walking* (see Appendix 2). There are also many on-line walking forums that can be accessed by search engines.

Chapter 4 Topographic maps

1   There are many kinds of maps including
- street maps
- geological maps
- historical maps
- road maps
- maps of public transport
- political maps
- topographic maps (these are the maps used by walkers)

2   Some maps, such as street maps, road atlases, and topographic maps attempt to be as accurate as possible within the limitations of scale. Other maps, such as those of the London Underground are stylized and although wildly inaccurate in the sense that they are not to scale, they serve their purpose admirably.

3   The maps used by walkers are called topographic (from the Greek meaning a 'drawing of place') and they attempt to show on a two-dimensional sheet of paper a three-dimensional bird's-eye view of the features on the surface of the earth as accurately as possible within the limits of scale.

Features of topographic maps

4   The following features are found in topographic maps
- scale
- a coordinate system (often referred to as a 'grid')
- contours

Scale

5   Scale is the relationship between a map and the section of the world's surface that it depicts. An easy way of grasping the concept of map scale is to appreciate that it is expressed as a ratio:
   a) In the example of a map with a scale of 1:50,000
- the first figure represents the unit on the map
- the figure after the colon represents the number of units on the ground

Thus, the map is 1/50,000th of the size of the area of the area that it covers.

b) All the topographic maps of the British Isles used by walkers are now metric so it is useful to express the scale of a 1:50,000 map as
- one centimetre to 50,000 centimetres (which is 500 metres)
- or, more conveniently, two centimetres to one kilometre

(Imperial measure *can* be used but 1 inch on the map is 50,000 inches on the ground which converts to 0·7891413 miles which is not a convenient conversion!)

6 The most popular scales on maps used by walkers in the British Isles are:

a) 1:50,000 or 2 centimetres to the kilometre or 1 millimetre to every 50 metres which are used by the following map series
- the *Landranger* series published by the Ordnance Survey (see 5:25-8)
- AA *Leisure maps* (see 5:35-6)
- the *Discovery* series published by the Ordnance Survey of Ireland (see 16:8-9)
- the *Discoverer* series published by the Ordnance Survey of Northern Ireland (see 16:8-9)

b) 1:40,000 or 2·5 centimetres to the kilometre or 1 millimetre to every 40 metres
- the *Walker* series published by Harvey (see 5.40)

c) 1:30.000 or 3 centimetres to the kilometre or 1 millimetre to every 30 metres of the Republic of Ireland published by
- Harvey (see 16:21-2)
- EastWest mapping (see 16:18-20)

d) 1:25,000 or 4 centimetres to the kilometre or 1 millimetre to every 25 metres
- the *Explorer* series published by the Ordnance Survey (see 5:29-33)
- AA *Walker* series (see 5:35)
- Geographia *A-Z Adventure Atlases* (see 5:36)
- the Harvey *Superwalker* series (see 5:38-9)
- the *Activity* series published by the Ordnance Survey of Northern Ireland (see 16:41-2)
- the Ordnance Survey Ireland *Leisure* series (see 16:17)
- the States of Jersey *Official Leisure Map* (see 17:10)

e) 1:15,000 or 6 centimetres to the kilometre or 1 millimetre to 15 metres
- *Official Map of Guernsey* (see 17:9)

7   As can be seen from the above pattern, the easy way to remember what one millimetre on the map measures on the ground is to use the first two figures after the colon. Thus

- 1 millimetre on a 1:50,000 map represents 50 metres on the ground
- 1 millimetre on a 1:40,000 map represents 40 metres on the ground
- 1 millimetre on a 1:30,000 map represents 30 metres on the ground
- 1 millimetre on a 1:25,000 map represents 25 metres on the ground
- 1 millimetre on a 1:15,000 map represents 15 metres on the ground

8   The expressions 'small-scale map' and 'large-scale map' are relative terms. The Ordnance Survey describes its 1:50,000 and 1: 25,000 maps as 'small scale' and reserves the term 'large scale' to the 1:10,000 and scales above this. The *higher* the number after the colon the *smaller* the scale of the map.

Grid systems

9   All the maps of the British Isles used by walkers (with the exception of Jersey in the Channel Islands which uses latitude and longitude) employ an artificial grid system comprising vertical and horizontal lines which form one-kilometre squares on the map. Grids serve a purpose similar to latitude and longitude but are much easier to use. They allow the identification of a location to within 100 metres on 1:50,000 and 1:40,000 maps and, if you use a romer (see 6:70-1), you can give an eight-figure grid reference accurate to within 10 metres on 1:25,000 and 1:30,000 maps.

10   There are four separate and unrelated grid systems in use on maps of the British Isles used by walkers

- the National Grid is used on maps of Great Britain and the Isle of Man
- the Irish Grid is used on maps of both the Republic of Ireland and Northern Ireland
- the Guernsey grid used on the map of Guernsey
- latitude and longitude used on Jersey and Alderney

The National Grid

11   Although the National Grid appears only on maps of Great Britain and the Isle of Man, the area it covers is far wider and includes parts of France, Germany, Scandinavia and Iceland. This region has been divided into twenty-five 500-kilometre squares lettered A to Z but omitting the letter I (see Fig. 1). Great Britain and the Isle of Man occupy only a fraction of this area located in sections of squares H, N, S and T.

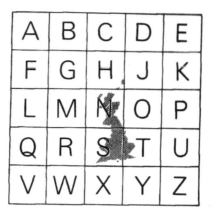

Figure 1   The 500-kilometre sqaures of the National Grid

12   The 500-kilometre squares are divided into twenty-five 100-kilometre squares each of which has been given a second letter, e.g. P, which is always used in conjunction with the letter of the 500-kilometre square as in SP (see Fig. 2). These two-letter 100-kilometre squares are the ones that are of interest to map-readers in Great Britain and the Isle of Man.

13   Maps are further divided into 10-kilometre squares and then one-kilometre squares with the numbered lines running almost exactly due south to north and west to east.

14   The grid lines that interest us are spaced at one-kilometre intervals and are used for providing an exact reference to any point on any map used by walkers, and also for taking compass bearings (see 6:50-6).

How to give a grid reference

15   To give a grid reference accurate to within 100 metres on maps of the British Isles with scales between 1:50,000 and 1:15,000:

   a)   Establish from the key to the map the letters which designate the 100-kilo-metre square in which the map falls e.g. SP. Note that some maps may cover the edges of two adjacent 100-kilometre squares so you must ensure that you designate the correct letters for the feature to which you wish to assign a grid reference. This information is shown in diagrammatic form on the key to the map.

   b)   Find the kilometre square that contains the feature to which you wish to assign a grid reference (see Fig. 3).

   c)   Find the first vertical grid line to the west (left) of the feature.

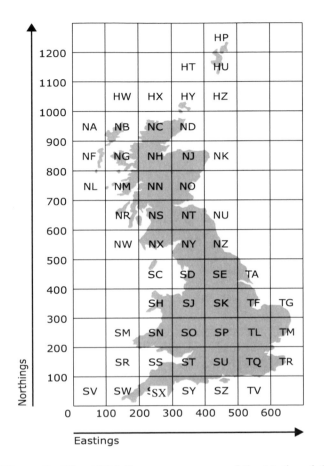

Figure 2   The 100-kilometre squares of the National Grid

d) Follow this vertical grid line either to the bottom or top of the map, whichever is closer, where a two-figure number will be found. This should be
   written down. Note that on the four corners of Ordnance Survey maps another figure in smaller superscript type that precedes the larger two-figures
   e.g. [2]80 will be found. These smaller figures relate to a pre-1951 referenc-
   ing system and should be ignored. Also, on some maps, the grid line numbers are repeated at intervals along the grid so that it may not be necessary
   to follow the line to the edge of the map.

e) Follow the grid line back to the square that contains the feature and either
   use a romer (see 6:70-1) or estimate the number of tenths of a grid square
   along the horizontal line on which the feature lies, and write it down.

f) You now have half of your grid reference consisting of three figures known as an 'easting'.

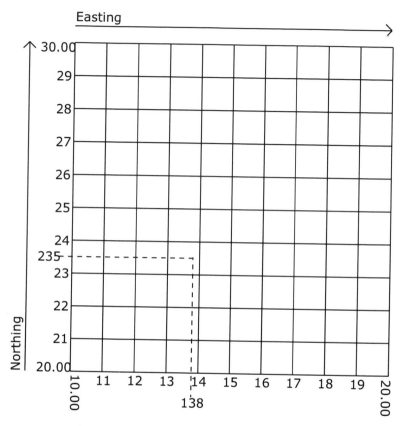

Figure 3   A six-figure grid reference (SP 136235)

16   To find the other half of the grid reference:

a) Return to the kilometre square which contains the feature.

b) Identify the horizontal grid line immediately south (below) the feature.

c) Trace this horizontal grid line either to the left or right margin of the map, whichever is closer, where a two-figure number will be found. This should be written down.

d) Trace the grid line back to the square that contains the feature and either use a romer (see 6.70-1) or estimate the number of tenths of a grid square along the vertical line that the feature lies, and write down the number.

e) You now have the other half of your grid reference which is known as a 'northing'. The reference for the point in Fig. 3, for example, is SP 136235.

17   A six-figure grid reference, which is accurate to within 100-metres, is adequate for most purposes. However, if you use a romer (see 6.70-1) in conjunction with a 1:25,000 map you can give an eight-figure grid reference, accurate to within 10 metres, by estimating the number of hundredths of a grid square beyond the tenths on both the eastings and the northings (see Fig. 4).

18   It is essential to find your eastings before your northings; if you don't, the grid reference will be inaccurate. There are two mnemonics to assist in remembering the correct order:

   a) E comes before N in the alphabet (but you must include the grid letters).

   b) Name the house (the grid square letters), walk in the front door and go along the hall (the easting) and up the stairs (the northing).

   Grid references are an example of a Cartesian coordinate x,y system.

19   There is an explanation of the National Grid on all Ordnance Survey and Harvey maps used by walkers.

20   Grid references are useful for establishing meeting places. It is better to meet at SP 707212 than at 'the gate near the railway bridge on the Quainton road'.

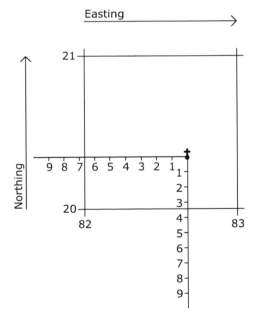

Figure 4   How to estimate an eight-figure grid reference (SP 82682033)

21   Sometimes, a grid reference is shortened by omitting the letters of the 100-kilometre square e.g. 707212. This can cause confusion because this same reference occurs in *every* 100-kilometre square. It is best to give a full grid reference because that location occurs only once in Great Britain and the Isle of Man.

22   Before the introduction of the *Explorer* maps, it was common practice to substitute the distinctive *Landranger*, *Pathfinder* or *Outdoor Leisure* sheet number for the letters of the 100-kilometre grid square. This practice is to be deplored because it is now impossible to find a location when using a map of a different series. The sheet numbers of both the old *Pathfinder* series and the *Outdoor Leisure* maps had distinctive prefixes of 'P' and 'OLM' respectively, but most maps in the *Explorer* series which replaced them have sequential numbers starting at 101 which could easily be confused with a *Landranger* number.

23   For example, the sheet number followed by a six-figure grid reference (e.g. 184/035286) gives the following locations that are 150 miles apart
   • SU 035286 near Salisbury, Wiltshire on *Landranger 184*
   • TM 035286 near Colchester, Essex on *Explorer 184*
It is better to be pedantic and avoid any possible confusion by *always* including the letters of the grid square. An additional advantage is that you can find the location on every map that uses the same grid.

24   Note that the National Grid uses an alphanumeric notation so, although it is standard practice to describe a grid reference in terms of the number of *figures*, the grid *letters* should always be included. Thus
   • SU 035286 is a six-figure grid reference accurate to 100 metres
   • SU 03521863 is an eight-figure grid reference accurate to 10 metres
   • SU 0352418637 is a ten-figure grid reference accurate to 1 metre

The Irish Grid

25   The Irish Grid covers the whole of the island. It is an artificial grid, similar to, but not related, to the National Grid used in Great Britain and the Isle of Man.

26   Ireland is covered in twenty-five 100-kilometre squares lettered from A to Z but omitting I. These are further subdivided into 10-kilometre squares and then one-kilometre squares.

27   The method of calculating a grid reference is the same as that used on maps published by the Ordnance Survey (see 4.15-17).

Grids used in the Channel Islands

28   The following grids are used
  - Guernsey uses its own grid as well as latitude and longitude, and Universal Transverse Mercator (UTM)
  - Jersey and Alderney use latitude and longitude

Depiction of relief

Contours

29   The standard method of depicting relief on modern topographic maps is by drawing contour lines which indicate the third dimension, height, on the two-dimensional, length and width, surface of a map. This feature is the most difficult for beginners to grasp but once understood, it is easy to visualize the shape of the land from the configuration of the contour lines.

30   Contours are drawn at a uniform interval which is stated in the key to the map. A walker who was able to follow the line of a contour would remain at exactly the same elevation above sea level for the duration of the walk.

31   Fig. 5a shows two hills at sea level with contours sketched in. Assume that the three-dimensional model is made of ice, and the contours of thin wire. If it were possible to melt the ice, the wire contours would sink to the baseboard on which the model stands and look exactly like the contours of a map (see Fig. 5b).

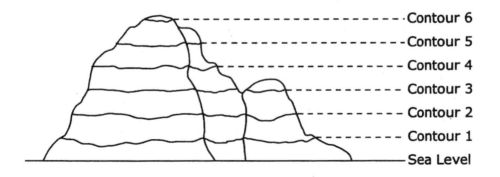

Figure 5a   The profile of a hill showing contour lines

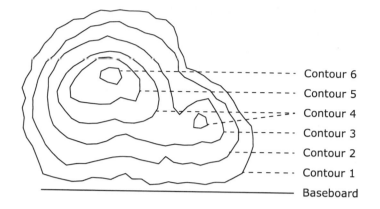

Figure 5b   How the contours would be shown on a map

32   The shape of hills and valleys can be reconstructed by projecting the contours as shown in Figs. 6a-d. No two features have identically shaped contour lines, but some fall into certain categories that it is helpful to be able to recognize (see Figs. 6a-d).

33   The elevation of contour lines is shown only at intervals and it is often necessary to trace the line of the contour for some distance to establish the elevation. Unless the elevation is traced, it can be difficult to decide whether a hill or a valley is depicted because the patterns are the same (see Fig. 6c). However, if a stream is shown it *must* be a valley and if there is no stream it is *likely* to be a hill (but be aware that dry valleys are quite common in chalk and limestone country). In such cases it is essential to trace the contour lines to establish their values. The figures indicating the elevation of contour lines always read *up* the slope so if the figures on the contours can be read you must be looking uphill.

34   Every fifth contour is shown as a thicker line and is known as an 'index contour'. The quickest way of calculating the elevation of a particular location is to
   • establish the contour interval from the map key
   • count the index contour lines and multiply by the interval between the index lines
   • count the number of thin contour lines at each end, multiply these by the contour interval and add to the figure obtained from the index lines

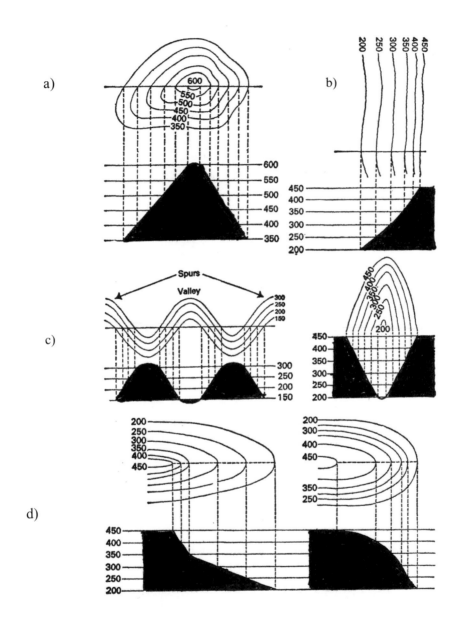

Figure 6   The shape of hills and valleys reconstructed by projecting contours:
a) hill; b) escarpment; c) valleys; d) concave and convex slopes

35   For example, Fig. 7 shows contours taken from an *Explorer* map. According to the key, the contour interval is 5 metres so the interval between the two index contour lines is 25 metres. Therefore the elevation is 25+ 3 thin contours (15 metres) giving a total of 40 metres.

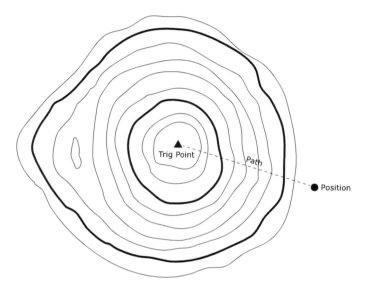

Figure 7   Counting contours

36   Contours depict the elevation of the land *at the point at which they are shown on the map;* they tell you nothing about the shape of the land between contours.

37   Contours spaced at regular intervals *generally* indicate a regular slope but between contours there may be, in theory, an almost vertical drop of
   • 14·9 metres on maps with a contour interval of 15 metres
   • 9·9 metres on maps with a contour interval of 10 metres (approximately the height of the roof of a two-storey house)
   • 4·9 metres on maps with a contour interval of 5 metres (approximately the height of the top of the parapet of a railway bridge that crosses a road)

38   Similarly, if a path is shown following, and occasionally crossing, the same contour it does not necessarily mean that the path is undulating significantly. It may only vary in elevation by a metre but it could fluctuate by as much as
   • 29·9 metres on maps with a contour interval of 15 metres
   • 19·9 metres on maps with a contour interval of 10 metres
   • 9·9 metres on maps with a contour interval of 5 metres

39   Theoretically, there could be a series of undulations between contours. If there were five this would amount to a cumulative ascent of

- 149·9 metres on maps with a contour interval of 15 metres
- 99·5 metres on maps with a contour interval of 10 metres
- 49·5 metres on maps with a contour interval of 5 metres

40   In practice, the laws of probability and natural topography, suggest that paths

- that do not cross a contour are reasonably level
- that cross a contour either climb or descend

Nevertheless, you should be aware of the limitations of contours.

Spot heights

41   Spot heights show the elevation at a particular point indicated by a tiny dot. Spot heights may be derived either from ground or aerial surveys.

Accuracy of topographic maps

42   There is a popular misconception that a good map should be absolutely accurate. This is an impossible ideal for many reasons of which the most obvious are given below.

43   Virtually all maps are inaccurate from the date of publication. This is because the survey on which the map was based took place some time before publication and during the intervening period changes to the landscape will almost inevitably have taken place. The only likely exceptions to this rule are uninhabited wilderness areas of inaccessible mountains, deserts and the polar regions.

44   A map is flat whereas the earth is an ellipsoid which is why a map of the world distorts significantly, especially at the poles. Thus, on most projections, Greenland appears to be larger than the United States although it is actually only one quarter of the latter's size. However, on any map used for navigation by walkers in the British Isles, the distortion caused by the curvature of the earth is so minute that it can be ignored.

45   Surveyors and draughtpersons are human and occasionally make errors. When reported to the Ordnance Survey, the walker will receive a letter of thanks and the error will be corrected when the map is revised. Here are some examples:

a)   A spot height near Knole in Kent was given as 498 metres (the correct elevation is 152 metres) on *Explorer 147* (edition A).

b)   A seriously inaccurate depiction of a junction on a main road in Amersham, Buckinghamshire on *Explorer 172* (edition A).

46   Some map publishers incorporate minor inaccuracies, known as 'fingerprints', into its maps in order to assist in the detection of copyright infringements. Fingerprints are chosen carefully and used sparingly so they should not affect the map-reader. Fingerprints are commercially sensitive secrets but they are rumoured to include

   • non-existent farm buildings

   • non-existent minor tributaries of streams

   • tiny kinks on rivers

   • exaggerated curves on roads

   • deletion or addition of apostrophes

   • assigning names to anonymous features such as woods, crags and hills

47   The Ordnance Survey denies that it ever uses fingerprints. The only known case of copyright infringement involving a suspected fingerprint turned out to be the reproduction of a genuine error made by the Ordnance Survey itself. In a more recent instance, the Ordnance Survey won a case for copyright infringement based on stylistic and other grounds, not on fingerprints.

Selection and omission

48   For a map to be completely accurate it would have to be the same size as the area that it was attempting to portray, and the scale would be shown as 1:1. A paper map on this scale would be impossible to make (it is, in theory, possible to make a 1:1 digital map) but it serves to illustrate the point that as soon as a reduction in scale is made, some detail is inevitably lost. Because of the limitations of scale, it is not possible to show every feature and so a selection has to be made.

49   Until recently, the boundaries of military land were shown on Ordnance Survey maps but sensitive buildings were omitted which resulted in some curious anomalies. The most prominent building in the North York Moors National Park is the early warning radar station at Fylingdales (grid reference SE 866967), but as it was not on the map it could not be used to take a compass bearing.

Distortion and simplification

50   Certain essential features are distorted ('displacement' is the term favoured by cartographers). This is done in the interests of map-readers because, even though there may be a departure from absolute accuracy, the effect is to make the map easier to read, understand and use:

   a) On *Explorer* maps, a road that is less than four metres wide is depicted by a line that is 0·5 millimetres wide, yet 0·5 millimetres represents 12·5 metres on the ground. If the road were drawn to scale it would be almost invisible.

The knock-on effect of this displacement is that the fields, gardens, buildings etc. on either side of the road will be shown as marginally smaller than they actually are.

b) The displacement of roads results in a general smoothing of bends and curves making them appear less acute than they actually are.

c) The width of the symbol for a public bridleway on *Explorer* maps measures 0·3 millimetres which represents 8·3 metres on the ground. This is unlikely to cause displacement but sometimes puzzles walkers using handheld satnavs because public rights of way were not always plotted accurately (see 5:23) which, when combined with any inherent inaccuracy of the satnav (see 9:38), can result in a discrepancy of as much as 15 metres between the route shown on the satnav screen and the path on the ground (see also 9:39).

d) On maps of upland areas, a certain amount of simplification takes place when showing precipitous slopes.

Date of survey

51 A map can only be accurate at the time of the survey and the countryside is constantly changing. For example
- new roads are built and old roads are realigned
- canals are filled in
- reservoirs created
- building development takes place
- farmers grub hedges and erect new barns
- woods are felled and forests planted
- footbridges are washed away
- pubs and public conveniences may close

The map-user must always think of the possible changes which may have happened since the date of the survey whenever the map appears not to agree with the terrain.

In conclusion

50 The study of maps can greatly enhance your walking experience. Instead of being led as part of a group, or slavishly following instructions in a footpath guide, the close examination of maps will enable you to plan your own routes to suit your particular interests. Authors of footpath guides do not always choose the best routes. For example, a careful reading of the map can significantly improve on Alfred Wainwright's deservedly popular Coast to Coast Walk both scenically and also by avoiding some sections of road walking (see http://walkwithwestacott.com/the-coast-to-coast-walk).

Select bibliography

The information given in this chapter can be supplemented with some of the books listed in the bibliography in Chapter 5 (5:45-64).

Chapter 5   Maps used by walkers in the British Isles

1   This chapter describes the maps used by walkers in the British Isles. Note that:

   a)   The Ordnance Survey has licensed the Automobile Association and Geographia to publish a selection of maps at scales of 1:50,000 and 1:25,000 (see 5:35-6). They are

- the AA *Leisure* series with a scale of 1:50,000
- the AA *Walker* series with a scale of 1:25,000
- the Geographia *A-Z Adventure Atlases* with a scale of 1:25,000

   As these are, in effect, reproductions of Ordnance Survey mapping, whenever a reference to, or a description of, Ordnance Survey maps is made, it will apply equally to maps of the same scale published by the Automobile Association and Geographia *unless a specific exception is made.*

   b)   The maps covering other parts of the British Isles are mentioned here but described in more detail in the chapters dealing with the walking opportunities in each individual country.

2   The topographic maps of the British Isles are among the best in the world. The bodies responsible for mapping include:

   a)   The Ordnance Survey is the government agency responsible for the mapping of

- England
- Scotland
- Wales
- the Isle of Man (*Landranger* map only)

   b)   The Ordnance Survey of Northern Ireland (OSNI) is the government agency responsible for the mapping of Northern Ireland.

   c)   Harvey Maps is a commercial publisher that markets maps for walkers covering selected areas of Great Britain and Ireland (see 5:37-40).

   d)   The Ordnance Survey of Ireland (OSi) is the government agency responsible for the mapping of the Irish Republic.

   e)   The Crown Dependency of the Isle of Man is mapped at 1:50,000 in the Ordnance Survey *Landranger* series (sheet 95), but publishes its own 1:25,000 map (17:5).

f) The Crown Dependencies of Jersey and Guernsey are responsible for their own mapping (see 17:7-10).

Ordnance Survey maps

3 **IMPORTANT NOTE:** The Ordnance Survey publishes several helpful free leaflets that can be downloaded from its website. Readers are strongly advised to download the following to be used in conjunction with this chapter and Chapters 6, 7 & 8:

a) The keys of *Landranger* and *Explorer* maps from www.ordnancesurvey.co.uk/education-research/resources/map-symbol-sheets.html

b) The Ordnance Survey *Guide to Map Reading and Navigation* from www.ordnancesurvey.co.uk/docs/ebooks/map-reading.pdf

4 The Ordnance Survey gives its map series for walkers distinctive titles
  • *Landranger* (scale 1:50,000)
  • *Explorer* (scale 1:25,000)

5 Maps in both these series are revised regularly and this information, together with the copyright date of the edition, is shown on the key. The extent of the revision is indicated by a code made up of a letter followed, in some cases, by a number:

a) When a sheet is fully revised, the edition letter is advanced, e.g. from A to B, and the copyright date is changed. Note that even a fully revised edition does not necessarily mean that all field boundaries are updated; some may date from surveys made thirty years ago.

b) When a sheet is revised with significant changes the edition letter is unchanged but a number is added or advanced, e.g. A to A1 or B2 to B3, and the copyright date is changed.

c) When a sheet is reprinted with minor changes the edition is underscored, e.g. A2 to A2, and the copyright date remains unchanged.
  STOP PRESS: a new system of numbering will be introduced in June 2015. Full details are at www.ordnancesurvey.co.uk/docs/collateral/ordnance-survey-leisure-map-catalogue.pdf.

d) Note that the copyright date alone appears on the 1:50,000 and 1:25,000 maps published by the Automobile Association and Geographia.

6   Information about the latest edition of any *Landranger* and *Explorer* map may be obtained from the on-line map catalogue www.ordnancesurvey.co.uk/docs/collateral/ordnance-survey-leisure-map-catalogue.pdf. Walkers who are interested in the edition history of Ordnance Survey maps can find the information at www.watsonlv.addr.com/os-maps.shtml.

7   Both *Landranger* and *Explorer* maps are general-purpose maps and include some 'invisible' features that are normally of little interest to walkers. These tend to clutter the map and make it more difficult to read. Examples are the administrative boundaries of
- countries
- counties
- unitary authorities
- districts
- metropolitan districts
- London boroughs
- civil and community parishes (on *Explorer* maps only)
- parliamentary and European constituencies (on *Explorer* maps only)

8   Other boundaries that are more relevant to walkers are those of
- national parks
- forest parks
- National Trust and National Trust for Scotland properties
- access land (on *Explorer* maps only)

9   Rights of way that follow the line of two or more boundaries that coincide can be masked and make the details on the map difficult to read. Harvey maps do not show administrative boundaries

10   In order to understand a map properly it is necessary to be able to interpret the symbols used which will be found in the key on the map. These symbols vary slightly depending on the scale and map series. The most common can be learnt quickly, but be aware that some have variants that look similar at a first glance. On *Landranger* maps the symbols for a place of worship lacking a tower, spire, dome or minaret and a site of a monument can look similar and cause confusion. It is necessary to check the key constantly until you are thoroughly familiar with all of the symbols.

11   An indication of the amount of detail shown can be gained by comparing the keys of the *Landranger* and *Explorer* series. As is shown below, the two series have their own key but within each series every map has a standard key contain-

ing all the symbols and features used in the whole series. Thus, the key to a map covering the Yorkshire Dales will include information about coastal features.

12   It is annoying to have your home or favourite starting point for local walks located on the edge of a map which could involve the purchase of as many as four sheets to cover the area in which you want to walk. The Ordnance Survey will print you special editions, known as *OS Select*, of both *Landranger* and *Explorer* maps centred on any point that you choose in either folded or flat format. The cost is approximately twice that of the standard edition plus post and packing. Copies can be ordered from the on-line map shop (www.ordnancesurvey.co.uk/mapshop) or from selected Ordnance Survey stockists.

Ordnance Survey conventions

13   Many walkers assume that all the information they require about Ordnance Survey maps is contained in the key of the map series. This is not so and there is some useful information that is not published about the following
     • field boundaries
     • electricity transmission lines
     • water features
     • tourism and leisure facilities
Walkers should be aware that Ordnance Survey draughtpersons are allowed some leeway in what is included in the map on which they are working, providing it is done in the interests of clarity.

Field boundaries

14   Field boundaries are shown on *Explorer* maps (but not on *Landrangers*) although there is no mention of them in the key. A field boundary may be a fence, wall, berm or hedge and they may easily be recognized on *Explorer* maps as a pattern of thin black lines. Walls that are out of repair and less than 0.3 metres high are not depicted, nor are straggly hedges containing gaps (see also 5:5(a).

Electricity transmission lines

15   The pylons (known in the industry as 'towers') and poles of electricity transmission lines on *Explorers* are plotted accurately so navigators can use them to help fix their position.

16   On *Landranger* maps the transmission lines are plotted accurately but the supporting pylons are spaced conventionally and so their positions are not reliable *except* where the transmission line changes direction. Poles are not depicted.

Water features

17   On both *Explorer* and *Landranger* maps, watercourses (i.e. canals, rivers and streams) more than 5 metres wide are depicted with double blue lines and are plotted accurately within the limits of scale, but some smoothing of meanders (bends) may take place.

18   On both *Explorer* and *Landranger* maps, watercourses less than 5 metres wide are depicted with a single blue line of standard width. Some smoothing of meanders (bends) may take place.

19   All footbridges are depicted on *Explorer* maps whereas on *Landranger* maps only those footbridges over watercourses more than 5 metres wide are shown. This is an important piece of information because walkers using *Landrangers* may assume that if a footbridge is not shown then it does not exist.

20   Bodies of water (i.e. ponds, lakes, llyns, lochans, lochs, tarns etc.) have to be at least
   • 10 metres wide to be depicted on *Explorer* maps
   • 50 metres wide to be depicted on *Landranger* maps
This has implications for map-reading. For example, at Blackbeck Tarn (grid reference NY 201129), east of Haystacks in the Lake District, *Explorer OL4* shows another five small, unnamed tarns within an area measuring 350 metres by 250 metres; *Landranger 89* depicts Blackbeck Tarn alone. Thus, a walker who had gone astray and was trying to relocate using the *Landranger* map could be confused if unaware of the 50-metre convention.

Tourist and leisure information

21   Tourist and leisure information on maps used by walkers is usually indicated by symbols:
   a) *Explorer* maps employ the most comprehensive set of symbols which, in most cases, indicate the exact location of the feature. The major exception is the beer mug symbol which denotes a public house. They are shown in rural areas only (i.e. villages, hamlets and in isolated locations) presumably on the grounds that all towns have at least one pub. You should be aware that in villages and hamlets the beer mug symbol (which is not to scale and appears to measure 90 metres square) on *Explorers*, and the abbreviation PH on *Landrangers*, merely indicates the presence of at least one pub, but its location may only be approximate. For example, on edition A of *Explorer 133*, in Jane Austen's village of Chawton in Hampshire (grid reference SU 708375), the symbol was shown some 250 metres from the pub's actual location. In later editions, the same pub is shown much nearer to its correct location.

b) Car parks and public conveniences on both *Explorers* and *Landrangers* are shown in rural areas only with, if necessary, the exact location indicated by an arrow.

c) The symbols depicted on *Explorer* maps include
   - viewpoints
   - picnic sites
   - walks and trails
   - cycle trails
   - horse riding
   - preserved railways
   - theme and pleasure parks
   - cathedrals and abbeys
   - castles and forts
   - buildings of historical interest
   - museums
   - English Heritage properties
   - country parks
   - gardens and arboreta
   - nature reserves
   - water activities
   - fishing
   - slipways (for launching boats)
   - car parks
   - park and ride
   - public telephones in rural areas
   - information centres
   - visitor centres
   - recreation and sports centres
   - selected camping and caravan sites
   - golf courses
   - public houses in rural areas
   - public conveniences in rural areas

Landranger maps also show tourist information but with fewer categories.

Secondary sources

22 The Ordnance Survey relies on secondary sources, such as local authorities, for some of the information that is recorded on its maps. Examples include

- archaeological and historical information
- rights of way in England and Wales
- boundaries of access land, national parks, National Trust and National Trust for Scotland properties

23 Rights of way for maps of England and Wales are incorporated from Definitive Maps (see 14:7-12) but even though they are legal documents they were sometimes compiled in a haphazard and sloppy manner showing routes that few walkers have ever used. Where black pecked lines appear running close to rights of way on maps of upland areas, these generally depict the route actually visible on the ground.

24 For example, the *Explorer* map of the broad, flat summit of St. Sunday Crag (grid reference NY 369134) in the Lake District south west of Patterdale, shows the right of way heading north east. However, the route generally used by walkers can only be found by walking due north across a stony area, on which no path is visible, to a cairn which marks where the steep descent commences. It is only at that point that black pecked lines appear on the map. The right of way depicted on the map is rarely used.

Landranger maps

25 This series covers the whole of Great Britain and the Isle of Man in 204 sheets each covering an area measuring 40 km x 40 km. The Ordnance Survey aims to ensure that, on average, each sheet is revised every three years and never longer than every six years. Minor revisions to take into account significant changes, especially to the road system, are incorporated whenever the map is reprinted. Every sheet is identified by a sequential number which starts at 1 for the northern tip of the Shetland Isles and ends at 204 at The Lizard in Cornwall.

26 Some *Landrangers* covering popular tourist areas are now available as *Landranger Maps – Active*. They are printed on durable, waterproof paper that can be marked and highlighted with a washable ink pen.

27 *Landranger* maps show public rights of way in England and Wales distinguishing between

- roads
- footpaths
- bridleways

- roads used as public paths (RUPPs)
- byways open to all traffic (BOATs)
- restricted byways
- other routes with public access (except in urban areas)
- selected, named long-distance paths

28   The only significant feature essential for walking in lowland areas that is lacking are field boundaries. These maps are suitable for navigating in mountainous
and moorland regions, and are useful for the initial planning of routes in lowland areas. Many walkers prefer to rely on the more detailed *Explorer* series
when actually walking, although the shape of the land in upland areas often
stands out better on *Landranger* maps, as does the symbol for paths in Scotland.

Explorer maps

29   These superb 1:25,000 maps show the countryside in great detail and are essential for navigating in lowland areas because they show field boundaries (see
5:5(a). They are numbered from 101, starting in the Isles of Scilly, and finishing
at 470 in the Shetland Isles (they do not cover the Isle of Man, the Channel
Islands or Northern Ireland). The 34 discontinued *Outdoor Leisure* maps have
been incorporated into the *Explorer* series but are not part of the sequential
numbering system; they are prefixed by the letters OL.
STOP PRESS: a new system of numbering will be introduced in June 2015.
Full details are at www.ordnancesurvey.co.uk/docs/collateral/ordnance-survey-
leisure-map-catalogue.pdf.

30   Single-sided *Explorer* sheets cover an area measuring 30 kilometres by 20 kilometres and double sided maps cover an area 20 kilometres by 20 kilometres on
each side. The Ordnance Survey aims to ensure that, on average, each sheet is
revised every two-and-a half years and never longer than every six-and-a half
years. Some *Explorer* maps covering popular walking areas are available in a
special *Active* edition printed on waterproof paper. The contour interval is

- 5 metres on the 333 sheets that cover lowland areas
- 10 metres on the 70 sheets that cover upland areas

31   An examination of the key to an *Explorer* map will reveal the extraordinary
amount of information that each map contains. For example, the following types
of vegetation are depicted

- coniferous trees
- non-coniferous trees
- coppice
- scrub

- orchard
- bracken, heath or rough pasture
- marsh, reeds or saltings

It takes time to become familiar with them all so it is comforting to know that they are available for reference on the key of every map in the series.

32 *Explorer* maps depict all categories of rights of way:

  a) In England and Wales
- roads
- footpaths
- bridleways
- roads used as public paths (RUPPs)
- byways open to all traffic (BOATS)
- restricted byways
- national trails/long distance routes and recreational routes
- other routes with public access (not normally shown in urban areas)
- permitted footpaths
- permitted bridleways
- off-road cycle routes

  b) In Scotland
- Long Distance Routes
- Great Trails

33 The most important feature for navigating in lowland areas is the field boundary (hedge, wall or fence) which allows walkers to follow the true line of the path and to recognize immediately the field that they are in. There is no mention of field boundaries on the key to these maps but they are easily recognized as a pattern of black lines.

Other Ordnance Survey maps

34 Two other map series, which can often be found locally in large public libraries, estate agents and surveyors' offices are useful for occasional reference especially by those involved in protecting rights of way:

  a) 1:10,000 (1 centimetre to 100 metres) is the basic map from which both the *Explorer* and *Landranger* series is derived. These maps can be useful for establishing the true line of the path where it is not entirely clear on the smaller-scale maps.

b) 1:2500 (1 centimetre to 25 metres) gives Ordnance Survey field numbers which are sometimes referred to in planning applications and proposals for diverting and extinguishing rights of way.

Other maps used by walkers

35 The Automobile Association has published two series of maps licensed by the Ordnance Survey which are, in effect, clones of *Explorer* and *Landranger* maps respectively:

a) The 1:25,000 *Walker* maps cover popular areas of the country. This enables the maps to be centred on the region which often reduces the number of sheets required. For example, three *Explorer* maps cover the Chilterns Area of Outstanding Natural Beauty, whereas one double-sided *Walker* map encompasses it completely. The format is considerably larger than *Explorers* which makes map-reading in the field more difficult in windy weather so it may be helpful to cut each sheet in half.

b) The 1:50,000 *Leisure* maps are also centred on selected, popular areas.

36 Geographia publishes a series of *A-Z Adventure Atlases* containing 1:25,000 Ordnance Survey maps of popular areas for those who prefer their maps in a book rather than conventional sheet format. This allows the inclusion of a comprehensive index to towns, villages, hamlets, natural features, nature reserves, car parks and youth hostels. Each index entry has a page reference and a six-figure grid reference. Each atlas covers an area of countryside popular with walkers and has the same footprint of a folded *Explorer* map.

Harvey maps

37 Harvey publish maps especially designed for walkers, cyclists and horse-riders at scales of 1:40,000 and 1:25,000. These are based on their own surveys supplemented by aerial photography and are comparable to the Ordnance Survey *Landranger* and *Explorer* series respectively. They cover the most popular walking areas in the uplands of Great Britain and Ireland, and the company also publishes strip maps to some long distance paths. Harvey maps show the National Grid, are printed on waterproof paper and come with the covers separate from the map in a plastic slip case. They are more convenient to handle than Ordnance Survey maps.

Superwalker maps

38 This series has a scale of 1:25,000 and is of particular interest to walkers. The design differs in many ways from Ordnance Survey *Explorer* maps and the overall effect is perhaps not quite so pleasing.

39   There are significant differences between *Superwalker* and *Explorer* maps:

a)   As these maps are designed specifically for walkers some of the non-essential information found on *Explorer* maps, including administrative boundaries, is omitted.

b)   Contours are at 15-metre intervals, so the shape of the land stands out better than it does on *Explorer* maps. The larger interval has the effect of smoothing out minor hillocks and depressions so an 'auxiliary interval' is used if considered necessary.

c)   Colour is used to show different types of vegetation which improves clarity when compared with the Ordnance Survey use of symbols.

d)   Rocky outcrops are indicated by changing the colour of the contour lines from brown to grey which again obviates the need for symbols and makes the map easier to read.

e)   Rights of way in the form of footpaths and bridleways are shown on maps of England and Wales but roads used as public path (RUPPs), byways open to all traffic (BOATs) and restricted byways are all depicted as bridleways.

f)   An interesting feature is that a distinction is made between paths that are visible on the ground and those that are not. The depiction of the latter is not always accurate because sections that are visible on the ground are sometimes inexplicably omitted. For example, the alternative Coast to Coast route above Easedale in the Lake District that runs over Calf Crag (NY 302204), Gibson Knott (NY 318099) and Helm Crag (NY 326093) before descending to Grasmere is a clearly visible path all the way and is depicted as such on the *Explorer* map, but the *Superwalker* map shows the route with sections missing.

g)   Permissive paths are also shown together with other paths that are not rights of way. Long distance paths are neither named nor given a special symbol.

h)   An important omission is the field boundaries across farmland in upland areas which are so helpful when map-reading. Boundary walls and fences are only shown on mountain and moorland beyond the limits of cultivation. A useful distinction is made between walls and fences that are maintained, and those in disrepair.

Walker maps

40   This series has a scale of 1:40,000 and serves the same purpose as *Landranger* maps at a slightly larger scale which gives a good overview of the upland regions that they cover. *Walker* maps, unlike *Landranger* maps, show field boundaries but only those located beyond cultivated land.

Care of maps

41   Maps need to be treated with care and protected from the elements. Ordnance Survey maps will last longer, and fold more easily in a map case if the covers are removed. Some walkers cut their *Explorer* maps in half which makes them easier to fold and fit into a map case.

42   Map cases can be purchased from outdoor shops but, with a few exceptions, they are rarely waterproof for long and soon tear. They are designed to be worn round the neck which, apart from looking odd, can be a nuisance in a strong wind so many walkers prefer to carry maps in a self-sealing freezer bag that can be slipped into a convenient pocket, or tucked securely into the waist-strap of a rucksack or bum bag.

43   Maps can be made waterproof by painting them on both sides with clear matt varnish purchased from hardware stores. The maps take on a slightly brown tinge but become highly water-resistant and can still be marked with a pencil. This method is much less expensive than buying document sprays from stationers, or laminating them. All Harvey maps are printed on waterproof paper and there are waterproof editions of some *Explorer* and *Landranger* maps covering popular walking areas.

Non-paper maps

44   There are a number of Ordnance Survey and Harvey maps available on-line. Information about using maps with computers and handheld satnavs can be found in Chapter 9.

Select bibliography

45   In the last few years the Ordnance Survey has discontinued the *Pathfinder* and *Outdoor Leisure* series and replaced them with the *Explorer* series which, to all intents and purposes, are the same but in a larger and more convenient format. Some of the titles listed in this bibliography were published before this change took place so wherever the term *Pathfinder* or *Outdoor Leisure* is used, substitute *Explorer*.

46   Brotherton, Lyle, *The Ultimate Navigation Manual.* HarperCollins, 2011. This is an exceptionally detailed treatise covering all aspects of the subject except lowland navigation. It should be read in conjunction with the list of amendments published on the author's website http://micronavigation.com/wp-content/uploads/Important-corrections-to-first-print-of-the-UNM.pdf.

47   Cliff, Peter, *Mountain Navigation* 5th ed. Published by the author at Ardenbeg, Grant Road, Grantown-on-Spey PH26 3LD.

48   Forte, Carlo, *Navigation in the Mountains: the Definitive Guide for Hill Walkers, Mountaineers & Leaders: the Official Navigation Book for All Mountain Leader Training Schemes.* Mountain Training UK, 2012.

49   Harley, J. B., *Ordnance Survey Maps: a Descriptive Manual.* Ordnance Survey, 1976. This scholarly work is no longer in print but it can be found in many large public reference libraries. It does not cover 1:25,000 maps published since 1974 but is still useful to those interested in cartography for the description of the principles on which Ordnance Survey maps are compiled.

50   Hawkins, Pete, *Map and Compass: the Art of Navigation* 3rd ed. Cicerone Press, 2003. The title indicates that it covers all kinds of navigation but it concentrates almost entirely on navigation for hillwalkers.

51   Hawkins, Pete, *Navigation; Techniques and Skills for Walkers*. Cicerone Press, 2010.

52   Higley, Chris, *Old Series to Explorer; a Field Guide to the Ordnance Map.* The Charles Close Society for the Study of Ordnance Survey Maps, 2011. This is a history of those maps with scales ranging from the 1:126720 to 1:25,000 published by the Ordnance Survey.

53   Keay, Wally, *Land Navigation* 2nd ed. Duke of Edinburgh's Award, 1999. A good general introduction to navigation for walkers. Lowland navigation is treated in a single chapter.

54   Langmuir, Eric, *Mountaincraft and Leadership* 4th ed., Mountain Leader Training Board, 2013.

55   Marsh, Terry, *Map-reading Skills: an Introduction to Map-reading and Basic Navigation.* Jarrold, 2007.

56   Mee, Pat and Mee, Brian, *Outdoor Navigation; Handbook for Tutors.* Harvey, 2010.

57   Monmonier, Mark, *How to Lie with Maps* 2nd ed. University of Chicago Press, 1996. A fascinating book that describes some of the problems and pitfalls of cartography.

58   Owen, Tim, & Pilbeam, Elaine, *Ordnance Survey; Map Makers to Britain since 1791.* Ordnance Survey/HMSO, 1992. The latest history of the Ordnance Survey.

59   Saunders, Colin, *Navigation and Leadership; a Manual for Walkers* 2nd ed revised by Julian Tippett. Ramblers' Association, 1994. This, the best guide to lowland map-reading, is a teaching text. It is out of print but a copy containing some revisions in manuscript can be downloaded from www.ramblers.org.uk.

60   Seymour, W. A., *History of the Ordnance Survey.* Dawson, 1980.

61   Tippett, Julian, *Navigation for Walkers.* Cordee, 2001. An excellent introduction to the subject that deals with both lowland and upland techniques.

62   Walker, Kevin, *Mountain Navigation Techniques.* Constable, 1986.

63   Walker, Kevin, *Navigation; Finding Your Way on Mountain and Moorland.* Frances Lincoln, 2007.

Websites

64   Much useful information about maps and mapping is available on-line at
   • Harvey Maps: www.harveymaps.co.uk
   • Ordnance Survey: www.ordnancesurvey.co.uk

Chapter 6 Map-reading and basic navigation techniques

1   Map-reading and navigation is a complicated subject in which experts some-times employ techniques that the majority of walkers will probably never use. Nevertheless, there are some basic techniques that are easy to acquire and with which every walker should be familiar.

2   Many walkers are content to enjoy the countryside either in the company of others who are responsible for route-finding, or they will use a guidebook. However, the pleasures of walking can be greatly increased if you are a compe-tent map-reader because you can work out your own routes to suit your particu-lar interests. You learn to understand the shape of the land; and if something on your walk intrigues you, then you can make a diversion to satisfy your curiosity.

3   The essentials of map-reading are easily acquired and one of its delights is that you never stop learning. Indeed, many walkers find that the pleasure of plan-ning a new route from the map is almost as enjoyable as the walk itself. Most instruction manuals treat lowland and upland navigation techniques as separate subjects notwithstanding that the principles are exactly the same. The only dif-ference between them is that hill-walkers may use some techniques that are not employed in lowland countryside. This book treats map-reading and navigation as one subject regardless of the location. In this chapter, all the basic techniques useful in both lowland and upland areas are described and in Chapter 8 those advanced methods that are mainly applicable to upland areas are discussed.

4   Walkers can learn to map-read from a manual, by attending navigation classes, or can be taught by a friend. The National Navigation Award Scheme (www.nnas.org.uk) sets national standards for a syllabus at three levels - bronze, silver and gold and keeps a register of centres which offer approved courses. Map-reading classes are also organized by some education authorities, and the Ramblers' Association.

5   Whichever method you choose, consider learning map-reading skills in the safety of lowland countryside where you are rarely out of sight of a road or human habitation for more than a few minutes. You can gain confidence in your skills before practising them in the more demanding environment of moorland and mountain.

6 Map-reading in lowland countryside is often more difficult than it is in upland areas. Mountain and moorland paths are more likely to be

- clear on the ground
- the path network is less dense
- there are likely to be fewer obstructions

7 Some of the most difficult areas in which to navigate are popular lowland locations such as the Devil's Punch Bowl, Leith Hill and Box Hill in Surrey, and the New Forest. This is because they

- are well-wooded
- have a dense network of paths and tracks that are not rights of way which have been created organizations such as the National Trust. Many of these non-definitive routes are not depicted on Ordnance Survey maps
- contain fire breaks
- have trails made by foresters

But you are unlikely to come to any harm if you go astray because you are unlikely to be far from a road or habitation, whereas, even in fine weather, it can be a serious matter if you get lost in remote, upland countryside.

8 The following instructions are based on using Ordnance Survey *Explorer* maps but much of the information will also apply to all 1:25,000 and 1:30,000 maps covering the constituent countries of the British Isles.

Making a start

9 A good way of starting to learn the basics of map-reading is to buy a copy of the *Explorer* map of your home area. Familiarize yourself with the most important symbols shown on the key and walk around your neighbourhood with map in hand. Townies should plan and follow a route that includes side roads, alleyways and parks and note the amount of detail that the map shows. Canals have towpaths that are well worth exploring to note the path junctions, bridges etc. on your map. Once you have become used to map-reading it is time to go further afield and explore some real countryside. If you live in a rural area you probably already know some of the local paths so you should follow them whilst constantly referring to the map.

10   The basic technique of lowland map-reading in England and Wales is to follow rights of way from feature to feature on your route. A feature is something obvious that is marked on the map such as

- roads
- field boundaries (hedges, walls and fences)
- farms and buildings
- woods
- reservoirs
- lakes
- watercourses (canals, rivers etc.)

11   Between features, you are most likely to be walking through fields whose boundaries are depicted on the map, so you will be using hedges, walls and fences to guide you on your way. In popular walking areas such as the Cotswolds, the Chilterns and the North and South Downs, most of the paths will be visible on the ground, but in remoter, less popular parts of the country some of them may be so little used as to be invisible. You still have an absolute right to use them, but it does make accurate map-reading more critical.

12   Work out a circular route at home and mark it on your map with a highlighter pen. Examine the route carefully and break it down into sections which are referred to as 'legs'. A leg is a stretch of path that runs between two distinctive features. For example, your path is almost certainly going to start from a road and it may then cross several fields to another feature such as a farm or a wood. The next leg might take you to a lane. This pattern should be followed until you return to your starting point. This system ensures that reaching the obvious feature at the end of each leg confirms that you are following the route correctly.

13   The first thing you should do when you arrive at the start of the walk is to orientate your map so that it lines up with all the features on the ground. There are two methods:

a)   Hold the map in front of you with the top (north) edge farthest away from you. Place your compass on the map and turn your body until the north-seeking compass needle is pointing to the top of the map.

b)   If you do not have a compass then you should align the map to features that you can identify on the ground, such as a church tower. Be sure that you know your present position and place a pencil on your map along a line linking your position to your chosen landmark. Then turn your body until the pencil is pointing at the landmark (see Fig. 8).

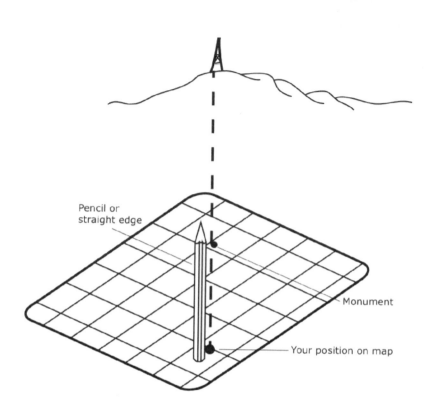

Figure 8   Orientating the map

14   If there is no convenient landmark you can use a reasonably straight stretch of road. The map is now 'set' or orientated and you are ready to walk! (Chapter 7 gives a practical demonstration of map-reading in lowland countryside.)

15   Most walkers like to hold the map in front of them orientated in the direction in which they are walking. This means that they turn the map whenever the path makes a major change of direction.

16   If following a complicated route, such as when navigating through a series of fields that all look the same, it is useful to employ a technique known as 'thumbing'. Mark the tip of your thumbnail with a felt-tip pen or nail varnish. The map is gripped with your thumb on the position at which you last examined the map so that the next time that you look at it you don't have to spend time searching for your previous position. Another method is to fashion and cut a small arrow from a self-adhesive 'Post it' note, attach it to your last position and move it every time that you consult the map. Ensure that the shaft of the arrow protrudes slightly beyond the adhesive so that it is easy to move. One arrow will last for several walks and will reduce the time spent on map-reading.

17   Walkers who use two trekking poles can find map-reading awkward because they have to slip one hand from their wrist strap and prop the pole precariously against their body, a tree, wall or fence. One solution, which is particularly useful in lowland countryside where frequent reference to the map is often necessary, is to make a map case from a suitably-sized lid from a plastic food container. Bolt a couple of spring clips onto the lid, drill holes for two horizontal and one vertical length of small-diameter shock cord to secure the map inside a freezer bag and clip the contraption to the shaft of one of your poles.

18   Some of the technical terms used in the following pages are known by more than one name (a baseplate compass is also known as an orienteering compass).

Aids to navigation

19   There are several devices that can assist in map-reading, route-planning and navigation including
   • maps which are essential for route-finding and are usually more satisfactory than footpath guides (see 10:9)
   • compasses for calculating and following bearings (see 6:51-6)
   • opisometers (map measurers) for measuring distances of more than a kilometre on maps (see 6:69)
   • romers for calculating grid references and measuring distances of less than a kilometre on the map (see 6:70-1)
   • magnifying glasses for examining the detail of a map (often incorporated into compasses)
   • route cards (see 8:23)
   • altimeters (see 6:102-4)
   • stop-watches (see 6:98)
   • handheld satnavs (see Chapter 9)
   • pedometers (see 6:105-11)
   • tachometers which can be used for counting paces but are rarely used except by orienteers
There are expensive wrist computers that incorporate an altimeter, barometer, stop-watch and a satnav.

20   The only *essential* item of navigational equipment required by those whose walking is confined to lowland countryside is a map, but many walkers find that a compass is also useful. All hill-walkers should carry a map and a compass *and know how to use them* and, as they gain experience, may find stop watches and altimeters useful. Those who regularly walk off-path should consider investing in a handheld satnav but *it should not be considered a substitute for competence with map and compass* (see Chapter 9).

Compasses

21   There is much confusion about the names given to some of the technical terms associated with compasses and their use. Scientists, compass manufacturers, cartographers, and walkers often use different terms to describe the same thing. For example:

a)   The type of compass used by most walkers, and described in 6:27-32, is variously known as
- a **baseplate compass** (the term used in this book)
- an orienteering compass
- a protractor compass
- a Silva-type compass (after the Silva company which manufactured the first model)

b)   The angle between grid north and magnetic north (see 6:39-42) is variously known as
- the '**grid magnetic angle**' (GMA) which is the term used throughout this book
- the Ordnance Survey and the British Geological Survey treat 'magnetic variation' and 'declination' as synonymous terms and use them interchangeably
- the National Geophysical Data Center of the United States uses 'declination'

c)   The term '**deviation**' is used in this book to describe anything, such as ferrous metals and electrical interference, that causes the compass needle to deviate from magnetic north. (It should be noted that some walkers and navigation manuals use the term 'deviation' to describe *anything* that causes the compass needle not to align with magnetic north. This includes the grid magnetic angle and the effects of ferrous metals and electrical interference).

22   Many walkers never bother with a compass in lowland areas, despite its obvious usefulness, and rely solely on their map-reading skills. However, those who walk in mountainous or moorland country must be competent in the use of both and understand the several ways in which they can be employed. Theoretical

knowledge obtained from reading a manual such as this is no substitute for practical skills. Every opportunity should be taken to practise and master these techniques in good conditions so that, when you really need to use them, they come as second nature.

23   A compass has a free-swinging magnetized needle which, using the earth's natural magnetism, always points to the north in the northern hemisphere and to the south in the southern hemisphere. (From now on in this book, it is assumed that the navigator is in the northern hemisphere, but the principles apply equally in the southern hemisphere.) This remarkable property gives navigators a reference point that allows them to move with precision in any direction that they wish and, when used in combination with an accurate map, can take them unerringly to their destination.

24   However, the compass needle does not point to true north (i.e. the North Pole) but to magnetic north which lies some distance from it and which moves according to a reasonably predictable pattern. The grids on topographic maps of the British Isles (see 4:9-10) are, for practical purposes, aligned to true north.

25   The Earth is an ellipsoid, whereas maps are flat, so it is obvious there is only one line on any grid that has vertical lines that are exactly parallel and which can be aligned to true north. However, the difference is so minute that it is of no concern to walkers and, in practice, all the vertical lines of the national grids used in the British Isles can be treated as aligning to true north.

26   A compass, when used in conjunction with the map, allows you to walk in the direction that the path you wish to follow runs. For example, if walking in an area where paths are poorly defined on the ground, the use of a compass, as described below, will enable the route to be followed with pinpoint accuracy. An expert can navigate at night through unfamiliar fields using this technique and have no difficulty in finding the stiles and gates on the path.

Baseplate compasses

27   A baseplate compass (also known as an orienteering compass, a protractor compass and a Silva-type compass) is the most suitable type for walkers because it combines the functions of a compass and a protractor. This obviates the need to orientate the map when taking bearings. The great advantage that the baseplate compass has over the conventional compass is that routes, complete with bearings, can be plotted without orientating the map. It can even be done in the comfort of your home.

28   There are several brands and many models of baseplate compasses but they all have the same essential features and the type illustrated in Fig. 9 is typical. There are more sophisticated and expensive types such as sighting and mirror versions but they all work on the same principle and most walkers find that one of the simpler models is adequate for their purposes.

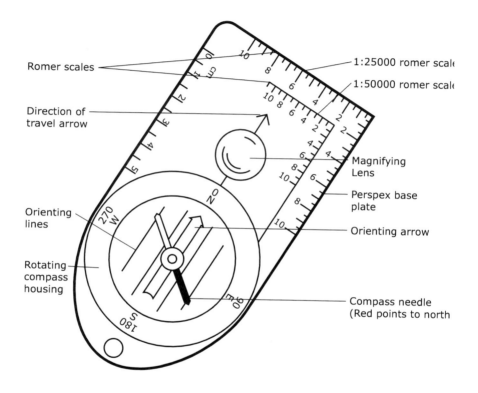

Figure 9   A baseplate compass

29   A baseplate compass is mounted on a transparent perspex base which often incorporates a magnifying glass and a romer (see 6.70-1). The compass housing, in which the needle swings, can turn on the perspex base and has 360 degrees marked on its outer face, and an arrow with parallel lines on the bottom.

30   Compasses used by the military are graded in 6,400 mils instead of 360 degrees but these are rarely used by walkers. When choosing a compass ensure that it is marked with degrees otherwise it may be difficult to calculate bearings accurately from a map, and you will be unable to exchange bearings with other walkers.

31 Most baseplate compasses purchased in the northern hemisphere will not work in the southern hemisphere, but there are universal versions that have two small magnets mounted on either side of the plastic needle that ensures that they will work anywhere in the world.

32 On the perspex base plate of the compass will be found romer scales for 1:50,000 and 1:25,000 maps, which are used for measuring short distances and for calculating grid references (see 6:70-1 and Fig. 9). The lanyard is used to prevent loss by attaching the compass to the shoulder strap of a rucksack or the buttonhole of a shirt.

33 Some walkers carry a simple wrist or thumb compass as well as a baseplate compass because they find it useful for orientating their maps and establishing at a glance which route to follow when several paths meet. These compasses are inexpensive and can obviate the need to fumble in your pocket to find, and then adjust, your baseplate compass, but they are no substitute for the real thing when maximum accuracy is required. Wrist compasses should not be worn next to your watch.

Factors affecting compass accuracy

34 Every compass has its own individual compass error (ICE) but this is so minute that it is of no concern to walkers.

35 When taking bearings, compasses should be kept well away from
- ferrous metals
- the photoelectric cells of cameras
- pylons and electricity transmission cables
- iron gates and fences
- the hinges and latches of wooden gates

36 The only place in the British Isles where magnetic rocks can make your compass unreliable is in the Cuillins on the Isle of Skye. Some walkers believe that Bowfell in the Lake District has rocks that can affect compasses but this myth has been disproved.

37 A bubble may occasionally form in the liquid of the compass housing in which the needle swings. This sometimes happens at altitudes above 1,000 metres but it often disappears once lower levels are reached. Compasses in which large bubbles persist should be replaced.

38 The compass needle can suffer from reversed polarity which causes the north-facing (red) needle to point to the south. This happens when the compass is affected by a magnetic field such as those surrounding electricity transmission lines, ferrous objects and magnets. The cure is to restore the correct polarity by stroking the north (red) end of the needle with a magnet, and then checking it against a compass known to be accurate. Some compass manufacturers will correct reversed polarity without charge.

How to use a baseplate compass

39 Before using a baseplate compass, certain fundamental principles have to be understood. On the topographic maps used by walkers in the British Isles, three norths are shown (see Fig. 10)

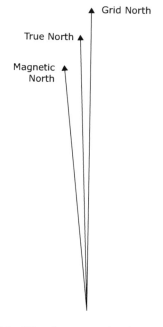

Figure 10   The three norths depicted on all Ordnance
Survey maps published *before* 2014 (see 6:55)

Magnetic north: the north to which the compass needle points and which changes slightly from year to year according to a predictable pattern.

Grid north: the north pointed at by the grid lines on the map and which is almost identical with true north.

True north: the actual North Pole which is almost identical with grid north but is of no practical interest to walkers and may be ignored.

40 The various norths are shown in diagrammatic form on the map key together with a statement of the angle between magnetic north and grid north and may be expressed in one of two forms:

a) The easier to use is when degrees alone are employed as in *'Magnetic north is estimated at 3° west of grid north in 2005 decreasing by about 1° in four years.'* Round the result to the nearest full degree.

b) On some maps it is expressed in degrees and minutes for example *'Magnetic north is estimated to be 4°10' west of grid north for July 2004. Annual change is approximately 12' east'*. This is more difficult to calculate and you have to remember that there are 60 minutes in a degree. Round the result to the nearest full degree.

41 You must be clear under what conditions you should use grid or magnetic bearings and describe them as such:

a) When giving a bearing that is to be used within a few weeks as, for example on a route card, then it can be described as *'X° mag'* because magnetic variation will not change perceptibly during the period that it will be used, and it will save the reader the trouble of converting the bearing.

b) Bearings given in guidebooks should be described as *'X° grid'* because someone may use the book several years after it was published during which time the grid magnetic angle will have changed. Guidebooks should state the date on which the bearing was calculated so that the reader can refer to a map and calculate the present grid magnetic angle.

42 The baseplate compass can be used in a number of ways, each of which should be mastered by practising the techniques in lowland countryside before venturing into upland areas where your safety may depend upon its accurate use. It can be used to

- stay on course
- plot a course from the map
- find your exact position on the map

How to stay on course

43 This technique (see Fig. 11) is the most basic use of the compass because it does not involve the map. It is used mostly in upland areas and may occasionally be employed in lowland countryside but it only works when the loss of visibility is temporary.

44 Let us suppose you are on a hillside following an indistinct path. You know your position on the map and your destination is the summit of a hill that you can see some way ahead. You notice some low cloud coming down that will temporarily obscure your destination. With your compass:

a) Point the direction of travel arrow at the summit.

b) Turn the compass housing until the arrow on the base of the housing points in the same direction as the north (red) end of the compass needle.

c) Keep the compass needle and the arrow on the base of the housing in line and walk in the direction to which the direction of travel arrow is pointing.

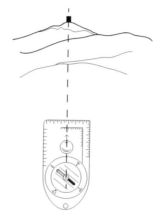

Figure 11   How to stay on course

45   Do not keep your eye glued to the direction of travel arrow but find an objec such as a tree or rock on the line of the path somewhere near the limit of visibility and walk towards it. Repeat the process until the destination is reached.

46   By using these techniques you should arrive at your destination, but cross-winds and side slopes tend to make you drift off-course so you will get only to within striking distance of it. Even an experienced walker cannot expect to follow a bearing with an accuracy better than 4°. Nor can you be certain whether you have deviated to the left or right of your intended course. Errors of deviation per thousand metres will result in being off-course by the following distances

4°	70 metres
5°	87·5 metres
6°	105 metres
7°	122·5 metres
8°	140 metres
9°	157·5 metres
10°	175 metres

47   The distance by which you could be off-course can be found by:

a)   Multiplying the distance travelled by the sine of the angle of deviation. The sine of 1° is 0·0175 so the equation is
distance travelled x angle of deviation x 0.0175.

b)   An easier calculation is to apply the 1 in 60 rule which states that over a distance of 60 metres you will be 1 metre off-course for every 1° of deviation. Thus, if you deviated from your bearing by 2° over a distance of 500 metres you would be 16·6 metres off-course.

48   You should be aware that if visibility remains poor, you may be unable to find your destination by the deduced-reckoning (the modern term for dead-reckoning) technique described above. You probably won't even know whether your destination lies to the right or left and you may have to employ other methods to reach your destination (see Chapter 8).

49   If you can take backbearings you may be able to improve your accuracy (see 8:14) and a handheld satnav will take you unerringly to your destination if you key in the grid reference.

Plotting a course from the map

50   Paths usually follow relatively straight lines between well-defined features; they rarely curve significantly across a field, and even in mountainous country they are often quite straight unless climbing steeply or following a natural feature such as a stream.

51   Using a suitable map and a baseplate compass it is possible to plot your course beforehand by noting down the compass bearing at each point that the path changes direction (see Fig. 12). The method is as follows:

a)   Place the map on a flat surface. It is *not* necessary to orientate it (i.e. position it so that the northern edge faces north).

b)   Estimate to within 90° the bearing of the path that you wish to follow. For example, if it lies in the quadrant between
• north and east it will be between 0° and 90°
• east and south it will be between 90° and 180°
• south and west will be between 180° and 270°
• west and north it will be between 270° and 360°

52   Place the edge of the perspex base of the compass along the line of the path to be followed making sure that the direction of travel arrow is pointing in the direction you want to go.

53 Without moving the base, turn the compass housing until the arrow engraved on the bottom of the housing points towards the north (top) edge of the map and the lines are exactly parallel to the north-south grid lines on the map.

54 Remove the compass from the map. You now have a grid bearing (i.e. a bearing aligned on grid north) but your compass needle points to magnetic north so you have to make an adjustment. This is where you have to be careful. For more than 200 years magnetic north has been *west* of both true north and grid north but in January 2014, the extreme west of Cornwall became *east* of grid north.

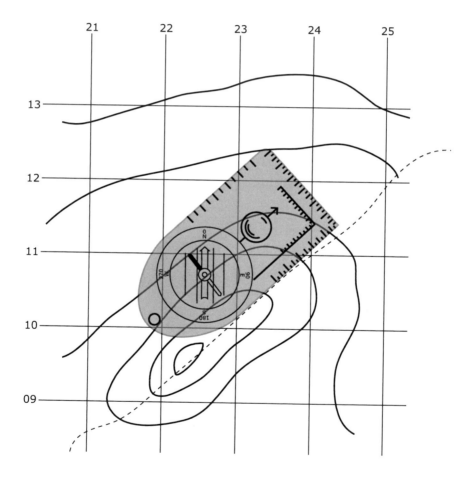

Figure 12   Plotting a course from the map

55   Adjust the difference between grid north and magnetic north (see the map key and it is also available for the United Kingdom from the British Geological Survey website www.geomag.bgs.ac.uk/data_service/models_compass/gma_calc.html)

- if the magnetic bearing is **WEST** of grid north **ADD** the appropriate number of degrees
- if the magnetic bearing is **EAST** of grid north **SUBTRACT** the appropriate number of degrees

a)   Check the bearing to ensure that it is within 90° of the estimate you made in 6:51 above. If it is not, then you have made an error. Check that your original estimate was correct and that you have not made an error of 180° by

- pointing the direction of travel arrow towards your present position instead of towards the point where the path changes direction again
- turning the compass housing so that the arrow at the bottom points to the south instead of to the north

b)   Read off the bearing from the point indicated on your compass and note it down. When reaching the point in the walk for which you set the bearing, hold the compass in your hand and turn your body until the red arrow in the compass housing is in line with the north-pointing needle.

c)   The line of the path runs where the direction-of-travel arrow on the perspex base plate of the compass is pointing.

56   The above method illustrates the principles of using the baseplate compass and the relationship between grid north and magnetic north. Once they are grasped, it is possible to make a short cut in the method. Instead of adjusting the magnetic variation (e.g. +3°) to the grid bearing, point the compass needle to 357° instead of 360° (magnetic north). Some of the more expensive compasses have an adjustable pointer or scale known as a declinometer which you can set to correct the grid magnetic angle. Another method is to stick a strip of sticky paper to the underside of the compass to mark the difference between grid north and magnetic north. The method of plotting a course now becomes:

a)   Place the perspex base of the compass along the line of the path with the direction of travel arrow pointing in the direction you want to walk.

b)   Without moving the base, turn the compass housing so that the arrow in the housing points towards the north end of the map and exactly parallel to the north-south grid lines.

c)   Remove the compass from the map and, holding the compass in front of you, turn your body until the north (top) edge of the compass needle points to 357° (or the appropriate grid magnetic angle, as it varies slightly in different parts of the country and from year to year).

d)   The line of the path runs where the direction-of-travel arrow is pointing.

Finding your position on the map

57 You are walking along a path that is depicted on the map and, although you are not lost, you wish to know your precise position (see Fig. 13). It can be found as follows:

a) Select a feature such as a building, the edge of a wood or a field boundary that can be identified with certainty both on the ground and on the map.

b) Point the direction-of-travel arrow at this feature.

c) Turn the compass housing so that the arrow on the base lines up with the north-facing needle.

d) Adjust the difference between magnetic north and grid north by moving the compass housing the correct amount.

e) Place the base of the compass on the map with the straight edge touching the feature on which the bearing was taken.

f) Without altering the position of the compass housing, turn the perspex base plate on the map until the arrow on the base of the compass housing points to the north (top) edge of the map and is exactly parallel to the vertical grid lines.

g) Your position is where the edge of the base plate intersects with the path.

There is a variation of this technique which, theoretically, can be used to locate your position when walking off-path. It involves taking bearings on two, and

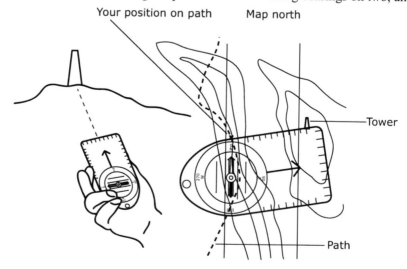

Figure 13 Finding your position on the map

preferably three, distant features as described above. Transfer each bearing onto the map by drawing a line along the compass base. Your position is where the lines intersect. (If using three bearings the lines are unlikely to meet exactly at one point, but your position will be somewhere inside the resulting tiny triangle). The procedure is known as a 'resection' but is not often used because it relies on being able to identify *with certainty* the features on which you are taking the bearings (one mountain can look very much like another). Nevertheless, it is a good training exercise in compass skills.

58 It is obvious that another short cut can be made. Instead of adjusting the magnetic variation, just point the direction-of-travel arrow to the landmark and then turn the compass housing until the north-facing compass needle is pointing at the corrected grid magnetic angle instead of 360°. The procedure then becomes:

   a) Select a feature that can be identified on the ground and on the map.

   b) Point the direction-of-travel arrow at the feature.

   c) Turn the compass housing so that the north-facing needle lines up with corrected grid magnetic angle.

   d) Place the perspex base plate of the compass on the map with the straight edge touching the feature on which the bearing was taken.

   e) Without altering the position of the compass housing, pivot the perspex base plate on the feature until the arrow on the perspex base of the compass housing points to the north edge of the map and is exactly parallel to the grid lines.

   f) Your position is where the edge of the perspex base plate intersects with the footpath.

59 The three situations described in 6:51-8 above are fundamental to the use of compass and map. All other conditions of use are variations on these themes; master them and you will quickly become adept and come to regard your map and compass as your best friends.

60 There is a useful technique, known as the 'brace position', and described by Lyle Brotherton in *The Ultimate Navigation Manual* (see 5:46), that will provide a stable platform for map and compass that will assist in the taking of accurate bearings :

   a) Go down on one knee and place your map folded so that the area in which you are navigating is visible (see Fig. 14), and your knee is pointing in the direction of the feature from which you want to take the bearing.

b) When taking the bearing ensure that your eyes are directly above the compass to avoid any risk of parallax error.

61   If it is not convenient to adopt the brace position:

Figure 14   The brace position

a) Hold your compass at waist level and slowly turn until facing the feature from which you want to take a bearing.

b) Bend your head so that your eyes are directly above the compass and take the bearing.

Measuring distances on the map

62   Distances cannot be measured on the map with absolute accuracy because a map is two-dimensional which makes it impossible to measure the extra distance travelled when climbing and descending hills. However, the extra distance is usually small so it can be ignored except in extreme conditions (see 6:108).

63   There are several ways of measuring distances on the map including
  • counting grid squares
  • using your fingers
  • thread
  • opisometers (map measurers)
  • romers
  • counting path symbols

Grid squares

64 This rough and ready method of estimating distance involves counting the number of grid squares that the route crosses
- the side of a square measures one kilometre
- the diagonal measures 1·4 kilometres (for ease of calculation assume it be 1·5 kilometres)
- if the route crosses a part of a grid square then estimate its length

Fingers

65 This method can be more accurate than counting grid squares because you can measure curves. Measure four centimetres from the tip of your little finger for 1:25,000 maps, and two centimetres for 1:50,000 maps, and note where this coincides with a joint or a crease in your skin. A variation of this method is to measure and use the width of your finger(s).

Thread

66 Lay a piece of thin thread along the route and then measure the thread against the scale printed on the map. A more satisfactory alternative is to mark or tie knots at four centimetre intervals on the lanyard of your compass. Four centimetres represents one kilometre on 1:25,000 maps so if you are using a 1:50,000 map multiply the number of knots counted by two.

Opisometers (map measurers)

67 These are useful for measuring significant distances on the map such as when planning a walk. They usually comprise a dial around which a pointer, activated by a wheel at the base of the instrument, turns as it is pushed over the map. The route is measured and shown on the dial in centimetres and inches, and the result has to be converted according to the scale of the map.

68 There are electronic opisometers into which the scale of the map can be keyed so that no conversion is necessary. The distance covered is shown on a tiny screen. They are not so convenient to use as the mechanical version because they continue measuring whether you push them forwards or backwards. If you make a mistake you cannot roll them back to where you went wrong as you can with the mechanical version; you have to measure the whole route again.

69 Opisometers do not always give consistently accurate results and are not suitable for the measurement of short distances for which a romer (see 6.70-1) is more accurate. It is difficult to measure the length of a path accurately because you have to follow every kink and curve, and in upland areas hairpin bends are

often shown conventionally rather than with absolute accuracy. Opisometers are normally only used to measure a walk to ensure that it is a suitable distance. In these circumstances accuracy to within 500 metres is normally acceptable.

Romers

70 Romers are named after Lieutenant Carrol Romer (1883-1951) who invented a device for calculating grid references on First World War military maps. A modern romer (see Fig. 15) is a piece of plastic or card on which is engraved or printed map scales of 1:25,000 and 1:50,000 divided into 100-metre divisions (there are also versions that incorporate protractors for calculating bearings). Most baseplate compasses have romers engraved on their perspex base.

71 Romers are useful devices for measuring distances of less than 1,000 metres. They can also be used for calculating grid references (see 4:15-17).

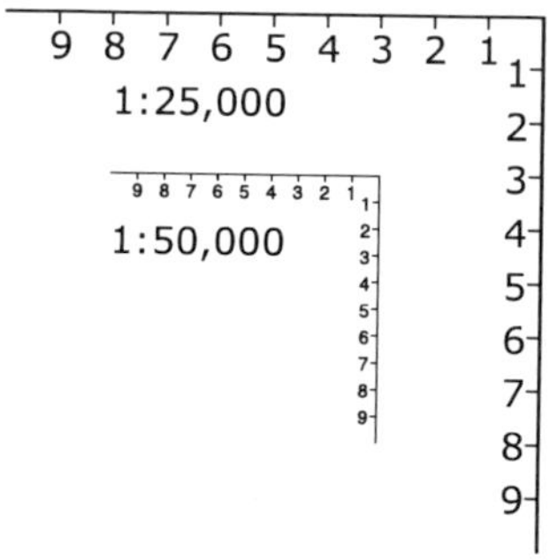

Figure 15 A romer

Path symbols

72 The dashes and dots that represent paths on some maps can be counted and used to measure short distances because every dot or dash, plus the space that follows it, represents a precise distance on the ground.

73 Walkers using Ordnance Survey maps can employ the '30-50-70-90 rule' which states that

- a short green dash indicating a public footpath on *Explorers* represents 30 metres as does the short red dash indicating a permissive footpath
- a short red dash indicating a public footpath on *Landrangers* represents 50 metres

- a long green dash indicating a public bridleway, and the long red dash indicating a public bridleway, and the black dash for a path on *Explorers* all represent 70 metres
- a long red dash indicating a bridleway on *Landrangers* represents 90 metres

74 Other symbols on *Landranger* maps that can be used for measuring short distances on the ground are

- a black dash and following space indicating a path represents 90 metres
- a black double-pecked line and following space indicating a track represents 70 metres

75 The same principle can be applied to other maps used by walkers in the British Isles providing that

- the path symbol is large enough
- the distance between the symbol and the following space is regular
- you are able to measure and calculate the distance that it represents

Estimating the time it will take to complete a walk

76 It is useful to be able to calculate the length of time that a walk will take. This information is often required in order to catch a bus or train, rendezvous with a car at a suitable pickup point, or to avoid being caught out after dark (known as benightment) on a winter afternoon. It is always better to overestimate the time it will take to complete a walk.

77 Many walkers believe that they can cover ground faster than they actually can and confuse the speed of their pace on level ground with their average speed. They may be able to walk at five kilometres per hour across a flat, firm field but they ignore the slowing effect of

- mud and boggy areas
- wind and rain
- hills
- climbing stiles and passing through gates
- taking photographs
- map-reading
- calls of nature
- adjusting clothing
- shopping for food

so that their average speed is considerably slower.

78   It is helpful to keep records of the time taken to complete walks making notes of variable factors such as

- the terrain
- the weather
- the number in the party

as this will provide data for calculating the time required to complete a range of walks in different kinds of terrain.

In upland country

79   The generally accepted method of calculating the time required to complete a walk is by using Naismith's Rule. The classic definition states

- allow one hour for every five kilometres measured on the map plus an additional half hour for every three hundred metres climbed

80   This is more usefully defined as:

a)   Allow 12 minutes for every kilometre measured on an *Ordnance Survey* map plus an additional minute for every 10-metres of contour crossed (many *Explorer* maps have contours at 5-metre intervals).

b)   Allow 12 minutes for every kilometre measured on a Harvey map plus an additional 1·5 minutes for every 15-metre contour crossed (it's easier to calculate if you add 3 minutes for every two contours crossed).

81   The total amount of climbing is the sum of all the ascents not just the highest point reached (see Fig. 15).

For example

     total distance measured on the map: 10 km
     total elevation climbed: 870 m

Therefore:

time required to walk 10 km (12 x 10)	120 mins
time required to climb 870 metres (870 ÷ 10)	87 mins
	Total 207 mins

Note that the average speed is 10 x 60 ÷ 207 = 2.9 kph
If the walk was level the average speed would be 10 x 60 ÷ 120 = 5 kph

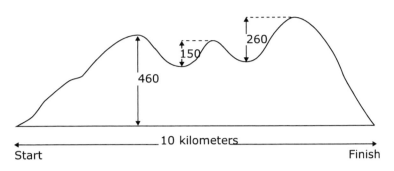

Figure 16   Calculating the total amount of ascent

82   Naismith's rule assumes average fitness and good conditions, so extra time should be allowed for
  • bad weather
  • difficulties in route-finding
  • heavy packs
  • uneven and boggy ground
  • river crossings
  • taking photographs
  • calls of nature
A group tends to be slower than a solo walker because of the time spent queuing for stiles.

83   If these factors have to be built in then it is usual to amend Naismith's Rule by reducing the number of kilometres covered in an hour. Many walkers wearing only a light pack find that, even in good conditions, it is more realistic to allow one hour for every four kilometres (15 minutes per kilometre). Backpackers should consider basing their calculations on one hour for every 2·5 kilometres (approximately 25 minutes per kilometre). Once you have made your calculation you have to add an allowance for meal breaks and other factors listed in 6:82. It is always better and safer to overestimate the time that a walk will take!

84   A refinement of Naismith's Rule, known as Tranter's Variations (see Appendix 6), is described in some walking manuals but it is rarely used and many walkers prefer to amend Naismith's Rule in the light of their own experience.

In lowland countryside

85   There is no generally accepted formula for calculating the time it will take to complete a walk in lowland countryside. Naismith's Rule does not work well because hills are not such a significant factor and there are far more stiles and gates than in upland areas. It takes an average of 12 seconds for a walker to cross a stile, and to open and close a gate, and in the case of stiles there is a knock-on effect for a group of walkers. The first person over will tend to walk a few steps and then either slow down or even wait for the rest of the party to cross. This has a significant effect on the average speed of a group. Gates do not slow down a group to the same degree, especially if there is a designated gate-shutter.

86   Westacott's Rule for calculating the time for completing a lowland walk works reasonably well for the lone walker, but extra time has to be built in for groups. In order to use Westacott's Rule you first have to work out your average speed through fields on reasonably level ground. This can be done by measuring a fixed distance of at least two kilometres and then timing yourself over the route walking at your normal pace. From this you can calculate your average speed per kilometre of ground.

87   The amount of time spent on map-reading varies considerably according to the type of terrain:

a)   On the well-defined tracks on the chalk downs of southern England, route-finding is easy and relatively little time is spent on examining the map.

b)   In a landscape of fields and woods, such as is found throughout the Midlands and southern England, close attention has to be paid to the map in order to follow the route. Walkers who are constantly referring to the map tend to walk more cautiously and their pace is often slower than it would be on familiar ground. Experiments show that in this type of countryside as much as three or four minutes per kilometre can be spent map-reading.

88   To establish the average time spent on map-reading, plan a walk of at least fifteen kilometres in unfamiliar countryside comprising fields and woods, and record the time taken to complete the walk, excluding stops for lunch etc.

89   You should now be familiar with the route so repeat the walk without referring to the map and record the time taken, excluding stops. Subtract the time of the second attempt from the time of the first and you have the time spent map-reading. Divide this figure by the distance covered to obtain the average time spent map-reading per kilometre. The formula now becomes

Multiply the length of the walk in kilometres by your average speed per kilometre and then add one minute for every 10 metres of significant ascent (i.e. a hill that will slow you down *not* an imperceptible slope that crosses the occasional contour). Then multiply your average time taken for map-reading per kilometre by the length of the walk and add this to the total.

Example

distance: 15 km

significant ascent: 280 m

average walking speed: 13 minutes per kilometre

average time map-reading: 3 minutes per kilometre

Calculation

time taken to walk 15 km: (15 x 13)	195 mins
time taken to climb 280 m (280 ÷ 10)	28 mins
time taken for map-reading (15 x 3)	45 mins
Total	**268 mins**

The average speed is 15 x 60 ÷ 268= 3·4 kph

If you were familiar with the route it would be 15 x 60 ÷ (268 - 45) = 4 kph

Measuring distances on the ground

90   There are situations when it is useful, sometimes essential, to be able to walk a specific distance accurately.

91   Imagine that you are following a poorly-defined headland path and looking for a stile in the overgrown hedge on your left. You can calculate from the map the distance from the last hedge that you crossed to where the stile should be either by using a romer (see 6:70-1) or, in England and Wales, by counting the path symbols (see 6:72-5), and then measuring the distance on the ground.

92   Similarly, imagine that you are walking along a featureless moorland path in poor visibility. You come to a gate in a wall and you know from the map that there is a fork in the path 2·25 kilometres ahead. It is vital that you find this junction to ensure that you take the correct route.

93   The two methods of measuring distances on the ground are by

• pacing

• timing

In normal circumstances, and with practice, both can be remarkably accurate. A handheld satnav (see Chapter 9) will do this more conveniently and accurately.

Pacing

94   Pacing is generally used for measuring distances up to 500 metres. When you walk at your normal speed on ground that is reasonably level, the length of your stride is constant. Thus, if you know how many double-paces you take to cover 100 metres, you can calculate the distance covered by counting the number of strides you take with your dominant foot (normally between 60 and 70).

95   In order to establish the number of double-paces you take you have to measure a set distance. The easiest way to do this is on a running track but if this not available the following method may be used:

a) Tie a tent peg to each end of a 50-metre length of string.

b) Using the string as a tape measure, place two pegs 200 metres apart.

c) Walk continuously at your normal pace five times between the pegs counting your double-strides (you will then have covered 1,000 metres).

d) Divide the number of double-paces by 10 to calculate the number of double-paces taken to cover 100 metres.

96   You take shorter steps when climbing hills so you should make allowances for this. Find a steep hill and measure the longest incline you can and count your double-paces.

97   Pacing is made easier if you only have to count the number of double-paces to cover every 100 metres. The following methods can be employed:

a) Use a tachometer.

b) Pick up the appropriate number of small stones and carry them in your left hand. Transfer one stone to the right hand after every 100 metres (this is safer than discarding the stone because, should you accidentally drop the stones in your left hand, you can still make the calculation).

c) Attach six cord grips to one end of your compass lanyard or a short length of nylon cord secured to the shoulder straps of your rucksack. After every hundred metres slide one grip to the other end of the lanyard or cord.

Timing

98   Timing is generally used for measuring distances greater than 500 metres. After you have counted your double-paces as described in 6:94-7, time yourself with a stop-watch over 1,000 metres whilst walking at your normal speed (it should take between 11 and 13 minutes).

99   Assuming that it takes you 12 minutes to walk 1 kilometre on level ground it should take you

12 x 3·25 = 39 minutes to reach the path junction described in 6:92

after 35 minutes you should be on the alert

after 43 minutes you are likely to have overshot it

100 You walk more slowly when going uphill so allowance has to be made for this. The generally accepted adjustment is to add

a) 1 minute for every 10 metres of elevation gain on *Landranger* and *Explorer* maps. Note that all *Landrangers* have a 10-metre contour interval whereas the interval on *Explorer* maps may be either 5 metres or 10 metres.

b) 3 minutes for every 2 contours crossed on Harvey maps.

101 In the examples above, if you had to cross 4 contours (40 metres elevation gain on Ordnance Survey maps of upland areas) before reaching the path junction, then the calculation becomes

$$12 \times 3\cdot25 + 4 = 43 \text{ minutes}$$

Other tools used in navigation

Altimeters

102 Before the use of satnavs became widespread, altimeters were an important navigation tool for walkers in upland areas. If you were following a path depicted on the map, or walking on a compass bearing, and also on a steep slope (indicated by the closeness of the contour lines), you could fix your position by matching your elevation to the appropriate contour line (see Fig. 17). A satnav will provide a much quicker and accurate fix. Most satnav's have an altimeter mode but the most likely purpose that it serves is when contouring (see 8:21-2).

103 Altimeters are available both as stand-alone instruments and in some multifunction watches. They work in the same way as a barometer by recording air pressure which declines at a rate of 1 millibar for every 10 metres of elevation gained above sea level. However, the accuracy of an elevation recorded on an altimeter depends upon a number of factors including

- the calibration interval of the instrument which can range from ±1 metre to ±5 metres
- fluctuations in air pressure
- the humidity of the atmosphere (air with a high water content is heavier than dry air)
- the temperature
- the spot heights and contours depicted on maps are subject to minor inaccuracies

Walkers must bear all these considerations in mind when using an altimeter especially when relying on them for navigating in extreme conditions. Further information can be found at www.hills-database.co.uk/altim.html.

104 Altimeters can *sometimes* be used to establish your position. If there are no features from which to take a compass bearing it may be possible to establish your position on a path or other significant feature such as a ridge. This technique can only be used on steep terrain otherwise the distance *on the ground* between contours is too great to be of use in determining your position:

a) If your altimeter has a stated accuracy of ±5 metres
- on a 10° slope angle (18% gradient) your position could be off by up to 29 metres in either direction
- on a 20° slope angle (36% gradient) you could be off by up to 15 metres in either direction
- on a 22° slope angle (40% gradient) you could be off by up to 13 metres in either direction

b) If your altimeter has a stated accuracy of ±1 metre
- on a 10° slope angle (18% gradient) your position could be off by up to 6 metres in either direction
- on a 20° slope angle (36% gradient) you could be off by up to 2·9 metres in either direction
- on a 22° slope angle (40% gradient) you could be off by up to 2·7 metres in either direction

105 When relying on an altimeter to fix your position it is essential to calibrate it against known heights as frequently as possible. This can be done from the contour nearest to any feature that can readily be identified on a map including
- trig points (these are few and far between)
- summits
- cairns
- bodies of water (lakes, lochs, tarns and loughs)
- footbridges
- junctions of paths
- walls that are crossed when following a path
- junctions of walls when in pathless terrain

106 To practise using an altimeter it is a good plan to plot a walk at least 10- kilometres long containing a number of hills with a height difference of at least 50 metres:

a) List the location and elevation of at least a dozen features.

b) Calibrate the altimeter to the correct elevation at the start of every walk.

c) Walk the route several times in various weather conditions and note the elevation recorded on the altimeter at every location
   • the first time, complete the walk without re-calibrating the altimeter at every location other than at the start
   • on subsequent walks, re-calibrate the altimeter at every location

By studying the results you will learn to appreciate the usefulness as well as the limitations of altimeters.

107 Figure 17 demonstrates how an altimeter can be used in poor visibility. Imagine that you are using a 1:50,000 map and have arrived at the cairn. Worsening conditions make it advisable to seek lower ground. The path is indistinct and it is essential that you make the turn at the 550-metre contour (for the sake of clarity only the 50-metre index contours are depicted). This is the procedure:

a) Note the stated elevation of the spot height at the cairn from the map and re-calibrate your altimeter to 712 metres.

b) Take a compass bearing from the map along the obvious route, sometimes referred to as the 'fall line', to the 550-metre contour.

c) When your altimeter indicates that you have reached the 550-metre contour, take another compass bearing from the map along the fall line that will take you to lower ground and safety.

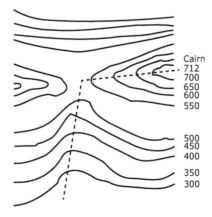

Figure 17 Navigating with an altimeter

108 If you only have a map and compass, you will have to rely on timing and/or pacing to reach the appropriate contour (see 6.94-101). However, you should be aware of the extra distance that has to be taken into account caused by a two-dimensional map attempting to portray the third dimension (elevation). On a map showing a slope angle of 27°, for every 100 metres measured on the map, the distance on the ground is actually 112 metres. Over a distance of 500 metres this discrepancy is significant and has to be taken into consideration. A credit card-sized tool for measuring the slope angle on 1:25,000 and 1:50,000 maps, and calculating the extra distance, is available from www.shavenraspberry.com.

Pedometers

109 These instruments can be used for measuring the distance covered on foot. They are not suitable for precise navigation because the information they record is not easily visible. When used intelligently they can be quite accurate.

110 Pedometers are usually clipped onto the belt and worn over the hip. A bob-weight counts the number of strides which are then converted mechanically or electronically onto a dial, scale or display that shows
   • the number of steps taken
   • the distance recorded

111 Some pedometers will give additional information including
   • overall average speed
   • average speed when moving
   • time taken
   • estimated number of calories burnt

112 For maximum accuracy, it is important for users to know the exact length of their stride which, unfortunately, varies according to walking speed, slope, terrain and conditions underfoot. The average length of your stride in Norfolk is likely to be significantly longer than it is in the Lake District or the Scottish Highlands. Similarly, when walking with a group, your speed is that of the group not your own natural pace and this can significantly distort the result recorded by your pedometer.

113 To use a pedometer properly, records of the number of paces and distance covered in differing kinds of country must be kept. The most accurate method of calculating the length of your stride is to choose routes of at least ten kilometres in the type of countryside in which you normally walk. Use a handheld satnav in odometer mode to measure the length of the walk and divide this by the number of steps recorded on your pedometer.

114 Other methods are less reliable. You can use an opisometer to measure the length of the walk and divide this by the number of steps recorded by the pedometer, or measure a fixed distance by using a tape (see 6:95).

115 Finally, what useful purpose does a pedometer serve? Theoretically, it could be used for counting paces (see 6:94-7) but they are not easy to read because most models have to be located over the hip so it is usually more convenient to use a tachometer or to count the number of double paces as described in 6:95.

Select bibliography

(See the list of titles in the bibliography for Chapter 5 (5: 45-64).

Chapter 7 A map-reading exercise

1 In this chapter, a short walk of just under five miles is described to illustrate most of the problems likely to be encountered when map-reading in lowland countryside.

2 The walk was described in the 1978 edition of *The Walker's Handbook* when much of the path network in England, especially in those rural areas unlikely to attract walkers from afar, was in a parlous state. In the last thirty years the condition of public paths has been transformed due largely to the work of
   • the Countryside Commission (now Natural England)
   • the Ramblers' Association
   • the Open Spaces Society
   • highway authorities
   • local activists

3 For example, there are three parishes in the north of Buckinghamshire containing a 20-mile network of public rights of way located in pleasant but unexciting countryside which is poorly served by public transport. In 1978, there was only one landowner who maintained his paths and it was only the most determined who could complete a walk. Problems included
   • fields ploughed and the path not restored
   • crops growing on the line of the path
   • gates and stiles missing or unusable through neglect
   • few roadside signposts
   • no waymarks

4 When the rights of way in these parishes were surveyed in 2010 by a pathchecker for the Ramblers' Association, only one serious problem, an old iron gate tied up with binder twine (subsequently replaced), was found. Every other public path met the following legal requirements
   • signposted from where it left a road
   • waymarked throughout its length
   • the path furniture, with the exception noted above, was in a serviceable condition
   • paths restored after ploughing and free from encroaching crops
This is a measure of how much the condition of England's path network has been transformed in the last thirty years.

5   Despite some of the misleading statements made by the Ramblers' Association
    (see Appendix 4), walkers in most parts of England can be reasonably confident
    that they will encounter only the occasional insuperable problem.

The walk

6   An imaginary route has been devised using only those features found on Ord-
    nance Survey maps and omitting, for the sake of clarity, contours (which are of
    no great significance in lowland countryside), and grid lines.

7   In practice, as mentioned in paragraph 5 above, it is unlikely that a walker
    would encounter so many problems in such a short itinerary. The purpose of
    including so many is to illustrate how, by using a map and compass, you can
    find your way when the path is not visible on the ground.

8   The walk is from Barchester to Puddlecombe-in-the-Slush. The *Explorer*
    1:25,000 map (see Fig. 18) will be used for navigation. This is not a popular
    walking area and is farmed intensively, so the paths are unlikely to be clearly
    defined on the ground and reliance must be placed on natural features to pin-
    point the route. The walk has been split into three sections subsequently referred
    to as 'legs', each bounded by a road, which will help to confirm our position
    before we start the next leg.

Leg 1

9   The walk starts from a gate which leads from the road onto a bridleway that
    runs alongside a picnic site at Fox Covert situated about two kilometres from
    Barchester. According to the map, the bridleway follows the edge of Fox Covert
    (this is a handrail as described in 8:4). We turn our map so that it is orientated to
    the bridleway and walk along the outside edge of Fox Covert to a gate and stile
    in the hedge at the end of the wood at point A (this is a tick feature which con-
    firms our position as described in 8:5). Here we find a huge field of gently wav-
    ing barley where the map indicates that there should be a very narrow field. Let
    us examine the map to work out what has happened.

10 There are only three possible explanations
    - the map is wrong
    - we have misread the map and gone astray
    - the terrain has been altered

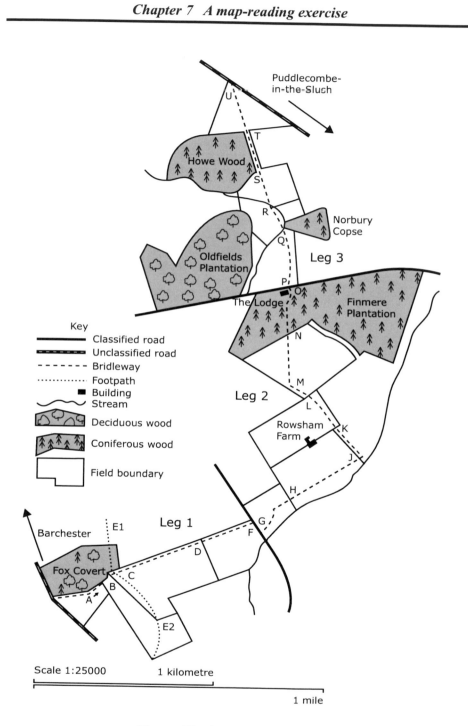

Figure 18   A map-reading exercise

11 Each possibility must now be considered:

a) It is very unlikely that the map was wrong *at the date of the survey.* The Ordnance Survey is not infallible but its errors are usually in minute details and it rarely makes mistakes of this magnitude.

b) Have we gone astray? This is unlikely, as Fox Covert is readily identifiable and there is no other wood on the map with which we could confuse it.

c) Has the terrain altered? Let us consider some of the changes that can be made to the landscape. They include
   - erection of buildings
   - demolition of buildings
   - realignment of roads
   - construction of new roads and tracks
   - construction of reservoirs
   - abandonment of railway lines
   - diversion of streams
   - planting of woods
   - felling of woods
   - realignment of field boundaries

12 In this case the most likely explanation is that some field boundaries have been removed and we now have to consider which ones have gone. As far as we can tell, the field now looks roughly the shape shown in Fig. 19.

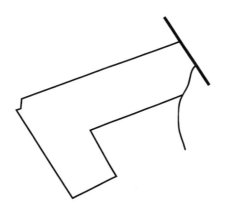

Figure 19 Present shape of field

13 The long hedge which runs towards the road is still there. This can be confirmed by taking a compass bearing along its line and plotting the result on the map. We appear to be standing at point A but we are suddenly struck by doubts when we realize that the edge of Fox Covert does not project beyond our hedge as shown on the map at point B. Let us consider the possibilities again

  • the map is inaccurate (this possibility can usually be discounted)

  • the hedge has been moved

  • part of the wood has been felled

An examination of the hedge shows that it is old, containing many varieties of shrubs and some well-established trees. This proves that part of Fox Covert has been felled.

14 We have now identified two hedges and from the size of the field we can deduce that the field boundary at point C, which formed one of the sides of the narrow field, has been removed. But even if we imagine our map without that field boundary, the shape of the field is still wrong, so we have to consider whether any other boundaries have been removed. We can see that the field is L-shaped and this gives us the clue, for we can now see that another boundary, at point D running at right angles to the bridleway, has been removed.

15 Although we do not plan to follow it, let us turn our attention to the map-reading problems involved in following the footpath E1 to E2 which crosses the bridleway (see Fig. 20). Anyone travelling in a southeasterly direction would expect to pass through Fox Covert and then to walk along the right-hand headland of a now non-existent field boundary (a headland is a path that runs beside a field boundary). When the boundary was removed, the landholder should have applied to divert the path along the other headland because the path makes for the corner of the field. Landholders, as well as recreational interests would be better served by a sensible diversion. Without accurate surveying instruments it would be impossible to follow the true line of the path, so in these circumstances it would be better to follow the headland route.

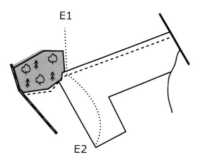

Figure 20 A map-reading problem

16   To return to our bridleway. We can now walk along the left-hand headland (a handrail) to a gate giving access to the road at point F (a collecting feature) which is also the end of the first leg.

Leg 2

17   At the start of the second leg, we orientate our map so that it lines up with the road, turn right and look for a bridleway sign on the left-hand side. There is no signpost but we can see a gate at point G which must be the one we want because it is roughly halfway from where we emerged onto the road and the bridge which carries the road over the stream. We orientate our map again and pass through the gate and walk diagonally across the field to a gate we can see in the hedge opposite at point H. The path now heads across the field to the junction of the hedge and stream where we find a wide gap leading into the next field at point J. Here we have to turn left and orientate our map to follow the hedge (a handrail). This field has been ploughed and the farmer has left only a narrow strip of undisturbed ground along the headland which, through lack of use, has become overgrown with vegetation that impedes our progress.

18   We confidently follow the left-hand headland to a gate at point K in a fence (a tick feature) which leads into the next field where the bridleway follows the right-hand headland (a handrail). At the top of this field at point L, we pass through a gate in a hedge (a tick feature), and follow the left-hand headland (a handrail) of another ploughed field. This has a slight rise followed by a dip which prevents us seeing Finmere Plantation. We cannot find any trace of a path running from the headland at point M to the boundary of Finmere Plantation at point N so we assume that the farmer has not restored the line of the path after ploughing.

19   The map indicates that the path should leave the headland at point M after about 125 metres so we estimate the distance as best we can by pacing (see 6:94-7). Next, we must decide the direction in which we must walk across the ploughed field. The easiest way to do this is to take a compass bearing (see 6:50-6). But we may be able to do it by aligning the hedge marked on the map with the hedge that we are following by placing a pencil on the map pointing along the line of the path from M to N (see Chapter 6, Fig. 8). We look along the line of the pencil to see if there is a prominent feature such as a tower, pylon, easily recognizable hill etc. on the same line of the path and which is also visible on the ground. If there is, then all we have to do is to walk towards the feature and we will arrive at the gate that leads into Finmere Plantation. Should we not have a compass, and there is no distinctive feature, then all we can do is to estimate the direction as best we can and walk towards the top of the rise.

20　Once there, we find that the gate at point N, which gives access to Finmere Plantation (a tick feature), is visible at the bottom of the dip and, if necessary, we adjust our direction. A couple of hundred metres later, a number of forest tracks, which are not marked on the map, meet at a junction (see Fig. 21). There are no waymarks or other helpful identifying features, so the only way of being certain of following the right of way is to take a compass bearing from the map which gives us a grid bearing of 2°.

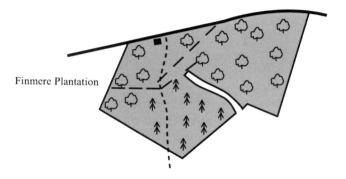

Figure 21　Identifying the route with a compass

21　The map key tells us that magnetic declination (grid magnetic angle see 6:55) is 3° so, as we are only using a compass to *identify* rather than to *follow* the route we can ignore the difference. (Note that when using a compass bearing to *follow* a route, you must *never* ignore the grid magnetic angle or you may end up several hundred metres from your destination.

22　After a few hundred metres, our confidence is rewarded when we reach a clearing at The Lodge (a tick feature). We keep it on our left and find a gate and bridleway sign on the road at point O (a tick feature). This marks the end of the second leg.

Leg 3

23　On the other side of the road we see a gate and bridleway sign at point P, so we follow the path along the headland (a handrail) to a gate and culvert which crosses the stream at point Q (a tick feature), and then follows it. According to the map, the path crosses the stream again at a footbridge at point R and, sure enough, we come to a wide farm bridge (a tick feature). Across the bridge there is a farm track running towards the right-hand corner of the field (see Fig. 22).

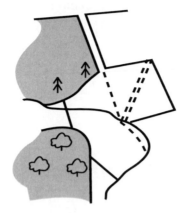

Figure 22 A map-reading problem

24   Before succumbing to the temptation to follow this track we first check that it is
on our chosen route. Our map reveals that our path runs along the edge of Howe
Wood and we can now see a gate and stile on the edge of the wood at point S (a
tick feature). Accordingly, we ignore the track and make for the gate and stile
and enter a narrow lane bordered by hedges at point S (a handrail) which leads
into a field at point T (a tick feature). The path continues in the same direction
to the corner of the field to a gate and stile in the hedge bordering the road at the
finish (a tick feature). Beside the gate and stile is a house, which causes us some
concern as it is not marked on the map. For a moment or two we wonder if we
have gone wrong. However, we can see that it is a new house which must have
been built after the survey for the *Explorer* map was made. We are now on the
outskirts of Puddlecombe-in-the-Slush and we turn right along the road and
walk into the village.

Conclusion

25   This imaginary walk demonstrates how to navigate through lowland countryside
using an *Explorer* map for guidance. The principle we followed was to walk
from feature to feature, using handrails and tick features, until we reached the
end of each leg and were thus able to confirm our position. The features we
used were

- field boundaries
- woods
- a stream
- roads
- buildings

26 We have learnt:

a) That a compass was helpful in confirming the route through Finmere Plantation, where we encountered some forest tracks that were not marked on the map, and also at point R where we could have been confused by the farm track.

b) Some techniques for resolving problems when the map seems not to match the terrain.

Select bibliography

The following titles deal specifically with lowland walking

27 Hawkins, Pete, *Navigation; Techniques and Skills for Walkers*. Cicerone Press, 2010.

28 Marsh, Terry, *Map-reading Skills; an Introduction to Map-reading and Basic Navigation*. Crimson Jarrold, 2007.

29 Saunders, Colin, *Navigation and Leadership; a Manual for Walkers* 2nd ed. revised by Julian Tippett. Ramblers' Association, 1994. This, the best guide to lowland map-reading is a teaching text. It is out of print but a copy containing some revisions in manuscript can be downloaded from www.ramblers.org.uk.

30 Tippett, Julian, *Navigation for Walkers*. Cordee, 2001.

Chapter 8   Advanced navigation techniques

1   Mastery of the techniques described in Chapter 6 will make you a competent fair-weather navigator but additional skills are required when
    • hill-walking
    • lost
    • visibility is poor

2   There are a number of techniques which can assist in following a route. These include
    • handrails
    • tick features
    • overshoot features
    • collecting features
    • transit points
    • attack points
    • aiming off
    • backbearings
    • boxing
    • aspect of the slope
    • contouring
    • route cards

3   Some walkers argue that the widespread use of handheld satnavs (see Chapter 9) has rendered many of the techniques described in this chapter redundant. However, not every walker either wants, or can afford, a handheld satnav and in any case the mastery of traditional paper map and compass navigation will give you a greater insight into the features of the landscape. Walkers of a nervous disposition should consider carrying a satnav but to use it to confirm their position *after* they have located themselves by employing traditional navigation techniques.

Handrails

4   A handrail is an easily-recognized linear feature that is marked on the map and can be followed to help guide you along your route. Handrails do not have to be

in close proximity to your route but they must be visible. Examples of handrails include

- paths that are visible on the ground
- field boundaries
- the edges of woods
- streams
- canals
- the shores of lakes, lochs and reservoirs
- power lines
- ridges
- valleys
- railway lines

Tick features

5   When following a route, mentally tick off the features marked on the map that confirm your location and progress as you pass them. Tick features include

- paths and roads that cross your route
- paths that join your route
- railway lines
- bridges
- triangulation pillars (but be aware that the Ordnance Survey has removed many in recent years, especially in lowland areas, so the absence of a 'trig point' is not necessarily significant)
- field boundaries
- woods
- sheepfolds
- buildings
- streams
- tarns, ponds, lakes, lochs and reservoirs
- outcrops and crags
- power lines

Overshoot features

6   An overshoot feature is something marked on the map that will indicate that you have gone too far and missed your turning. This technique is more commonly used in upland areas but can also be useful in lowland countryside.

7   Suppose that you are on a featureless moor looking for a path junction that is two kilometres ahead. You may use timing (see 6:98-101) to reach the junction

but it is also useful to be able to identify a feature that will indicate that you have gone too far and missed the junction.

8   Overshoot features are similar to tick features and include
- paths and roads that cross your route
- railway lines
- bridges
- triangulation pillars (but be aware that the Ordnance Survey has removed many in recent years, especially in lowland areas, so the absence of a 'trig point' is not necessarily significant)
- field boundaries
- woods
- sheepfolds
- buildings
- streams
- tarns, ponds, lakes and reservoirs
- outcrops and crags

When you reach an overshoot feature you will have to measure the distance back to the path junction and retrace your steps. (A handheld satnav obviates the need to identify overshoot features.)

Collecting features

9   When walking in upland country, it is useful to aim for an easily recognized feature that can be used to guide you on the next leg of your walk. Collecting features are always linear and can become handrails when you reach them. They include
- valleys
- ridges
- streams
- walls
- tracks
- roads

Note that in winter conditions, some of these features may not be visible.

Transits

10   Sometimes it is possible, especially when walking off-path on a bearing in good visibility, to line up two features such as a sheepfold and a pylon. By keeping them in-line you can walk towards them without having to use your compass again. The pub in Fig. 23 is hidden from view by a dip in the road. The easiest

way to reach it is to line up the sheepfold and pylon, walk to the road and turn right. Note that when crossing undulating terrain the features may disappear from time to time and you may have to line them up again. Such features are known as transit points and the route taken is a transit line.

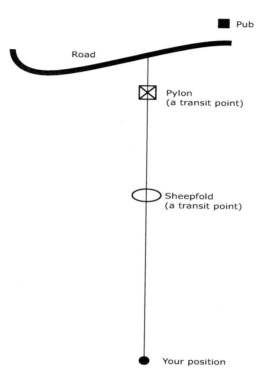

Figure 23   Transit points

11   The same principle can be employed to establish your position when following a handrail as when walking along a ridge. It is often possible to line up two features across the valley, such as a building and the edge of a wood, which will fix your position on the ridge (see Fig. 24).

Aiming off

12   There are some circumstances when it is helpful to build in a deliberate error, known as 'aiming off', when navigating over pathless country. For example, in Fig. 25, walkers making for the footbridge over the stream cannot see it, due to

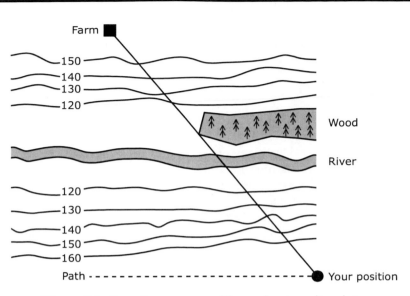

Figure 24   Locating your position using transit points

the lie of the land or poor visibility. If they walk on a bearing that will take them directly to the bridge, and cannot find it when they get to the river, they will not know whether it lies to the left or right (it may even be missing!). But if they take a bearing that will bring them to the river bank some distance to one side of the bridge they will know in which direction to turn to find it. When first employing this technique you should consider aiming off by 10° a figure which you can refine in the light of experience.

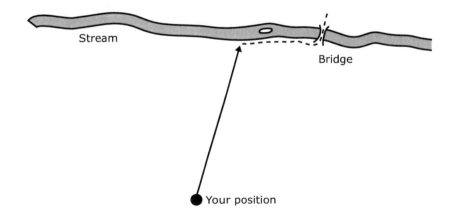

Figure   25 Aiming off

13 If you have a handheld satnav you do not need to aim off because you can key in the grid reference of the bridge. The receiver locks on to this location and will guide you there unerringly irrespective of the number of diversions you make (see Chapter 9).

Backbearings

14 When walking on a bearing (see 6:50-6), the direction of the wind and the angle of the slope can cause you to drift off-course. This can be corrected if your previous position, or an identifiable object on the line of your route, is still visible. Turn round and face the direction from which you have come and point the direction of travel arrow to the start of the leg or a feature that is on the line of your route. Turn the compass housing so that the south-facing (white) needle lines up with the arrow in the bottom of the compass housing. If the south-facing (white) compass needle is not over the arrow, then you are off-course. Move either to the right or the left until the needle and the arrow coincide.

Boxing

15 This is a useful technique when following a compass bearing and a diversion has to be made to avoid an obstruction such as a boggy area (see Fig. 26):

a) Take a compass bearing along the line of your route.

b) Turn 90° and count the number of paces taken to clear the obstacle.

c) Turn 90° parallel to the path and walk along the original compass bearing until you have cleared the bog and it is possible to make another 90° turn.

d) Count the same number of paces that you made in b) above, then take another 90° turn and you will be back on your original course.

This is where a handheld satnav becomes really useful. If you key in the grid reference of your destination it will lock onto the location and will guide you there irrespective of the number of diversions you make (see Chapter 9).

Aspect of the slope

16 The general direction and angles of slopes are sources of useful information when navigating. For example, if you are following a path with a downhill slope to your right but the map shows that the slope should be on the left, then you are either

- on the wrong path
- walking on the correct path but in the wrong direction

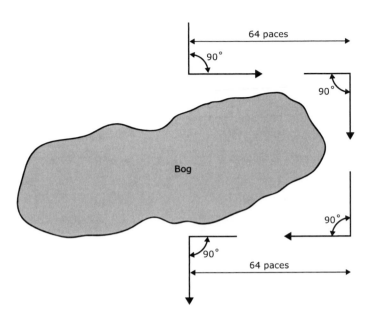

Figure 26   Boxing

17   In some circumstances it is possible to take a compass bearing down a slope to help to establish your position (see Fig. 27). This is referred to as 'taking the aspect of the slope' and can be done as follows:

a)   Face the slope holding your compass level, pressed firmly against your stomach and at right angles to a line between your shoulders.

b)   Keep your feet about 30 cm apart and directly under each shoulder.

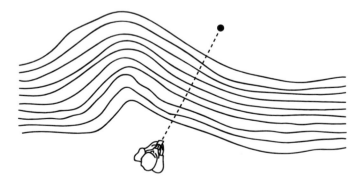

Figure 27   Taking the aspect of the slope

c) Adjust your position by shuffling your feet until the direction of travel arrow points exactly down the fall of the slope (i.e. the line that a ball would take when rolling down the slope). Tilt your compass until it is level, and read the bearing.

d) Convert to a grid bearing (see 6:50-6).

e) Place the compass on the map keeping the lines in the compass housing parallel with the grid lines on the map and with the arrow in the compass housing pointing to map north.

f) Push the compass along your route until the long side of the base plate crosses the contour lines exactly at a right angle.

g) Draw a pencil line along the side of the perspex base plate. You should be somewhere along this slope.

h) Establish your height with an altimeter (see 6:102-4) and you have the final piece of the jigsaw to confirm your position.

18 An even better fix can be obtained if you can find a small watercourse to straddle. Point the direction of travel arrow along the line of the stream and take a bearing. Follow the map procedures outlined above and you should obtain a fix that will include the stream.

19 In order to use this technique, you should know your position to within a few hundred metres or so. It is helpful if contour lines curve because if they run in a relatively straight line it is more difficult to be certain that you have obtained an accurate fix since you could be anywhere along the straight line. Repeat the procedure on a nearby slope that faces in a different direction to help confirm your position. A handheld satnav will establish your position much more quickly (see Chapter 9).

Contouring

20 Imagine that you are following a high-level path near the head of a valley. The path descends steeply into the valley and then climbs up the other side (see Fig. 28). It may be quicker and easier to walk round the head of the valley.

21 If you are walking off-path it is helpful to use an altimeter to keep you at a constant height. It is surprisingly difficult to maintain a steady height because you always tend to drift downhill but, by setting your altimeter to the appropriate height, the amount of drift can be much diminished.

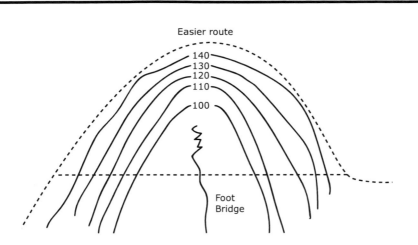

Figure 28   Contouring

22   You can use an altimeter for this purpose even if you have not reset it recently and are unsure of its accuracy. In this instance you are only interested in keeping level so it matters not what height it registers because the instrument will alert you if you drift downhill by more than 10 metres. (A handheld satnav obviates the need for a stand-alone altimeter.)

Route Cards

23   Some walkers prepare route cards (see Fig. 29). They are useful in lowland countryside and invaluable when walking in pathless terrain. They serve the following purposes:

a)   The discipline of examining the map to
- calculate distance
- calculate height gain and total cumulative ascent
- estimate time required to complete the walk
- where to aim off
- locate attack points

b)   Saving time by obviating the need for frequent reference to the map.

c)   They can be invaluable in bad weather when the wind may be so strong as to make consulting the map and taking accurate compass bearings difficult.

d)   A copy can be left with a responsible person so that the authorities can be alerted and a search made should the walker(s) fail to return.

e)   The back of the card can be used for recording the names, emergency telephone numbers and other personal details of members of the group.

f) The route card illustrated in Fig. 29 relates to a backpacking trip on Dartmoor using a compass and *Explorer OL 28*. The route follows rights of way and access land crossed by field boundaries.

ROUTE CARD

Start: Wild camp at Broad Hole SX 489782. **Finish:** Teigncombe SX 672871

LEG		MINUTES
1	BW E for 1·8km to West Dart River	25
2	Cross river & follow BW for 200m then b'ring 90° for 1·8km/+40 m to boundary	20
3	TL & follow boundary NE then NW for 4km/+70m to East Dart river	60
4	Cross river & after 50m TL on BW & head N for 3·8km/+95m to forest boundary	65
5	When BW enters forest leave BW & continue NNE along boundary & then NE for 1·7km/-40m	22
6	Follow bearing 232° for 1·7km/0m to Kester Rock	22
7	Follow bearing 350° for 1·3km/-60m to road	16
8	TR & walk 1·1km along road to Teigncombe	15
		Total 245

Figure 29 A route card

Abbreviations

b'ring = bearing   N = north
BW = bridleway   NE = north east
E = east   NNE = north northeast
km = kilometre(s)   NNW = north northwest
km/+m = distance and ascent   NW = north west
km/-m distance and descent   TL = turn left
m = metre(s)   TR = turn right

N.B. It is unusual to follow a bearing across open country lacking a handrail or intermediate landmarks for the distances given in legs 6 & 7. It is acceptable in this instance because there were two collecting features, a road and a wall, forming a horseshoe shape centred on Kester Rock that would funnel the walkers to the road near Teigncombe should they overshoot.

Foul weather navigation

24   Everyone who walks in the upland areas of the British Isles should be familiar with the techniques used in foul weather navigation. In bad weather, when visibility may be as low as 50 metres, and in the winter conditions of a white-out down to less than five metres, the only possible method of navigation where there is no path, apart from using a handheld satnav, is a combination of compass bearing and distance covered.

25   The first essential is to get an accurate fix *before* the bad weather sets in. Next examine the map carefully and decide whether it is wise to alter the original route to the destination. Consider the following points:

a)   Is it better to return to your starting point? (This may be the most mature and sensible decision.)

b)   Is the route dangerous in poor visibility? If it follows a knife-edge ridge or runs close to an escarpment an alternative route should be selected to obviate the risk of an accident.

c)   Is it possible to take an alternative route that will follow an obvious feature such as a stream, wall or track? This is the handrail principle (see 8:4).

Walking on a bearing

26   It is difficult to walk on a bearing accurately over a long distance in conditions of poor visibility. Members of a group have a significant advantage over the lone walker because they can employ the methods listed below that will assist in following the bearing accurately, and can correct any deviation by using the following signals

- raise the right arm horizontally to indicate 'move to the right'
- raise the left arm horizontally to indicate 'move to the left'
- raise both arms horizontally to indicate 'stand still'
- raise both arms vertically to indicate 'correction made'
- raise both arms vertically and beckon to indicate 'come forward'

27   The following methods are the simplest:

a)   This method (see Fig. 30a) will cover the ground fastest but is less accurate than b). It requires a minimum of three people and two compasses set to the same bearing. The leader walks in front followed a few paces behind by the second person who does not need a compass. The backmarker has a compass and sights through the second person to the leader. The leader stops at regular intervals so that the backmarker can indicate with arm signals if a correction has to be made.

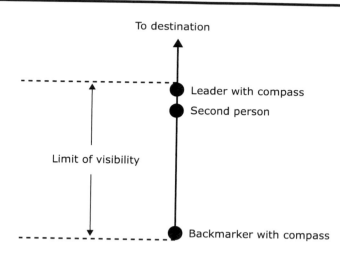

Figure 30a   Walking on a bearing: three people and two compasses

b) This method requires a minimum of two people, a leader and a backmarker, and one compass (see Fig. 30b). The leader should take a compass bearing from the map along the route to be followed. The backmarker remains stationary whilst the leader walks on the bearing to the limit of visibility and

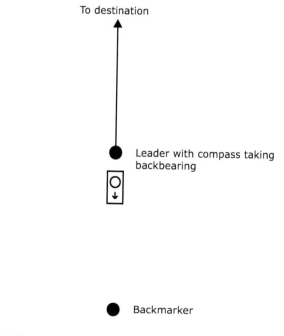

Figure 30b   Walking on a bearing: two people and one compass

then turns round and takes a backbearing (see 8:14) on the backmarker. If off-course, the leader adjusts the position accordingly before signalling to the backmarker and the rest of the group to come forward. The process is repeated as frequently as is necessary. This method is more accurate than that described in a) above but more than doubles the amount of time required to complete the walk.

c) A lone walker has no choice but to walk unaided on a compass bearing. This will be made more difficult if there is a strong cross-wind, or when traversing a slope because under both conditions it is difficult to keep a straight line and avoid drifting to one side. If there is snow on the ground it may be possible to take backbearings (see 8:14) on your footprints which will help to correct your position. Depending on circumstances, it might be better to make a diversion and aim for a collecting feature (see 8:9) that will guide you to your destination.

28 If you have a handheld satnav, then you should have no difficulty in navigating to your destination, but you must ensure, by checking the map, that you will not be walking into dangerous terrain.

Attack points

29 In poor visibility, or when searching for an inconspicuous object such as a tent in featureless moorland, it is often quicker and easier to aim for something nearby that is marked on the map such as

- a junction of walls
- a confluence of streams
- a plantation
- a tarn

These are known as attack points (see Fig. 31).

30 Once the attack point has been reached, a bearing should be taken direct to the object. The advantage of this technique is that the attack point can be used as a mark and returned to if the objective cannot be found at the first attempt. In poor visibility it may be necessary to conduct an area search (see 8:32).

31 If you have a satnav you can record the position of your tent or car as a waypoint. Then, when you return to it, you could turn the waypoint into a GoTo and the satnav will lock onto this location and guide you there (see Chapter 9).

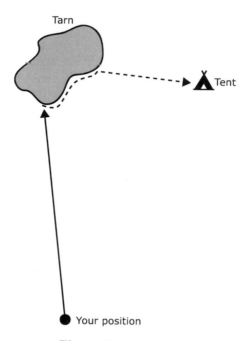

Figure 31   An attack point

Area searches

32 In foul weather it may be necessary to conduct a search to find a small object such as a tent. You navigate to get as close as possible by using a combination of techniques including

- attack points
- compass bearings
- pace-counting

but you still cannot see it. There are two methods of finding it. A sweep search is the quicker and more reliable method but can only be used if there are several walkers in the group. The solo backpacker has to employ an expanding square search (see 8:35).

Sweep searches

33 When you reach the attack point, you should calculate the bearing to be followed, and the number of paces required to reach the object.

34 Members of a group should walk on the bearing in line abreast each one at the limit of visibility from his or her neighbour. The leader should be in the centre counting the paces (see Fig. 32). This should find the tent.

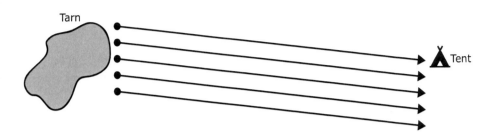

Figure 32   A sweep search

Expanding square searches

35 This technique (also known as a box search, square search, spiral search, and extended square search) can be used in poor visibility by lone backpackers to locate their tent once the attack point has been reached (see Fig. 33):

a) On reaching the attack point, calculate the bearing to be followed and the number of paces required to reach the object and walk towards it

b) If the object is still not visible, decide how many paces you can walk and still remain comfortably within the limit of visibility from your starting point which, for the purpose of this example, we shall assume to be 10 paces. Using your compass go

- north for 20 paces
- east for 30 paces
- south for 40 paces
- west for 50 paces
- north for 60 paces

and so on until the tent is found.

Figure 33   An expanding square search

Relocation

36 Relocation is the technical term used for establishing your position when you are lost

37 There is a difference between making a navigational error and being lost. If you make an error of navigation, realize your mistake and correct it, you are not lost because you have been able to work out your position. When you are lost you have no idea where you are. This can be a scary experience in upland areas, especially in poor visibility.

38 Relocating yourself after getting lost is normally a simple matter in lowland countryside because you are rarely out of sight of a house or road for more than a few minutes. If you are unable to relocate by examining the map, it is usually only a matter of retracing your steps until you reach a point where you know exactly where you are.

39 Being lost in the upland areas of the British Isles can be a serious matter, especially in bad weather, so it is important to keep a constant check on your progress by identifying the features depicted on the map. You are most likely to get lost in conditions of restricted visibility when the problem of relocating is made more difficult by the inability to see more than a hundred metres or so. The most difficult terrain in which to have to relocate is moorland because it is often featureless and it is difficult to follow a straight line. *Once you are assailed by doubts, stop immediately and assess the situation. Do not continue in the hope that you will recognize a landmark.*

40 You should do everything possible to avoid getting lost by following procedures that include:

a) Examining the route on the map carefully before setting off.

b) Completing a route card (see 8:23) because it forces you to describe the route in detail, helps you to pinpoint any route-finding problems and form an overall picture of what the route is like. Make a note of suitable escape routes in case you encounter foul weather. (An escape route will take you to lower ground from where you can find a safer route such as a road.)

c) Divide the walk into sections, often referred to as 'legs', using, as far as possible, features that you cannot cross without being aware of them. They include:
  • roads
  • tracks
  • walls, fences and hedges
  • valleys

• tarns, ponds, lakes, lochs and reservoirs

• woods

• ridges

• significant streams

• power lines

41 This breaks the walk down into a series of areas which you concentrate on in turn so that, should you go astray, you should have no doubt in which area you are. This technique makes relocation easier:

a) Make certain that you identify your starting point correctly before you set off. This may seem obvious but it is quite easy, especially if the walk begins from an isolated roadside path, to start the walk in the wrong place, especially when two paths leave a road within a short distance of each other. If one is signposted and the other is not, it is easy to assume that the signposted path is the one you want. Always confirm that you are starting at the correct path by identifying a nearby feature, or by taking a compass bearing along its line to confirm that it is running in the correct direction. This is yet another reason for ticking off the features that you pass; if the map and terrain do not match then you may have started from the wrong place.

b) Backpackers who are leaving their tent for a day's walk should ensure that they know the exact location of their pitch before setting off.

c) Note on your route card, the margin of your map, or a piece of paper, the time that you started walking together with the arrival and departure times at the end of every leg.

d) You should pay close attention to your compass (except, possibly, in the Cuillins on the Isle of Skye where magnetic rocks may be encountered), to ensure that you are travelling in the right direction, and mentally tick off features and landmarks as you reach them.

42 These precautions make navigation sound simple, and it often is when you are fresh, but as the day wears on and tiredness sets in you will become less alert and tend to make mistakes and to jump to conclusions. Foul weather can be demoralizing and seriously affect your ability to think clearly.

43 For example, every year thousands of people walk the Coast to Coast Path which, for much of the way, follows unwaymarked paths that are clear on the ground. However, in conditions of restricted visibility it is easy to get lost in the Lake District between Rosthwaite and Grasmere:

a) The route from Rosthwaite to the summit of Lining Crag (NY 283112) presents no problems but between Lining Crag and Greenup Edge (NY 285105) the path, although cairned, can be difficult to find in the broken and boggy terrain. The path descending from Greenup Edge is steep and broken but generally easy to follow. Halfway down there are a number of parallel routes that have developed because of heavy use and conditions underfoot.

b) It is easy for walkers go astray when they reach the beck in the basin at the bottom of the descent because they assume that it is a steady descent from the summit of Greenup Edge to Grasmere village. But close examination of the map shows that the path climbs for forty metres to a low, unnamed saddle (NY 295102) before making the final descent to Grasmere.

c) In good visibility it is difficult to go wrong, but walkers who cannot see the path running up to the saddle (grid bearing 110°), and do not check the direction with a compass, then the 'Wythburn trap' is sprung and they continue to descend (grid bearing 42°). Should they not realize their mistake they will continue for four kilometres until reaching the road at Wythburn (NY 322128).

d) As they will have descended 300 metres, visibility will probably have improved and they should be able to see the reservoir at Thirlmere which they may assume to be the lake at Grasmere. When they have relocated, they will find that they are now six kilometres north of Grasmere. This mistake could easily have been avoided had they noted the 40-metre ascent on the map, and kept their eye on their compass.

Relocation techniques

44   Begin by gathering all the clues that you can in a logical sequence:

a) Make a note of the time.

b) Orientate the map with a compass.

c) Ask yourself the following questions and write down the answers on a piece of paper or on the margin of your map. Are you in a valley on a hill, or a plateau?

d) *Explorer* maps give information about vegetation so check the ground underfoot with the key. Are you surrounded by bracken, heath, or rough grassland?

e) When you listen carefully can you hear traffic which would indicate a road? If so, try to locate the direction of sound.

f) Can you recall the last feature that you are certain was on the correct route? If so, mark it on the map.

g) Can you take a backbearing (see 8:14) towards this last feature, or at least attempt to determine the general direction in which you have been travelling? If so, can you make an estimate of the time that has elapsed between leaving that particular feature and your present position?

i) Roughly pencil an arc on your map, using as the radius the estimated distance you have travelled from the last identified feature, and centred on the approximate direction (see Fig. 34). The arc is the probable limit of travel and you should be somewhere inside it. If you know the general direction in which you have been travelling, put a cross on your best estimate of your position taking into account the answers to the questions you have written down.

j) If you have an altimeter, and you have checked its setting against known heights during the walk, you should be able to determine your altitude with reasonable accuracy. Adjust your estimated position accordingly.

k) Examine the map again. Is there a linear feature such as a wall, lake, patch of woodland, road, track etc. close to your estimated position? If visibility is poor and you cannot see the feature, consider taking a compass bearing to the feature and walking a short distance to see if you can locate it. If found, it should be possible to take a bearing along the linear feature, convert it to grid, and slide your compass over the map to find a match.

l) Is the feature still there? A map is only accurate at the date of its survey. Streams and small lakes can disappear during a long spell of dry weather, and woods can be felled. Have you walked far enough to find it?

45   When you have gathered this information together, you should have some idea of where you are. You now have to decide your next move which will be one of the following:

a) Plan a new route to reach your destination. If you make this choice, you should draw up a list of tick features (see 8:5) to confirm that you have identified your position accurately and are now following the correct route.

b) Return to your original route and start again from the point at which you went astray. The nature of the terrain in which you find yourself, for example, a dangerously steep descent or a river crossing, may make this your only rational choice.

In conclusion

46   Navigation is a fascinating subject which, to the newcomer, must appear daunting after reading Chapters 4-8. The secret of becoming a competent navigator is to practise constantly to hone your skills. It is not sufficient merely to have theoretical knowledge learned from a book because your confidence is likely to ebb when you find yourself lost in thick mist in mountainous country.

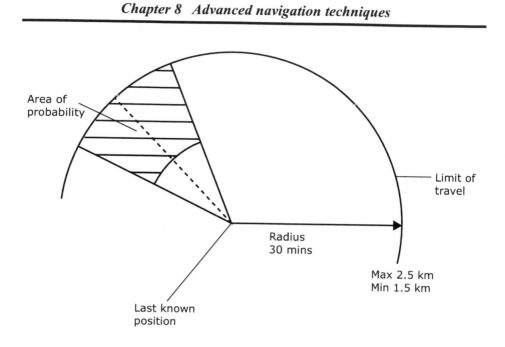

Figure 34   Area of probabilty

47 If you live far from upland areas, you may find it difficult to practise foul-weather navigation, so you should seize every opportunity to explore unfamiliar lowland routes in conditions of low cloud, mist, and at night. Bear in mind that:

a) Searching for stiles and gates whilst navigating from field to field, or following a public right of way through wooded areas criss-crossed with animal paths, fire breaks and foresters' tracks on a moonless night, can provide a challenging experience.

b) Your equipment should include a head torch and a compass with a luminous dial. The countryside at night has an eerie atmosphere especially when your torch picks up the eyes of sheep that glow in the dark.

c) Take particular care to ensure that there is not a bull present when passing through a field containing cattle.

d) Experiencing navigation at night in lowland countryside can stand you in good stead when you come to explore areas of mountain and moorland in poor visibility.

48 All competent navigators have occasionally got lost; it's part of the learning process. If an experienced walker tells you that he (and it will always be a man) has never got lost, he is lying!

Select bibliography

See the list of titles in the bibliography for Chapter 5 (5:45-64).

Chapter 9 The Global Navigation Satellite System

IMPORTANT NOTE

The development of global navigation satellite systems and their associated technologies is moving so fact that only a general outline can be given here. For the latest information readers are advised to make internet searches.

1 The development of navigation systems using satellites is the most significant advance in navigation aids to occur in recent years and is comparable in importance to the invention of the compass and radio direction finding. Handheld instruments have been developed that can receive signals from satellites which can be then be used by walkers as aids to navigation.

Definition of terms

2 The terms used in connection with satellite navigation systems have not yet been standardized and are sometimes confusing and self-contradictory. Those used in this book are defined here:

   a) **The Global Navigation Satellite System (GNSS)** refers to the system of circulating satellites and the signals that they transmit. They are transmitted from the satellites of
   - the **Global Positioning System (GPS)** operated by the United States
   - **GALILEO** operated by the European Space Agency
   - the **Global Navigation System** (GLONASS) operated by the Russian authorities
   - **BDS** (formerly known as Compass and Beidou-2) operated by the Chinese authorities

   Note that signals from all four systems are compatible and can be received by most satnavs, smartphones etc. Other countries are also developing navigation satellite systems.

   b) The handheld instrument that receives signals from the satellites of the Global Navigation Satellite System is described as a **handheld satnav** (derived from 'satellite **nav**igator') or the abbreviation 'satnav'. Note that a satnav may be described in other publications as a
   - GPS. This can cause confusion with the Global Positioning System (GPS) operated exclusively by the United States.

- •gps. This is an attempt, by using lower case letters, to distinguish the instrument (a satnav) from the Global Positioning System (GPS) operated exclusively by the United States
- GPS receiver. This term suggests that the instrument only receives signals from the Global Positioning System (GPS) operated exclusively by the United States, whereas the device may also pick up signals from other systems
- GPS compass. This term also suggests that the instrument only receives signals from the Global Positioning System (GPS) operated exclusively by the United States, whereas the device may also pick up signals from other systems
- GNSS receiver

c) Waypoints (WP) and points of interest (POI) are sometimes used interchangeably. In this book
- a **waypoint** is defined as a set of coordinates that identify a specific location, usually a grid reference in the British Isles (except in Jersey), or latitude and longitude in Jersey and world-wide
- a **point of interest** is a waypoint that identifies a specific feature such as a bridge, a trig point or building which is important to the person navigating, and to which a name or symbol can be assigned

Description of the Global Navigation Satellite System

3   The satellites of the four organizations, the Global Positioning System (GPS), GALILEO, GLONASS and BDS that make up the Global Navigation Satellite System transmit signals that can be picked up by a handheld satnav that converts the information into geographical coordinates. These will, depending on the sophistication of your handheld satnav, enable you to:

a) Establish your position anywhere on the earth's surface to within 5 metres.

b) Establish a series of coordinates from a map, and input them into a handheld satnav and then navigate to each one in turn.

c) Record a route you are walking, and then to save it and use it again later.

d) Plot the route on a computer mapping system to see where you have been.

e) Share routes with others via computers.

f) Download maps from a computer into your handheld satnav and follow a route in real time.

4   The accuracy of the signals picked up by handheld satnavs used by walkers is generally 5 metres or better for 95 per cent of the time.

5   There are two supplementary systems that receive satellite signals and improve their accuracy for use in civilian handheld satnavs. These Satellite-Based Augmentation Systems (SBAS) use a network of ground-based stations in fixed locations to calculate the locally-received errors. Corrections are transmitted to the satellites which then broadcast the corrected signals to handheld satnavs

   • WAAS (Wide Area Augmentation System) which covers the United States and Canada

   • EGNOS (European Geostationary Navigation Overlay Service) which covers Europe and the British Isles and extends for hundreds of miles into the Atlantic and as far north as Greenland

6   WAAS, EGNOS, GLONASS and BDS are compatible systems. Providing that your handheld satnav is either WAAS or EGNOS-enabled then accuracy is likely to be as good as 1·5 metres for 99 per cent of the time. Note that most handheld satnavs are manufactured by American companies which means that when setting one up for the first time you can normally only specify WAAS in the menu option. However, when specifying WAAS in European countries you will automatically be tuned to EGNOS.

7   Variations in signal accuracy caused by factors such as:

   a)   The number of satellites 'visible' to the handheld satnav; the more satellites the greater the accuracy.

   b)   Satellite constellation geometry; the wider the angle between them, up to a maximum of 90°, the more accurate the signal. Satellites on the horizon have poor signal strength.

   d)   Ionosphere and troposphere delays as the signal passes through the atmosphere (automatically corrected if the handheld satnav is WAAS/EGNOS-enabled).

   e)   Clock errors which happen because it is not practical to fit an atomic clock into a handheld satnav (automatically corrected if the handheld satnav is WAAS/EGNOS-enabled).

   f)   Minor orbital errors of the satellites (automatically corrected if the handheld satnav is WAAS/EGNOS-enabled).

Handheld satnavs

8   There are several makes and numerous models of satnavs. It is a technology that is developing rapidly so it is only possible to describe them in general terms. There are two main types:

a)   Entry-level satnavs that indicate the direction of travel between coordinates by means of a pointer on the 'Compass Page'. On what is usually called the 'Map Page' there is a diagram of the route which shows your progress by means a symbol that moves along it as you walk.

b)   Satnavs that display a topographic map on the screen showing your route and your progress along it.

c)   Note that satnav functions are available on many smartphones and tablet computers but it is not advisable to use them in the outdoors, unless they are properly protected, because they are neither as robust nor as weather-proof as dedicated handheld satnavs.

9   Most satnavs have a screen and a number of buttons that perform various tasks. Satnavs are powered by batteries, usually AA or AAA, and have a claimed life of 10-20 hours but be aware that manufacturers' forecasts are often optimistic. Battery life is also dependent on how the satnav is used because some functions consume more power than others. Some satnavs have a 'Battery save' mode.

10   The screen has several modes, often referred to as 'pages', which display information through which the user navigates. Each page often has several options which display additional information or perform particular tasks. There are usually pages showing

- satellite reception, signal strength, and current accuracy
- current position expressed as coordinates
- bearing in real time of the direction in which you are actually moving
- bearing of destination
- a topographic map or a diagram that shows your progress
- a navigation page that has a compass-like pointer that indicates the direction in which to travel
- distance covered from your start (odometer). This is normally as the crow flies between coordinates but in trackback mode, and when the route is downloaded from mapping software, the distance actually covered is measured
- distance still to go to your final destination
- current speed
- average speed

- trip time
- elevation which is normally derived from a conventional built-in altimeter which works on changes in air pressure so it has to be calibrated (scc 6:102 1)
- waypoints
- routes
- tracks

Using a handheld satnav

11   Signals cannot be picked up unless there is a clear view of the sky. Satnavs cannot be relied upon to work properly

- indoors
- inside a vehicle
- under dense tree canopy

But they seem unaffected when covered with light clothing. Nor is the accuracy of signals affected by darkness, cloud, fog, rain or snow but there may be a diminution in strength.

12   Switch on the satnav and ensure that it is set to the appropriate local map datum and grid:

a)   The datum is a set of reference points on the surface of the earth against which position measurements are made for geodetic and cartographic purposes. Some datums, such as WGS84, are worldwide; others cover a single country, such as OSGB36, which is the Ordnance Survey's datum for Great Britain and the Isle of Man. Information about the datum is normally given on the map and it is essential that you set your satnav to it.

b)   A grid is a system for locating points on a map. In Great Britain it is the Ordnance Survey National Grid (see 4:11-14). It is assumed in this chapter that you are using your satnav in Great Britain

- the Isle of Man uses the Ordnance Survey National Grid
- Northern Ireland has its own datum and grid which it shares with the Republic of Ireland (see 4:25-7)
- Guernsey uses its own unique grid as well as latitude and longitude, and the Universal Transverse Mercator (UTM) grid
- Jersey uses latitude and longitude

13   Take your satnav into the open in order to initialize it to receive signals from the satellites. If this is the first time that it has been used, or you have travelled several hundred of miles from the location where it was last used, the initialization process may take several minutes. This is known as a 'cold start'.

14   In order to navigate with a satnav you have to input location information which may be sourced from

- satellites
- paper maps
- mapping software installed on your satnav
- mapping software installed on your computer and downloaded to your satnav

15   The most basic function of your satnav is to locate your present position. Press the appropriate button and a 10-figure grid reference will be displayed on the screen which will look something like SU 87463 69282.

16   The letters indicate the 100-kilometre grid square and is followed by the figures of the easting and then the northing. In the example SU 87463 69282 the letters and figures for the easting break down as follows

- SU is the 100-kilometre square
- 8 is the 10-kilometre square
- 7 is the 1-kilometre square
- 4 is the 100-metre square (not shown on map so use a romer (see 6:70-1)
- 6 is the 10-metre square (not shown on the map so use a romer and esti-mate). Note that this can only be measured on 1:25,000 maps
- 3 is the 1-metre square (which is too small be measured on the map)

17   *A grid reference is a useless piece of information until it is related to a map.* This can be achieved in one of two ways depending on the capability of your satnav:

a) By transferring the grid reference to either
- a paper map with the aid of a romer (see 6.70-1)
- mapping software installed on your computer

b) If mapping software is installed on your satnav the grid reference will be displayed and your present position will be indicated on the map on your screen.

18   You can navigate using your satnav by creating

- waypoints
- routes
- tracks

Waypoints

19   A waypoint is a location identified by a grid reference. The procedure for inserting a waypoint manually requires the walker to key in the letters of the 100-kilometre square followed by a ten-figure grid reference. It is only possible to identify an eight-figure grid reference accurately when using a 1:25,000 map, but you are likely, depending on the make of satnav, to be required to key in ten digits for which there are two methods:

a)   If you make the final digit on both the easting and the northing a zero, you will know that you will arrive at the south-west corner of the imaginary 10-metre square so your location of interest should theoretically, assuming that your satnav is WAAS/EGNOS enabled, lie in a box that is no more than 10 metres square. This is the accepted practice.

b)   An alternative method is make the final digit of both the easting and the northing 5. This, on the balance of probabilities, is likely to give the least inaccurate grid reference because it is the median digit between 0 and 9.

20   In good conditions, it will take a competent map-reader up to two minutes to establish the grid reference using a romer, plus a further three minutes to key in the waypoint, making a total time of approximately five minutes.

21   The grid references of waypoints can be entered into most satnavs by using mapping software installed on your computer.

22   Waypoints can be saved and stored in your satnav for future use.

23   It is important for users to grasp that, in most modes, the satnav calculates direction of travel, bearings, distances, speed etc. in straight lines between waypoints. This means that if you are following a winding path, the information given on the screen will be based on the shortest distance between your current position and the next waypoint. Your satnav will let you know when you reach the waypoint but if the path winds about, the satnav will indicate the most direct line to take which may well be at variance to the direction of the section of path that you are following. Thus, it is important to place your waypoints carefully.

GoTo

24   A GoTo is a single waypoint which has been selected from the waypoints saved on your satnav and is an invaluable feature in certain circumstances. For example, you are navigating off-path in difficult terrain and are walking towards a bridge over a stream. Using a map and compass you would have to aim off to one side of the bridge to ensure that you could find it (see 8:12-13). But with a satnav you can key in the grid reference of the bridge and walk towards it guided by the satnav which has targeted the location. Not only will you arrive much closer to the bridge than you would using map and compass but, no matter how far you deviate from a straight line to avoid bogs and rocky outcrops etc., the pointer on the satnav's screen will direct you unerringly to the bridge. You will no longer have to take compass bearings, aim off or allow for diversions from the direct route. When using this technique you have to examine the route carefully to ensure that it is safe and that you will not walk over the edge of a cliff or fall into a bog. This precaution is particularly important in conditions of poor visibility.

Routes

25 A route is a sequential list of waypoints created to form a walk. Routes can be saved and used again, and can also be shared with other walkers via computers.

26 Be aware that the placing of waypoints to form a route is critical because a satnav normally directs the user to the nearest waypoint which may not be the next one in sequence. Thus, it is a good plan to break a circular walk into two semicircular routes.

Tracks

27 A track is a recording of the route that you have walked. Your satnav records a sequence of points in your route which are taken at specified intervals and which it displays on the screen as a 'breadcrumb' trail. The record of a completed walk is known as a 'tracklog'. Tracklogs allow you to
   • save the route of the walk
   • walk the route in reverse
   • follow the walk again at a later date
   • upload the walk into a computer
   • share the route with other walkers

Maps and mapping software

28 Entering waypoints and devising routes manually into a satnav is tedious and the process is much easier, faster and more accurate when it is done with mapping software. Data is transferred between computer and satnav by means of the GPS Exchange Format (GPX) files using a USB connection.

29 Most satnavs can use at least some of the features of mapping software installed on a computer:
   a) Some of the more expensive satnavs come with maps already installed.

b) Other satnavs can download, and display on their screen, third-party maps which have been installed on a computer.

c) Entry-level satnavs that cannot display topographic maps on their screen can download waypoints, create routes and most of the information listed in 9:10. They rely on a pointer to show the direction of travel between waypoints on the compass page, together with a diagram of the route and your progress along it on the map page.

30   Ordnance Survey and Harvey maps in a variety of scales are available for installing on your computer from such companies as

- Anquet (www.anquet.co.uk)
- Fugawi (www.fugawi.com)
- Garmin (www.garmin.com/en-GB)
- Harvey Maps (www.harveymaps.co.uk)
- Mapyx Quo (www.mapyx.com)
- Memory-Map (www.memory-map.co.uk)
- Tracklogs (www.tracklogs.co.uk)

31   OziExplorer (www.oziexplorer.com) allows you to work on the computer screen with suitable maps that you create from scanned or digital maps. You cannot upload maps to satnavs but you can plot routes on your computer screen and transfer waypoints, routes and tracks to most brands of satnavs. ViewRanger (www.viewranger.com) allows you to download Ordnance Survey and Harvey maps to mobile phones.

32   Before purchasing mapping software you must ensure that it is compatible with your computer's operating system. At the time of writing (2014), only RouteBuddy mapping software will run natively on all Macintosh computers. However, Macs with Intel chips, and with Boot Camp installed, can run all Microsoft Windows programs providing that you first purchase the Microsoft operating system.

33   Mapping software provides much more than the image of a map and may include such features as the ability to

- download maps and routes to satnavs and other portable devices such as smartphones and tablets
- print maps in a variety of formats including relief shading
- follow your route with real-time positioning
- save waypoints, routes and tracks and share them with other walkers
- calculate distances

- calculate cumulative height gain (the amount of uphill walking) determined by averaging the elevation within a grid (typically 50 metres), *not* individual map contours so the information is not reliable and can even be wildly inaccurate
- access hundreds of ready-made walking routes
- view 3D images of the landscape through which your route runs (often referred to as 'fly through')

34 Note that the contour interval on Ordnance Survey *Explorer* maps installed on a computer or satnav is *map-sheet specific* (see 5:30). This means that the contour interval on *Explorer* mapping software can change without warning. Thus, when using a satnav on the borders of upland and lowland countryside you should be aware of the possibility of a sudden change in contour intervals. For example, if enter grid reference SK 01753 79992 into your mapping software, you will see that the 225-metre contour suddenly stops at the 800 northing grid line that separates sheets OL1 and OL19 that cover the Peak National Park.

35 This remarkable technology comes at a price, The satnav itself can cost several hundred pounds (second-hand models are available much more cheaply from eBay and other on-line sources). The cost of the mapping software also has to be taken into consideration.

36 There are several sources of free or inexpensive mapping software including:

a) Where's the path? is a free, on-line resource that can be accessed at http://wp2.appspot.com/wheresthepath.htm. It shows 1:50,000 and 1:25,000 Ordnance Survey maps however the latter is not true *Explorer* mapping but an enlarged version of the 1:50,000 map so field boundaries are not depicted. An interesting feature is that it is possible to have Google Earth images side by side with the map. As you move the cursor over the map a corresponding movement will be seen on the Google Earth image allowing you to see aerial views of paths except when they are obscured by tree cover. This can be useful when, for example, the map does not depict a bridge across a stream that runs through a wood. If the path is visible both entering and leaving the wood in the aerial photograph, that is a good indication that there is a bridge *in situ.* You can also
- find the location of bus stops
- find 10-figure grid references
- create waypoints and routes and generate information about the length of your route
- view a height profile
- create a route card (see 8:23)
- print A4-size map extracts including route information

- import and export waypoints and routes as GPX files between your satnav and computer
- view out-of-copyright 1:63,360 maps dating from the 1930s, and 1:25,000 maps dating from the 1950s

b) Grough (pronounced 'Gruff') is an on-line source which, for a modest subscription, extracts from the complete range of Ordnance Survey *Explorer* and *Landranger* maps can be downloaded to your computer from http://route.grough.co.uk. You can
   - find 10-figure grid references
   - create waypoints and routes and generate information about distance and height gain
   - print A4 size map extracts
   - create a route card
   - import and export waypoints and routes between your satnav and a computer
   - share routes with others

c) Ordnance Survey *Getamap* (www.getamap.ordnancesurveyleisure.co.uk) offers a free and a subscription service. The free service gives you access *to Landranger* and *Explorer* mapping from which you can
   - view aerial mapping
   - plot & save routes
   - create route cards
   - import and export GPX data to and from satnavs
   - print A4 maps for a fee
   - download recommended routes for a fee

   For an annual subscription you have all the above facilities and can print and download an unlimited number of maps and routes.

d) Mapyx Quo allows you to download the free software and then purchase the Ordnance Survey digital maps you require. It also has the standard features of mapping software.

Limitations of handheld satnavs

37 Information supplied by the Global Positioning Satellite System needs to be used intelligently. It would be unwise to enter a route into a satnav and assume that you can dispense with a map of your walk. You should always use your satnav in conjunction with an on-screen or paper map of an appropriate scale
   - 1:25,000 in lowland areas
   - 1:25,000, 1:40,000 or 1:50,000 in upland areas

38 Be aware that GNSS signals are sometimes jammed locally during military exercises.

39 Most satnavs are normally reliable to within five metres. But this level of accuracy in lowland countryside will not necessarily tell you on which side of a hedge you should be.

40 In order to follow a route in lowland countryside without reference to a map, either paper or on-screen, and relying solely on the pointer of your satnav to guide you, the path has to be visible on the ground throughout its length, and every gate and stile must be waymarked (an ideal that does not always exist). Here are some real-life examples that illustrate the point:

a) A walker was following a route with which she was not familiar but which had been recorded as a track onto a satnav by a friend (see Fig. 35a). At one point, the right of way was a farm track running beside a hedge. After two hundred metres there was an unwaymarked gate in the hedge. The farm track continued along the southern side of the hedge in a westerly direction, but the right of way passed through the gate to the north side of the hedge and then continued in a westerly direction parallel to the farm track but a few metres distant separated only by the hedge. The satnav was not sufficiently sensitive to record that the right of way had gone through the gate, so she continued along the farm track for several hundred yards and entered a wood. Shortly afterwards, the track turned sharply to the south but the pointer on the satnav indicated that she should continue westwards through dense undergrowth. And all the time the right of way was a few metres away running outside the wood in the adjacent field.

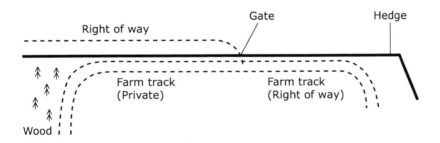

Figure 35a A satnav error

b) You have entered a field and are walking on a right of way that is not visible on the ground towards a junction of hedges (see Fig. 35b). When you arrive at **point A** you are confronted by two gates one on either side of the hedge that you have to follow. Unless one of the gates is waymarked, you cannot tell which side of the hedge the right of way runs without consulting your 1:25,000 map. Note, too, that this example demonstrates how important field boundaries are when navigating in lowland countryside. When faced with situations like this, 1:50,000 maps, which do not depict field boundaries, are of little use.

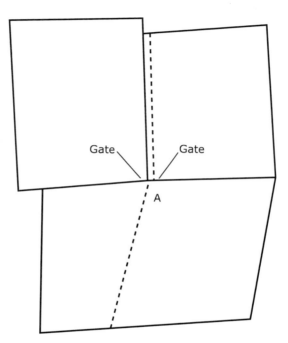

Route of path not visible on the ground

Figure 35b A satnav error

41   These examples demonstrate that it is essential to interpret the information given by the satnav by frequent reference to a map. In lowland countryside it is difficult to navigate reliably without a 1:25,000 on-screen or paper map.

42   If you are constantly referring to the satnav then you have to carry it in such a way that the built-in antenna is not masked. Padded cases designed so that the antenna can still receive signals inside the case are available for some models. When the instrument is not being used for navigation, but you wish to record your journey, it should be clipped as high as possible onto the shoulder strap of your rucksack; you may lose the signal if you wear it on your belt. Some satnavs allow an external antenna to be used which can be attached to your rucksack. There are also satnavs that can be worn on your wrist like a watch.

43   It takes time to learn how to use a satnav. The two most basic and useful functions, locating your position and keying in a grid reference, are soon acquired but others involve navigating through numerous menus and sub-menus which can be confusing.

Summary

44   Walkers discussing the Global Navigation Satellite System sometimes take up entrenched, even extreme, positions:

   a)   Some maintain that the use of satnavs has rendered traditional navigation techniques, relying on map and compass, obsolete.

   b)   Others argue that using satnavs is merely adding an unnecessary layer of expensive technology on top of a proven and cheap method of navigation. Furthermore, there is a risk of batteries failing and of signal jamming.

45   In fact, the truth lies somewhere in between the two extremes as the examples in the next paragraph demonstrate. *A satnav is merely a tool, just like a map and a compass, and has many uses, but it is unusable as a navigation aid unless it can be related to a compatible map.*

46   Imagine that you are in mountainous country in conditions of low visibility, a howling gale and torrential rain. Consider the following two situations which demonstrate that total reliance on either map and compass or a satnav is an unwise and blinkered approach, and that there is much to be said for using a combination of the traditional and the modern:

   a)   You are lost and relying on a map and a compass. It will take you a considerable amount of time to work out your position, as described in 8:43-4, before planning a suitable escape route. With a satnav you would be able to establish a ten-figure grid reference at the touch of a button allowing you to fix your position on the map quickly and accurately.

   b)   You have no paper map or stand-alone compass and are using a satnav with maps installed. The tiny satnav screen shows your position but you have to plan a route to escape from the atrocious conditions. Your only method is to scroll the map on the screen, but so little of the map can be viewed at any one time that this proves difficult. It would be much easier if you were able to use a paper map.

47 The decision to use a satnav is also a matter of temperament and personal preference which depend on whether you

- are content to follow your routes on a tiny screen
- are a technophobe and find it difficult to use of complicated instruments
- are a technophile who enjoys collecting and manipulating route data and statistics
- prefer a paper map because it shows a much larger area of countryside

48 The Global Navigation Satellite System is a giant step forward in navigation techniques but for walkers *it should be treated as a supplement to, not a substitute for, traditional map-reading and compass skills.* Hill-walkers who would be well-advised to carry a satnav include

- members of mountain rescue teams
- walks leaders (mainly as an insurance against claims that they were not properly equipped)
- those who regularly venture off-path
- those who require the additional security provided by a satnav and a mobile phone

Select bibliography

49 Brotherton, Lyle, *The Ultimate Navigation Manual.* HarperCollins, 2011.
This is an exceptionally detailed treatise covering all aspects of the subject except lowland navigation. It should be read in conjunction with the list of amendments on the author's website
http://micronavigation.com/wp-content/uploads/Important-corrections-to-first-print-of-the-UNM.pdf

50 Hawkins, Pete, *Navigating with a GPS; Effective Skills for the Outdoors.* Cicerone Press, 2008.

51 Judd, Peter & Brown, Simon, *Getting to Grips with GPS; Mastering the Skills of GPS Navigation and Digital Mapping.* Cordee, 2006.

52 Thomas, Clive, *GPS for Walkers; an Introduction to GPS and Digital Maps.* Jarrold, 2006.
An excellent introduction to global navigation satellite system navigation.

Chapter 10   Footpath guides

1   Footpath guides should more properly be known as 'walks guides' because some of the routes are likely to include bridleways and restricted byways. But, as the term 'footpath guide' is in almost universal use, it will be employed in this chapter.

2   Footpath guides are published:

   a) In book format by
- mainstream publishers
- rambling clubs and walking organizations
- individual authors (self-published)

   b) On-line from a number of websites from which walk descriptions can be downloaded. Some have GPX files of the walks which can be downloaded to a handheld satnav. New sites appear from time to time so rather than list them here, walkers are advised to enter 'Walk websites' into a search engine.

3   A good footpath guide can be useful for several reasons:

   a) They enable walkers whose map-reading skills are poor to explore the countryside.

   b) It is reasonable to assume that authors are familiar with the walks described and have chosen the best routes in the area that the guide covers.

   c) The routes were likely to have been free from obstructions and other problems *at the time that the walk was surveyed.*

   d) Routes that are described in guidebooks are likely to become better used than other routes in the area and the paths are more likely to visible on the ground and easier to follow.

   e) They are likely to contain information that supplements maps including
- snippets of local history
- the location of pubs and places of refreshment
- parking and public transport
- accommodation lists (in guides to long distance paths)

   f) A footpath guide is virtually essential when following a long distance path that is not depicted on maps by a special symbol.

Useful features

4   Footpath guides sometimes have to withstand rough handling and need to be protected from the elements. It is helpful if the design of guidebooks is portrait rather than landscape as this format usually allows them to slip into a map case when the book is open at a double-page spread. Guidebooks with a paper or soft cover will generally fit more easily into a map case than will a hard cover.

5   Most footpath guides include a map of each route which may be:

a)   A reproduction of the Ordnance Survey map of the route. Permission to reproduce these maps has to be obtained from the Ordnance Survey. The fees can add considerably to the publishing costs making short print-runs expensive. Most guides containing Ordnance Survey mapping appear under the imprint of established publishers and cover popular walking areas.

b)   A redrawn version based on the Ordnance Survey map as exemplified in the popular Wainwright guides. Copyright fees are payable to the Ordnance Survey but at a lower rate than for reproduction.

c)   A simple sketch map of the route which cannot be used for navigation. Such maps do not normally incur copyright fees.

6   Other desirable features include:

a)   A general map that locates the starting point of each walk.

b)   The length of each walk together with the total elevation gain (i.e. the total amount of uphill walking).

c)   A brief description of the nature of the terrain and the degree of difficulty.

d)   The sheet numbers of the topographic maps that cover each walk.

e)   An index to all the place-names mentioned in the text. This feature may not be required in a local guide such as *Walks around Puddlecombe-in-the-Slush,* but readers find it useful in guides to long-distance paths and those that cover a large area as in *Fifty Best Walks in the Peak District.* Place-name indexes were pioneered in the Wainwright guides.

How to judge a footpath guide

7   The single most important feature of a footpath guide is the route description which should be

- accurate at the time that the routes were surveyed
- unambiguous
- easy to comprehend and follow

8   Methods of satisfying these requirements may include:

a) Giving precise instructions such as *Follow the lane for **60 metres** to a foot-path sign and a stile on the left-hand side of the road...* **NOT** *Follow the lane **and you will come** to a footpath sign and a stile on the left-hand side of the road...* If the signpost were missing and/or the stile replaced by a gate, the walker following the first description stands a reasonable chance of identifying where to turn left. But it would not be clear to the walker following the second description, especially if there were another footpath sign and a stile on the left-hand side 150 metres farther along the lane. (Note that even though footpath signs and path furniture are not depicted on *Explorer* maps, there are other clues, in addition to the distance travelled, such as the location of paths in relation to field boundaries.)

b) It is often helpful to break the text into paragraphs each of which covers a short leg (see Chapter 7). This makes it easier to track your progress along the walk and to retrace your steps should you go astray.

c) Snippets of information interspersed with the route description can be distracting and are probably better kept separate.

Limitations of footpath guides

9   Walkers who explore the countryside with the aid of a footpath guide should be aware of the limitations of the medium. Some of the factors that can affect their usefulness have already been indicated in the paragraphs above. Others include significant changes made to the countryside since the walks were surveyed (fewer changes take place in upland countryside). Changes that can occur are best illustrated by examples:

a) Changes to path furniture, waymarks and signposts.

b) Landholders sometimes remove hedges and fell woods (see Chapter 7) and it is usually more difficult to work out what has happened when using a guidebook. If using a map, it is generally relatively easy because there are clues such as the alignment of field boundaries and the location of more distant obvious features such as prominent buildings, beacons, pylons etc.

c) If you misunderstand the instructions and go astray, it is usually more difficult to relocate than when using a map. In most cases you have to retrace your steps until you are certain that you have regained the correct route.

d) It is helpful to carry a suitable map *and know how to use it* in upland areas. In lowland countryside you are rarely far from a road, but if the weather suddenly deteriorates in the mountains and on the moors you may need to plan an escape route for which a map is essential.

How to write and publish a footpath guide

10   In a single chapter it is only possible to give an outline of the processes involved in producing a self-published footpath guide. More detailed information about self publishing is available on-line and also in the books listed in the bibliography at the end of this chapter.

11   Self-publishing has been greatly simplified with the advent of computers. Anyone who has access to

- computers
- word-processing programs
- scanners
- printers

has the tools with which to prepare a footpath guide ready for printing, or to upload to a website.

12   There is a considerable demand for footpath guides. The market for them in the most popular walking areas is saturated but there is still scope from local people in areas which have no special scenic qualities and which are unlikely to be visited by many walkers from outside the area. The publication of a footpath guide can often help to get local paths used.

13   Careful consideration should be given to the kind of guide required and the principles on which it should be compiled. Experience shows that circular walks of about ten kilometres are the most popular with the general public. If, from each starting point, two circular routes are described, this will provide a series of figure-of-eight walks which will cater both for those who want a short walk and those who prefer a longer route. (See 18:24-5 for information about devising a long distance path.)

Surveying

14   Every path must be surveyed and this will involve you in a great deal of work and walking. A book containing twenty 10-kilometre circular walks adds up to a minimum of two hundred kilometres. In addition, it will be necessary to note any difficulties such as missing footbridges and stiles, locked gates, obstructions etc., and take them up with the landholder or responsible local authority, which will result in further visits to check this the work has been done.

15   The following items are useful when surveying

- clipboard
- pencil attached to the clipboard by a cord

- pencil sharpener
- eraser
- *Explorer* map
- compass
- handheld satnav for following the route and for recording the route for subsequent conversion to GPX files
- recording device such as a cassette recorder, iPod etc.
- camera

16   Rights of way are shown on *Explorer* maps of England and Wales but it will be necessary to check the Definitive Map of rights of way to establish whether there have been any diversions or extinguishments since the *Explorer* map was published (see 14:13).

17   Walk each one of your chosen routes marking the map with all the features you intend to include, and amending the map where changes and development have rendered it inaccurate.

18   Record the route description as you walk and, if necessary, take photographs as an *aide memoire.* The recording will have to be transcribed and edited to make the printed version read properly.

The route maps

19   Information about Ordnance Survey copyright is given in 10:6 above. A good source of out-of-copyright 1:63,360 and 1:25,000 maps that can be used to draw routes is *Where's The Path* (http://wtp2.appspot.com/wheresthepath.htm). Permission to reproduce extracts must be obtained from the site owner.

Checking the routes

20   When the text and map have been finalized, someone unfamiliar with the route should be asked to walk it to check the accuracy of the description. It is helpful if this is done at a different time of year from the original survey because a walk surveyed in winter can look quite different when walked in summertime.

Preparing for publication

21 The next step is to decide on how the guide is to be published. Choices include:

a) Offering the guide to a commercial publisher that specializes in footpath guides such as

- Cicerone Press (www.cicerone.co.uk)
- Countryside Books (www.countrysidebooks.co.uk)
- Crimson Publishing (www.crimsonpublishing.co.uk)

A commercial publisher will only be interested in a guide that is likely to be popular enough to enjoy a long print run and is unlikely to be interested in guides such as *20 Short Walks around Puddlecombe-in-the-Slush.*

b) Paying a printer to publish the guide for you. There are a number of companies that specialize in this kind of self-publishing. Their services include

- designing the layout and art work
- obtaining an International Standard Book Number (ISBN)
- applying for copyright permissions
- satisfying the legal deposit requirements
- organizing distribution
- warehousing (storing unsold copies)
- conversion of text into eBook formats

It is not difficult, but time-consuming, to do most of these tasks and pay a printer to print the guide for you. If this appeals to you, the books on self-publishing listed in the bibliography will guide you through the process.

c) A variation of b) above is print on demand (POD). Instead of printing a specific number of copies, a POD company will, if necessary, print one copy at a time.

d) Publish the guide as an eBook. Most books on self-publishing will describe how this can be done.

e) Upload your routes to one of the on-line walks guides. This will not assist in publicizing local walks because most websites are general in nature and contain walks in many parts of the country. Nor will it bring any financial rewards.

Select bibliography

22   Baverstock, Alan, *The Naked Author; a Guide to Self-publishing.* Bloomsbury, 2011.

23   Pearce, Samantha, *Self-publishing; the Essential Guide.* Need-2-Know, 2012.

24   Rich, Jason R., *Self-publishing for Dummies.* Wiley, 2006.

Chapter 11 Safety, first aid, the weather, hazards & mountain rescue

1 Walking is one of the safest of outdoor pursuits. The number of walkers who become casualties is minute when compared with the millions who take to the countryside for their recreation. In the relatively densely populated lowland countryside of England and Wales, you are rarely out of sight of human habitation for long, or more than a mile or two from the nearest road, but in the upland regions of the British Isles, especially in Scotland, you can be a long way from help.

2 Everyone venturing into the upland regions of the British Isles should be aware there is an element of risk which can be minimized by:

a) Ensuring that either you, or someone in your party, has the necessary experience.

b) Dressing appropriately for the time of year and the prevailing weather conditions and carrying
- spare clothing
- gloves
- hat
- survival bag
- high-energy food for emergency use
- head torch
- first aid kit
- whistle

c) Carrying items of navigational equipment *and knowing how to use them in extreme conditions*
- map
- compass
- handheld satnav
- mobile phone

d) Carrying a survival bag or emergency shelter made of bright orange heavyweight polythene. It is designed to protect a casualty from wind and rain.

3   Most problems and accidents are minor and include misfortunes that can easily
be dealt with such as

- blisters
- ticks
- minor cuts from brambles and barbed wire
- bruises and grazes from falls

4   More serious problems include

- sprained ankles
- sunburn and windburn
- hyperthermia (heat stroke)
- hypothermia (exposure)
- dehydration
- fractures
- attacks by cattle
- lightning
- avalanches (see 12:12-13)

5   Other emergencies such as heart attacks and insulin deficiency are not specifically related to walking and are beyond the scope of this book.

First aid

Blisters

6   Blisters are a common cause of discomfort in walkers and unless remedial action is taken may develop into an abscess. Most blisters are caused either by ill-
fitting boots or by a foreign body such as a piece of grit or grass seed in the boot
or sock.

7   There are a number of specially formulated dressings for the care of blisters
which work like a second skin and are far superior to old-fashioned plasters.
They consist of a small sealed pouch containing a fluid sandwiched between an
adhesive backing and a protective outer layer. Most high street pharmacies and
supermarkets stock a range of dressings and remedies for blisters and other foot
problems.

8   The first warning that a blister might be forming is minor discomfort. If remedial action is taken at this stage it is often possible to prevent a blister forming
by removing the cause of the irritation which could be nothing more serious that
a rucked sock.

9 If a blister has formed:

a) Sterilize a needle in a match flame and gently prick it twice, once on each side.

b) Gently squeeze the fluid out with a clean tissue.

c) Apply a blister dressing according to the instructions that come with the product.

d) In extreme cases it may be necessary to relieve the pressure on a blister by applying a corn pad (*not* a corn plaster) or by cutting a hole in a piece of moleskin large enough to encompass the blister and applying it to the affected area.

Ticks

10 Ticks are bloodsucking anthropoids. There are many different species of tick living in the British Isles, some of which will feed on human blood.

11 A tick can be as small as a pinhead but its body becomes engorged after feeding and can become the size of a small pea. If not removed, it can continue to suck blood for several days. The bite is normally painless and the host only becomes aware of the tick when it is seen feeding.

12 Tick bites should be treated seriously because they may infect humans with
   • Lyme borreliosis (Lyme disease)
   • babesiosis (red water or cattle tick fever)
   • ehrlichiosis
of which the most common in the British Isles is Lyme disease.

13 Ticks which affect humans are commonly carried by deer and sheep. They fall off their host and are likely to be found in bracken and long grass from where they may attach themselves to humans. They prefer moist parts of the body so, although they may alight anywhere, they are most likely to be found in the armpits and the groin.

14 The risk of tick bites can be reduced by wearing
   • tops with long sleeves that fit closely to the wrist
   • trousers tucked into your socks
   • applying insect repellent

15 Ticks should be removed promptly to avoid the risk of infection. It is important remove them carefully so that neither its saliva nor the contents of its stomach are left in the wound:

  a) Tick-removal tools are sold in pharmacies and pet shops. Always follow the instructions carefully.

  b) If a tick-removal tool is not available
      • tie a single loop of cotton around its mouth and as close to the skin as possible
      • pull gently upwards and outwards
      • after removing the tick clean the bite site and the tweezers with anti-septic

  c) You should not
      • squeeze, crush or twist the body of the tick otherwise its head may be left embedded in your skin
      • use your fingernails to remove a tick
      • burn the tick off with a hot match head

16 Early symptoms of Lyme disease vary from patient to patient and can include
      • a general feeling of malaise
      • flu-like illnesses
      • erythema migraines (EM or bullseye rash)
      • headache
      • stiff neck
      • muscle pain
      • tender glands

Walkers exhibiting any of the above symptoms should be aware of the possibility of tick infection and mention it to their doctor even if they have not discovered a bite.

Sprained ankles

17 Sprains may be minor or severe. If it is minor, patients can usually continue walking after resting for a few minutes especially if they are relieved of their rucksack and use walking poles.

18 If the injury is severe then patients may be seriously incapacitated and evacuation may be necessary which, in upland areas, may involve the mountain rescue service (see 11:60). Some relief may be obtained by:

  a) Administering anti-inflammatory drugs such as aspirin and Ibuprofen.

b) A cycle of
- bathing the foot in cold water for 20 minutes
- removing the foot for 20 minutes
- bathing the foot another 20 minutes

Sunburn and windburn

19   A hot summer's day brings with it the risk of sunburn. Exercise increases the risk of sunburn because perspiration tends to irritate the skin made tender by the sun. The damage is often done before sufferers realize that they are affected and so it is advisable to be aware of the danger and to keep the limbs covered by light clothing. The application of sunscreen before the start of a walk is a wise precaution.

20   Windburn is another hazard, especially in upland areas, and usually makes the face tender and cracks the lips. Both sunscreen and lip salve will give relief.

Hyperthermia (heat stroke)

21   Hyperthermia occurs when the body has been exposed to excessive heat and can no longer control its rising temperature. Hard physical exercise on a hot day can generate heat beyond the body's ability to cool itself. Hyperthermia can be a life-threatening condition that requires immediate medical attention:

a) The symptoms of hyperthermia include
- hot and sometimes red, dry skin caused by the inability of the body to perspire
- swollen lips
- nausea
- vomiting
- headaches
- fainting
- dizziness

b) In severe cases the person may
- become confused
- be hostile
- appear to be intoxicated
- show an increase in the heart and breathing rate resulting in a pale or bluish skin colour

c) In extreme cases, the vital organs will begin to fail resulting in unconsciousness and death.

22   Remedies to counteract the effects of hyperthermia include
- resting in the shade
- removing clothing
- drinking water
- sponging the head, neck and trunk with cool water

The patient should respond in mild cases but acute conditions require urgent medical attention.

Hypothermia (exposure)

23   Hypothermia is caused by the body's surface being chilled sufficiently long for the core body temperature to be lowered to a point where it can no longer maintain the vital organs.

24   When the skin and the tissues immediately below the skin become cold, blood rushes to the surface to warm the affected area. If it is very cold, the blood itself is cooled and returns to the body core to be warmed again. This can quickly sap the energy of the patient and result in death.

25   One of the significant factors in hypothermia is the strength of the wind, which is known as the 'windchill factor' shown diagrammatically (see Fig. 36)

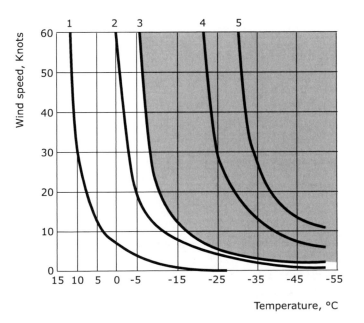

Figure 36   Windchill scale

- *line 1* indicates when the temperature feels cold
- *line 2* indicates when the temperature feels bitterly cold
- *line 3* indicates when exposed flesh is likely to freeze
- *line 4* indicates when flesh exposed to the air is liable to freeze in one minute
- *line 5* indicates when flesh exposed to the air is liable to freeze in thirty seconds
- the shaded area indicates when conditions are dangerous to survival

26   The diagram illustrates that a person standing in still air at -25°C is no more at risk than someone wearing similar clothes standing in a 30-knot wind when the temperature is -10°C.

27   Hypothermia can be avoided in most weather conditions by wearing the proper clothing. The risk is accentuated by fatigue and hunger.

28   The symptoms indicating the onset of hypothermia are not always obvious and are difficult to self-diagnose. The danger signals include
- stumbling
- a sense of unreality
- difficulty in making decisions
- slurring of speech

29   The remedy is to give the patient
- shelter
- rest
- warmth
- food, preferably hot
- hot drinks

30   Get the patient out of the wind and rain and into a tent, bivvy bag or emergency shelter into the lee of a wall or pile of rocks. Serious cases should be treated by wrapping them in dry clothes and, if possible, into a sleeping bag, preferably with another member of the party whose body heat will help warm the patient.

31   Never attempt to warm by rubbing or administering alcohol, for although spirits make a person feel warm they achieve this by encouraging the blood to go from the recess of the body to the surface, which has the effect of sending the cool surface blood into the body, thus reducing even further the body core temperature. Rubbing has a similar effect.

Dehydration

32   Dehydration occurs when the body excretes more fluid than it takes in. This upsets the balance of minerals in your body and affects the way that it functions.

33   Advice that everyone should drink a specific amount of fluid should be treated with caution because it is dependent on such factors as
- your body mass index (BMI)
- how hard you are exercising
- the ambient temperature
- the efficiency of your clothing
- the efficiency of your kidneys

34   Early warning signs of dehydration include
- thirst
- light-headedness
- excreting yellow or dark-coloured urine

Dehydration can be avoided by drinking small quantities of water at regular intervals.

35   Mild dehydration can usually be cured by resting and drinking water slowly. Acute cases can be life-threatening and require hospital treatment.

The weather

36   It is helpful to know the kind of weather likely to be experienced, particularly when walking in upland areas where conditions can be severe. Weather forecasts are available from
- radio and television stations
- the internet
- newspapers
- tourist information centres (TICs)
- national parks

37   A useful aid to weather forecasting is a barometer. There are portable stand-alone barometers and they are sometimes incorporated into multifunction watches and handheld satnavs.

38   Barometers work by recording air pressure:

a) If air pressure rises over a period of three hours, then the weather is likely to improve because high pressure is associated with fine weather.

b) If air pressure declines over a period of three hours, then the weather is likely to deteriorate because low pressure is associated with rain.

c) Note that air pressure changes with altitude so, in practice, your barometer has to remain at the same altitude for a minimum of three hours in order to give a reliable forecast.

39   Some of the old country weather sayings are based on sound observations:

a) *'Red sky at night, shepherd's delight'* is often true if the red sky is caused by the rays of the setting sun reflected on clouds high in the sky. This often indicates that a cold front has passed through and that there will now be a period of settled weather.

b) *'Red sky at morning, shepherd's warning'* is often true if the sun's rays are shining on high clouds. This often signals the approach of a warm front likely to bring rain with it.

c) *'Rain before seven, fine by eleven'* is based on the fact that unless the depression is very deep, which is indicated by thick, fast-moving, low-lying stratus clouds, it does not often rain for more than a few hours at a time in the British Isles.

40   The cross-wind rule will indicate if the weather will deteriorate, improve or remain unchanged. Stand with your back to the surface wind ensuring that it is not distorted by features such as hills, cliffs or mountains:

a) If the clouds are coming from the *left*-hand side, the weather is likely to deteriorate within the next few hours.

b) If the clouds are coming from the *right*-hand side, the weather is likely to improve within the next few hours.

c) If the clouds move on a parallel course, the weather is unlikely to change within the next few hours.

Lightning

41   An electrical storm in the mountains will make ice-axes and pack frames hum and cause the skin and hair to tingle. Lightning is caused by electrical activity ionizing the air allowing electricity to arc to earth. Lightning takes the shortest route to earth and will usually strike the nearest prominent feature.

42   A useful analogy to help appreciate the effects of lightning is to liken it to a quantity of water dropped from a height so that it splashes in all directions. Like water, electricity will follow the line of least resistance through gullies and cracks, and along the surface of wet rock.

43   If a human body offers the line of least resistance to the path of the current, then electricity will be attracted to it. A direct strike is the most dangerous and is often fatal, but ground currents which occur as the electricity is dispersing itself into the earth can also be dangerous.

44   Try to avoid being caught on ridges and the summit of mountains and hills during an electrical storm because these are the kind of locations that attract lightning strikes. It is safer to descend to lower ground.

45   Walkers caught in an electrical storm in the mountains should take the following precautions:

   a)   Try to find a prominent feature such as a large rock at least seven metres high. The area immediately around the rock, formed by a radius equivalent to the height of the rock, is an area of relative, but not absolute, safety.

   b)   Sit on a small boulder or stone well away from any cracks, crevices or gullies along which electricity might travel.

   c)   Insulate yourself as well as possible by sitting on a rucksack and spare clothing.

   d)   Reduce your contact with the ground by sitting with your knees up and your hands in your lap.

   e)   Never shelter in caves or recesses in the rock as these are likely to attract a lightning strike.

46   In lowland countryside there is less risk of a lightning strike but take the following precautions:

   a)   Avoid proximity to
       • metal gates
       • wire fences

   b)   In a field or open space do not shelter under trees because they may attract a lightning strike.

   c)   In woodland, find an open space or, if that is not possible, shelter under a short tree because a tall tree is more likely to attract lightning.

Fording rivers and streams

47   In upland areas there are innumerable small, narrow watercourses that are easy to cross by stepping from rock to rock. When they are in spate, it may be necessary search along the banks to find a convenient crossing point.

48   Most walkers will probably never have to ford a significant river in the British Isles and it is better to avoid doing so. Rivers on the line of a public path generally have bridges at crossing points which are marked on maps. When planning an off-path walk it may be possible to make a diversion from the direct route in order to cross at a road bridge.

49   If it is essential to ford a river the following considerations have to be taken into account

* the apparent depth of the water
* the speed of the current

The water is deeper and the current faster on meanders (bends), and where the river narrows. Examine your map and search for a wider section or a point where the river divides into two or more channels.

50   When you have found a suitable crossing point:

a)   Remove or roll up your trousers so that you have dry clothes to put on when you reach the opposite bank.

b)   Take off your socks and then replace your boots because wearing them will give you a firmer foothold and protect your feet from sharp stones. Wearing gaiters and/or supermarket plastic bags tied firmly below the knees can often prevent the inside of your boots from becoming completely saturated.

c)   Close all zips and tighten the straps of your rucksack to trap air to aid buoyancy should you be swept away.

d)   Undo the belt of your rucksack and loosen the shoulder straps so that you can remove your rucksack quickly should you be swept away.

e)   Trekking poles are helpful as an aid to balance and also for probing the bed of the river for hidden holes. A stick or branch makes a useful substitute.

f)   Be aware of the danger of being swept away. The most vulnerable part of your leg is the knee joint which can buckle if sufficient pressure is applied to the back of the knee, so it is important not to face downstream. Facing upstream will also enable you see any floating debris that could pose a threat.

Solo fording technique

51 Move forward slowly taking short steps and probing with your poles or a stick. When you feel the current getting stronger, face upstream and shuffle sideways.

Group fording techniques

52 There are three techniques for small groups to cross a river without the aid of a rope

- the huddle for three walkers of similar height
- the in-line abreast for two or more walkers
- the in-line astern for two or more walkers

Note that one person should be designated the leader of each group crossing so that the others can move in unison at the leader's command.

53 A huddle is formed by three walkers forming a circle by linking arms across the shoulders (see Fig. 37). The strongest person should face upstream so that the other two are approximately sideways to the current. They should then move slowly across the river at the command of the walker facing upstream.

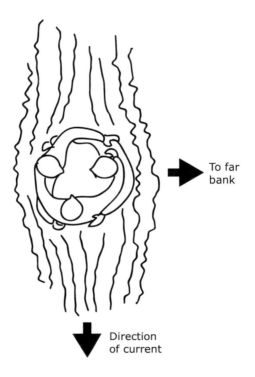

To far bank

Direction of current

Figure 37   The huddle

54 To cross in-line abreast, walkers should line up at the edge of the water, link arms and cross slowly on the command of the leader. A more secure version of this technique is for three walkers to link arms and grasp a single trekking pole or stick held across their trunks (see Fig. 38).

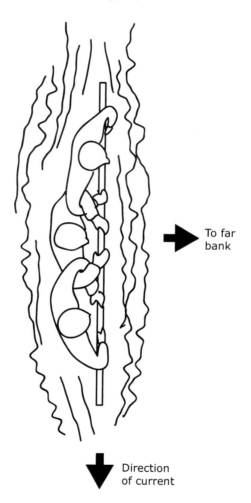

To far bank

Direction of current

Figure 38   In-line abreast

55 To cross in-line astern the strongest walker should face upstream, preferably with a pole to help balance, with the rest of the group grasping the waist of the person in front. The group then shuffles sideways at the command of the leader (see Fig. 39).

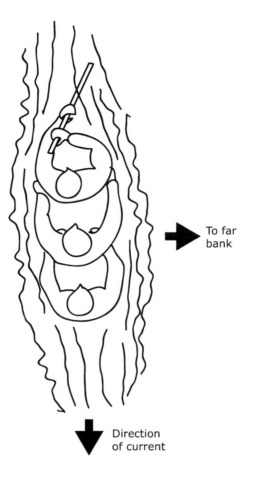

To far
bank

Direction
of current

Figure 39   In-line astern

Dealing with emergencies

56   Most emergencies occur in upland areas. In lowland countryside you are rarely
far from a road or a house and it is usually easy to summon help.

57   In the upland areas of the British Isles, particularly in Scotland, it may take
several hours for help to arrive. Emergencies include

- benightment (being caught out after dark)
- being lost
- injury

- illness
- exhaustion
- hypothermia
- hyperthermia

A combination of any of these circumstances.

58 The action to take depends on the nature of the emergency. Factors to take into account include the

- time of year
- weather
- time of day
- size and fitness of the group

59 The most experienced member of the group should take charge. Leaders of groups should try to exude an air of reassuring confidence. Their decisions might, according to circumstances, include:

a) Moving to lower ground to seek shelter such as a wall. In order to conserve heat, every member of the group should
- find something such as a thick mattress of heather that will insulate them from the ground
- put on all their clothes, including waterproofs
- cut a mouth-hole in their survival bag and pull it over their head
- place their feet, whilst still wearing their boots, into their empty ruck-sack and arrange it carefully under the skirt of the survival bag
- slip their arms out of the sleeves of their jacket as this will help to keep them warm
- huddle together

b) The international mountain distress signal is six consecutive blasts on a whistle repeated at one-minute intervals. At night flash a torch or a camera flash six times repeated at one-minute intervals.

c) Establish and write down the grid reference of the group's position, preferably using a handheld satnav, or a smartphone with which can give grid references, together with the time of arrival. If relying on a map and a romer (see 6:70-1), two persons should work independently and agree on the result.

d) If unable to establish the exact location, try to give the last known position together with the time that the group was there, and the general direction in which it walked. Also, write down a description of the area noting any particular features.

e) Write down the name, address and telephone number of every member of the group together with details of any injuries, symptoms and medication taken.

Seeking help

60 Mountain rescue services are co-ordinated by the police. Most people know that 999 is the number to use for contacting the emergency services but, if using a mobile phone, it is better to call 112. This is because 112 has been programmed into all mobile phones manufactured in the last decade and its use initiates a procedure that all global systems for mobile communications networks (GSMCs) recognize.

61 If you are unable to get a signal, try walking to higher ground from where it is more likely that a signal can be received.

62 If it is impossible to receive a signal, it will be necessary to go for help. Ideally, at least two of the party should set out together. Before departing they should:

a) Agree in the direction to go for help. This is a critical decision if they are unsure of their present position. Depending on the visibility and the nature of the terrain, following a stream downhill may be a good option.

b) Inform members of the group of the plan and assure them that help will be on its way but that it may take some time to arrive.

c) Instruct the group not to use any phones they may have in order to conserve battery power which may be needed later in the rescue.

d) Keep trying your mobile phone in the hope of getting a signal.

e) Once the police have been contacted, obey their instructions to the letter.

Search and rescue services

63 Search and rescue services (SAR) are provided free in the British Isles and are made up of volunteers who undertake such work for love of their fellow men and women. They have to spend hours, sometimes days, searching, often in bad weather, for walkers and climbers some of whom may have got into difficulties because of foolhardiness. Some of these volunteers actually lose wages as a result of their rescue activities. If you ever have to be rescued you should make a handsome donation to the work of the rescue team which may have saved your life. Note that search and rescue teams also operate in lowland countryside but their work is more likely to involve looking for confused persons who have gone missing rather than walkers.

64 The ever-increasing popularity of walking has resulted in more demands being placed on mountain rescue services. Accidents, such as a slip resulting in a broken limb, can happen to even the most experienced hill-walker, but too many of the calls that are made on the service come from walkers attempting routes for which they lack the requisite experience and/or essential equipment.

65 Most seasoned hill-walkers can relate tales of encountering walkers who were hopelessly lost, or attempting a walk that was far beyond their abilities. Examples include:

a) The party of university students who set out from Ambleside in poor visibility to walk a 16-kilometre circular route via Scandale Pass and Red Screes. They were greatly relieved when they emerged from the mist on the lower slopes of St. Sunday Crag to behold a lake that they assumed to be Windermere. But they were crestfallen when they discovered it was Ullswater some 16 kilometres from the northern end of Windermere.

b) The two ill-equipped young men who left Achintee at *noon* early in November to make the 17-kilometre return trip to the summit of Ben Nevis. They were met by a couple of walkers halfway to the summit and persuaded to return to Achintee.

Select bibliography

66 British Mountaineering Council, *Safety on Mountains.* British Mountaineering Council, 2010.

67 Carline, Jan D. and others, *Mountaineering First Aid; a Guide to Accident Response and First Aid Care* 5th ed. The Mountaineers, 2006.

68 Duff, Jim and Gormly, Peter, *Pocket First Aid and Wilderness Medicine* 11th ed. Cicerone Press, 2012.

69 *First Aid Manual; the Authorised Manual of St John's Ambulance, St Andrew's Ambulance Association and the British Red Cross* 9th ed. Dorling Kindersley, 2011.

70 Forgey, William, *Wilderness First Aid; a Falcon Basic Illustrated Guide.* Globe Pequot Press, 2010.

71   Hamblyn, Richard. *The Cloud Book; How to Understand the Skies.* David & Charles, 2008.

72   Langmuir, Eric, *Mountaincraft and Leadership* 4th ed., Mountain Leader Training Board, 2013.

73   Long, Steve and others, *Hillwalking; the Official Handbook of the Mountain Leader and Walking Group Leader Schemes.* Mountain Leader Training UK, 2003.

74   MacInnes, Hamish, *International Mountain Rescue Handbook* 4th ed. Frances Lincoln, 2005.

75   Murphy, Sam, *Get Fit Walking.* A & C Black, 2005.

76   Pedgley, David, *Mountain Weather; a Practical Guide for Hillwalkers and Climbers* 3rd ed. Cicerone Press, 2009.

77   Watts, Alan, *Instant Weather Forecasting* 3rd ed. A. & C. Black, 2007.

78   *Weather; a Collins Gem.* HarperCollins, 2004.

79   Wills, Katherine, *Outdoor First Aid; a Practical Manual: Essential Knowledge for the Outdoor Enthusiast.* Pesda Press, 2013.

Chapter 12 Walking in winter

1 Walking in winter has a magic all of its own especially on a bright, clear day when the countryside is blanketed in a covering of snow, but it is more demanding than walking in the temperate months of the year especially in upland areas. The factors and requirements that should be taken into account include

- the limited hours of daylight
- the weather
- the temperature
- the conditions underfoot
- clothing and equipment
- navigational skills

2 Calculate the available hours of daylight and consider tailoring your walk with a safety margin so that, given normal circumstances, you will complete your walk some time before darkness descends.

3 Conditions underfoot in lowland countryside are likely to be more treacherous than they generally are in summer. You are likely to encounter

- mud and surface water
- slippery conditions on slopes
- stiles and footbridges made slippery by frost, snow, ice, algae and mud

4 Soft snow will tend to slow your progress but, unless deep, should not prove to be hazardous. Melting snow that has become compacted is often slippery. Snow that has partially thawed, and then freezes, is dangerously slippery and should be avoided unless you are wearing crampons.

5 You should dress for winter weather employing the layering system (see 3:63-5) and in lowland areas are likely to require

- good quality waterproofs (see 3:36-8)
- gaiters (see 3:43-5)
- wicking base layer (see 3:54-6)
- wicking midwear (see 3:57-9)
- fleeces (see 3:57-9)
- warm headwear (see 3:92-4)
- waterproof gloves (see 3:95)
- extra warm clothing carried in your backpack

- a torch, preferably a head torch because it keeps the hands free and points in the direction in which you are walking, and spare batteries
- trekking poles to assist with balance (see 3:101-7)
- crampons for use in icy conditions (see 12:27-30)
- survival bag (see 11:2)

6   No additional navigation skills are required for lowland walking in winter but it should be remembered that even well-used paths may disappear under a mantle of snow.

Upland walking

7   *Walking in winter on the mountains and moors of the British Isles, especially in the Highlands of Scotland, should be treated as serious undertakings that require special skills. You can learn about the basic techniques required for upland walking in the temperate months of the year from an instruction manual, and then reinforce them by putting them into practice, but winter skills, such as the correct use of ice-axes and crampons, and especially self-arrest procedures, require tuition and much practice under the watchful eyes of a qualified expert. The following paragraphs are intended to do no more than outline some of the most basic skills that are required.*

8   The conditions and hazards that may be encountered include
- snow and ice
- gale-force winds
- blizzards
- reduced visibility including white-outs
- avalanches
- frostnip and frostbite

Snow and ice

Cornices

9   A cornice is a bank of snow that overhangs a precipitous drop (see Fig. 40). Cornices are inherently unstable and must be avoided. When a cornice fractures, the break may take place on firm ground some distance from the cliff edge so, when walking along a ridge, or plateau with a vertical drop, it is essential to keep well away from the apparent edge.

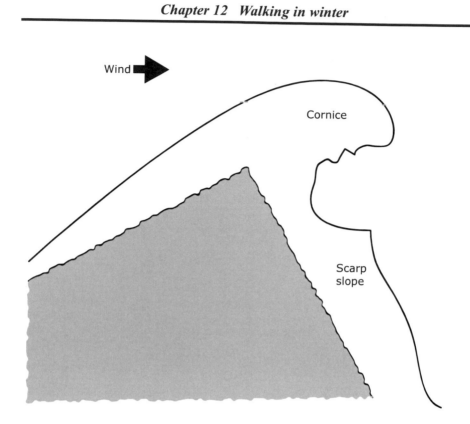

Figure 40   A cornice

Snow bridges

10   Frozen streams and bodies of water that are covered in snow may not always be readily visible especially when heavy snow has drifted to form irregular shapes on the normally smooth surface of the ice. Those who fail to recognize that they are walking on frozen water risk falling through the ice.

11   Fast-flowing streams are less likely to freeze and drifting snow can form bridges over them. Snow bridges can be difficult to see even in clear conditions so a close eye should be kept on the map in order to locate the existence of streams hidden beneath the snow. Snow bridges are best avoided for fear that they may collapse and plunge the walker into the water. They are particularly dangerous when sunshine may have weakened them. If it is essential to cross them, be sure to exercise extreme caution and only proceed if the bridge is very thick. Members of a group should cross one at a time.

Avalanches

12   Avalanches are a serious hazard especially in Scotland. They are most likely to occur on slopes with an angle of between 30° and 45°. Some of the more expensive compasses have a clinometer that will quickly establish the angle of slope. Most avalanches in the United Kingdom are slab avalanches which are triggered when the snow becomes unstable due to layers built up by winds coming from different directions. The layers do not bond well and the extra weight of a walker can cause them to slide.

13   Walkers should avoid steep snow-covered slopes. Information about the current avalanche risk can be obtained from the Sportscotland Avalanche Information Service (SAIS www.sais.gov.uk).

Blizzards

14   Blizzards are caused by a combination of strong winds and falling snow. The precipitation does not necessarily have to be heavy for conditions to be atrocious. It is the strength of the wind that is the more important factor. Forward progress may be virtually impossible and your snow goggles will rapidly become obscured by snow.

15   If there is no shelter nearby, the safest procedure is to turn your back to the wind and get to lower ground as quickly as is possible consistent with safety.

White-outs

16   A white-out occurs when snow and mist make everything, including the sky, appear to be white. This makes it impossible to see the horizon and visibility can be reduced to a couple of metres.

17   White-outs can occur suddenly as, for example, when they are caused by snow showers, and can just as quickly disappear, but they can also last for hours.

18   A severe loss of visibility causes a sense of disorientation and fear of what you might be walking into. It is essential to get an accurate fix of your position, preferably with a satnav, to ensure that you do not walk into a hazard such as a precipice.

Frostnip and frostbite

19   Frostnip and frostbite can occur anywhere in the body's extremities, such as the
- cheeks
- nose
- earlobes
- fingers
- toes

when the clothing worn in freezing conditions is insufficient to keep you warm.

20   Frostnip is a mild form of cold injury which, if not treated, can develop into the much more serious condition of frostbite. Frostnip is characterized by
- numbness of the skin
- itchiness and soreness
- the appearance of white, purple and yellow patches on the skin

The remedy for frostnip is gently to warm the affected areas. Do not rub as this can damage the skin.

21   Frostbite can develop from frostnip and is a much more serious condition:

a)   Ice crystals form in the body's cells causing them to rupture and die.

b)   The skin becomes insensitive, hardens and freezes and blisters will appear within a couple of days.

c)   In the final stage, muscles, tendons, blood vessels and nerves may freeze for which the only remedy is amputation.

d)   Medical help should be summoned immediately. The patient should not be rapidly re-warmed. Avoid touching hot or cold objects but cover the affected area with warm clothing. Do not rub.

Clothing

22   The risk of encountering the conditions described above require walkers to wear clothing which, in addition to the items listed in Chapter 3 is likely to include
- down vests and jackets (for the qualities of down see 20:21-8)
- salopettes
- four-season mountain boots
- gaiters
- winter-weight waterproof gloves
- headgear, such as balaclavas, to protect the head, cheeks and mouth

Equipment

23   Equipment used for winter walking in upland areas includes

- ice-axe
- crampons
- snow goggles
- head torch and spare batteries
- map and compass
- handheld satnav
- mobile phone
- survival bag
- personal locator beacon (their use is now legal in the United Kingdom)

Ice-axes

24   There are several kinds of ice-axe so it is important to select one that is suitable for hill-walking (see Fig. 41), and is of the correct length for your height. When the axe is grasped by the head with your arm full extended downwards, the pointed end of the spike should be somewhere between the top of your boot and at least two centimetres from the ground.

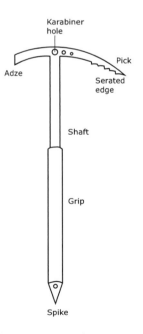

Figure 41   An ice axe

25   An ice-axe serves the following purposes:

a)   As an aid to balance. When contouring a slope, the ice-axe should be grasped by the head in the hand closest to the slope.

b)   Climbing a slope. The ice-axe should be held by the head in the uphill hand and driven into the snow. When zigzagging uphill it will be necessary to change the ice-axe to the uphill hand every time you change direction.

c)   Cutting steps when the snow is packed so hard that it is impossible to kick steps with your boot.

d)   Self-belay. This technique is used to prevent a simple slip turning into a disastrous slide requiring self-arrest. Throw your weight over your ice-axe to drive it into the snow to form an anchor (technically known as a belay) and then grasp the shaft of the ice-axe.

e)   Self-arrest. A life-saving technique which takes a great deal of practice to learn and can be used to stop a slide down a steep slope. As soon as you start to fall, roll over onto your chest keeping your feet up so that your crampons do not catch in the snow and cause you to somersault. Get the shaft of your ice-axe under your armpit and, leaning on the head, force the pick end into the snow (see Fig. 42).

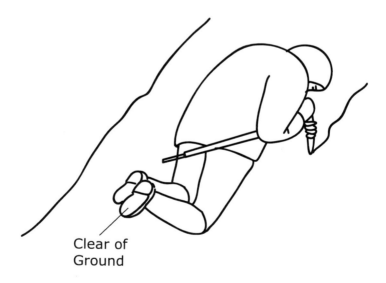

Clear of
Ground

Figure 42   Self-arrest

26 An ice-axe is a dangerous tool and must be carried safely so as to avoid injury to the person and damage to clothing. Protectors for both the head and the spike should be used. The way that the ice-axe is carried varies according to the design of your rucksack:

a) Some have a loop at the bottom of the pack through which the spike and shaft can be threaded. The shaft is then swung upwards so that the spike is pointing to the sky and the shaft secured by a strap near the top of the pack.

b) If your rucksack lacks side pockets the axe can be strapped, spike down, to the body of the pack.

c) Sometimes it can be slid down between your rucksack and your back with the head parallel to the width of your pack.

Crampons

27 Crampons comprise a series of spikes, known as points, attached to a pair of metal frames that are strapped to your boots to give a secure footing in ice and snow (see Fig. 43). Crampons have to 'match' the boot to which they will be fitted (see 3:81). There are several designs but those that satisfy a walker's requirement usually have

- 10 or 12 points
- 2 front-facing points
- an articulated frame that flexes with the boot

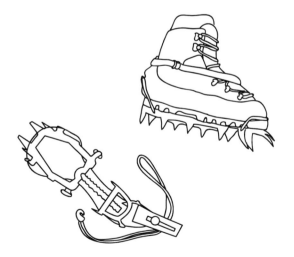

Figure 43   Crampons

28 It is important to learn how to walk whilst wearing crampons. Take short steps and keep your feet wide enough apart to avoid tearing your clothes and injuring your legs. You don't need snow to practise using them; a steep, grassy hill makes a good substitute for the real thing.

29 Snow tends to ball up under crampons but can usually be removed by tapping side of the crampons with an ice-axe.

30 When not in use, protectors should be fitted over the spikes and the crampons carried in a bag in or on the top of your rucksack.

Goggles

31 Goggles should be carried because they provide protection for the eyes from
- strong winds
- hail
- snow
- spindrift

Navigation

32 Snow can transform the appearance of a mountain landscape making familiar routes look entirely different
- paths can disappear under the snow
- rocks can take on strange shapes or disappear altogether
- hollows can fill with snow
- walls, gates and stiles can become obscured

Conditions such as these make accurate navigation of critical importance.

33 If you are relying on traditional map and compass techniques you must constantly check and confirm your position with the map. The sudden onset of heavy snow is not the time to get out your map to establish your position.

34 A handheld satnav, especially if loaded with a topographic map, will show your exact location but you should not rely solely on a satnav and always carry a map and a compass. If you have mapping software, consider printing out, on waterproof paper, two copies of that section of the map that contains your route. One copy can be used for map-reading, and the other kept in the rucksack in case the

first blows away. You should also carry the sheet map of the area in case conditions require you to alter your route.

Select bibliography

35 Cunningham, Andy and Fyffe, Allen, *Winter Skills; Essential Walking and Climbing Techniques: the Official Handbook of the Mountaineering Instructor Certificate and the Winter Mountain Leader Schemes.* Mountain Leader Training UK, 2007.

36 Langmuir, Eric, *Mountaincraft and Leadership* 4th ed., Mountain Leader Training Board, 2013.

37 Richardson, Alun, *Rucksack Guide to Winter Mountaineering.* A & C Black, 2009.

38 Shillington, Ben, *Winter Backpacking.* Heliconia Press, 2010.

Chapter 13   Walking in England and Wales

1   England has an area of a little over 50,000 square miles, and Wales covers 8,000 square miles. Within an area of a little under 60,000 square miles lies an extraordinary variety of scenery ranging from the beautiful coastal vistas of Cornwall and Pembrokeshire; the rolling chalk downland of southern England; the relatively level landscapes of the Midlands and the Welsh Marches; the reclaimed marshes of the Fens and the Somerset Levels; the bleak and atmospheric uplands of the Pennines to the exquisite miniature mountain landscapes of the Lake District and Snowdonia.

2   It has been said that it is difficult to travel more than ten miles in England and Wales without the character of the scenery and the vernacular architecture changing.

3   Despite the density of the population, especially in England, it is still possible to enjoy the countryside that surrounds many of our cities. Even parts of London still retain a surprisingly rural atmosphere as, for example, the walk along the Thames from Putney Bridge towards Richmond and Kingston. Canals frequently offer a quick and pleasant route from city centres to the countryside.

4   Both England and Wales are paradises for walkers. Within the two countries, there is a dense network of approximately 140,000 miles of public rights of way which is considerably more than the 103,000 miles of main and unclassified roads (excluding residential streets) in the whole of Great Britain.

5   The countryside in your neighbourhood may not contain any breathtaking views but it is likely to be pleasant and to make for attractive walks. For those who crave more exciting scenery, there are a large number of protected areas of landscape quality of which at least one is likely to be within a reasonable distance of your home. The three most important designations that indicate high landscape value are

   • national parks (NPs)
   • areas of outstanding natural beauty (AONBs)
   • access land

National parks

6 The world's first national park was the Yellowstone created in California in 1872. Great Britain waited until 1949 when legislation was introduced which enabled their creation. The national parks of England and Wales are not owned by the government, as are many national parks in the New World, but are areas which have been designated as having great natural beauty and a high value for open-air recreation with the land remaining in private ownership.

7 Each park is governed by its own national park authority which has the statutory duty *'to conserve and enhance the natural beauty, wildlife and cultural heritage of the area, and to promote opportunities for the understanding and enjoyment of the park's special qualities by the public'.*

8 National parks provide information and facilities in order to support the local economy including

- visitor centres
- accommodation bureaux
- guided walks
- lectures
- educational activities

9 Descriptions and information about all the national parks can be found are can be found at www.nationalparks.gov.uk

England

- The Broads (strictly speaking this is not a national park but has the equivalent status)
- Dartmoor
- Exmoor
- Lake District
- New Forest
- North York Moors
- Northumberland
- Peak District
- South Downs
- Yorkshire Dales

Wales

- Brecon Beacons
- Pembrokeshire Coast
- Snowdonia

Areas of Outstanding Natural Beauty

10   The primary purpose of the Area of Outstanding Natural Beauty (AONB) designation is to conserve natural beauty. Other purposes include

- recreation insofar as this is consistent with the conservation of natural beauty and the needs of agriculture, forestry and other users
- the safeguarding of agriculture, forestry, rural industries and the economic and social needs of local communities

11   Further information, including descriptions of individual AONBs, can be found at www.landscapesforlife.org.uk

England
- Arnside and Silverdale (Lancashire and Cumbria)
- Blackdown Hills (Somerset and Devon)
- Cannock Chase (Staffordshire)
- Chichester Harbour (West Sussex and Hampshire)
- Chiltern Hills (Bedfordshire, Hertfordshire, Buckinghamshire and Oxfordshire)
- Cornwall
- Bodmin Moor (Cornwall)
- Cotswolds (mostly in Gloucestershire and Oxfordshire)
- Cranbourne Chase and Wiltshire Downs (Dorset and Wiltshire)
- Dedham Vale (Essex and Suffolk)
- Dorset
- East Devon
- East Hampshire
- Forest of Bowland (Lancashire and North Yorkshire)
- High Weald (East Sussex and Kent)
- Howardian Hills (North Yorkshire)
- Isle of Wight
- Isles of Scilly
- Kent Downs
- Lincolnshire Wolds
- Malvern Hills (Worcestershire and Herefordshire)
- Mendip Hills (Somerset)
- Nidderdale (North Yorkshire)
- Norfolk Coast
- North Devon Coast
- North Pennines (North Yorkshire, County Durham and Northumberland)

- Northumberland Coast
- North Wessex Downs (Berkshire, Hampshire, Oxfordshire and Wiltshire)
- Quantock Hills (Somerset)
- Shropshire Hills
- Solway Coast (Cumbria)
- South Devon
- South Downs (Hampshire, East and West Sussex)
- South Hampshire Coast
- Suffolk Coast and Heaths
- Surrey Hills
- Tamar Valley (Cornwall and Devonshire)
- Wye Valley (Gloucestershire, Herefordshire and partly in Monmouthshire, Wales)

Wales
- Anglesey
- Clwydian Range
- Gower Peninsula (Swansea)
- Llyn Peninsula (Gwynedd)
- Wye Valley (Monmouthshire and partly in England)

Access

12   In many parts of England and Wales, walkers are required by law to keep to the rights of way and permissive paths that are depicted on Ordnance Survey maps. But there are also tracts of land comprising mostly of

- mountain (over 600 metres)
- moor
- heath
- down
- registered common land

where walkers can wander off-path.

13   These areas are known as 'access land' and are depicted on Ordnance Survey *Explorer* maps by a brownish/orange tint in open countryside and a distinctive green in woodland. Information about the location of access land can be obtained from

- Natural England
  (http://www.openaccess.naturalengland.org.uk)
- Countryside Council for Wales
  (http://www.ccw.gov.uk)

14   Landowners can restrict or prevent access for up to 28 days a year without special permission, and can apply for additional restrictions for purposes such as
land management, conservation and fire prevention.

Long distance paths

15   There is no formal definition of what constitutes a long distance path (LDP) but
it is generally accepted that it should
   • be at least twenty miles long (the majority are much longer)
   • be on rights of way and access land
   • have a distinctive name
   • have a guidebook

16   Some of the more popular long distance paths contribute significantly to the
local economy by encouraging the growth of rural businesses such as providers
of accommodation, pubs, and luggage transfers.

17   The Long Distance Walkers' Association
(http://www.ldwa.org.uk) has a database which, in 2015, contained a record of
more than 1,400 routes covering over 80,000 miles, and the list is constantly
growing.

18   Advice and information about choosing and walking long distance paths is contained in Chapter 18.

19   There are three main categories of long distance paths
   • national trails
   • recreational routes (also known as regional routes)
   • routes that lack any official recognition

National trails

20   National trails were established under the provisions of the National Parks and
Access to the Countryside Act 1949 and are funded by Natural England (NE)
and the Countryside Council for Wales (CCW).

21   National trails are generally kept in good condition and are well waymarked and
signposted. Problems are most likely to occur on coastal paths which are sometimes subject to cliff falls that may require a section of the route to be closed
until a suitable diversion can be negotiated.

22 A great deal of information about individual national trails can be found at the official website of each route(http://www.nationaltrail.co.uk/name of trail) including

- general description of route and terrain
- length
- start and finishing points
- guidebooks and maps
- accommodation
- luggage transfers

English national trails

23 This is a complete list of English national trails (note that some sections of Offa's Dyke Path cross into Wales)

- Cleveland Way: 110 miles from Helmsley North Yorkshire to Filey Brigg, North Yorkshire
- Cotswold Way: 102 miles from Chipping Campden, Gloucestershire to Bath, Somerset
- Hadrian's Wall Path: 81 miles from Wallsend, Tyne & Wear to Bowness-on-Solway, Cumbria
- North Downs Way: 151 miles from Farnham, Surrey to Dover, Kent
- Offa's Dyke Path: 177 miles from Chepstow, Monmouthshire to Prestatyn, Denbighshire
- Peddars Way & Norfolk Coast Path: 93 miles from Knettishall Heath, Suffolk to Cromer, Norfolk
- Pennine Way: 268 miles from Edale, Derbyshire to Kirk Yetholm just over the Scottish border
- Ridgeway Path: 86 miles from Ivinghoe Beacon, Buckinghamshire to Overton Hill, Wiltshire
- South Downs Way: 100 miles from Eastbourne, East Sussex to Winchester, Hampshire
- South West Coast Path: 630 miles from Minehead, Somerset to South Haven Point, Dorset
- Thames Path: 184 miles from source of the Thames near Kemble, Gloucestershire to the Thames Barrier, Greater London
- Yorkshire Wolds Way: 79 miles from Hessle, East Yorkshire to Filey Brigg, North Yorkshire

Welsh national trails

24   This is a complete list of Welsh national trails (note that some sections of Offa's Dyke Path cross into England)

- Glyndwr's Way: 132 miles from Knighton, Powys to Welshpool, Powys
- Offa's Dyke Path: 177 miles from Chepstow, Monmouthshire to Prestatyn, Denbighshire
- Pembrokeshire Coast Path: 186 miles from St Dogmaels to Amroth

Recreational routes

25   Recreational routes are long distance paths that are designated and promoted by a local authority. They are normally created by stringing together existing rights of way, giving the route a distinctive name, and then publishing a guidebook.

26   They are not as well-funded as national trails but are likely to receive more attention, in the form of waymarking and maintenance, than other rights of way.

27   When the Ordnance Survey is notified, recreational trails are depicted on *Landranger* and *Explorer* maps with the same lozenge symbol as national trails.

Other long distance paths

28   Most long distance paths in this category are created from existing rights of way either by individuals or by walking clubs. Some of them are themed walks connected, for example, to historical events or characters from literature.

29   Long distance paths of this type are not depicted on Ordnance Survey maps because they have no official sanction. This even applies to Wainwright's Coast to Coast Walk which is one of the most popular routes in the British Isles.

European long distance paths

30   There are eleven officially designated European long distance walking routes, known as E-routes, developed by the European Ramblers' Association. Two of them, the E2, and E8 are routed through the British Isles. Further information is available at http://www.traildino.com.

Select bibliography

31   There are innumerable footpath guides describing walks in every corner of the British Isles making it impossible to provide a meaningful bibliography. They may be sourced on-line from:

a)   Commercial publishers and distributors such as
- Cicerone Press (www.cicerone.co.uk)
- Crimson Publishing (www.crimsonpublishing.co.uk)
- Frances Lincoln (www.franceslincoln.com)
- Cordee (www.cordee.co.uk)

b)   Non-commercial organizations such as
- tourist information centres
- rambling clubs
- national parks
- areas of outstanding natural beauty
- local authorities ranging from parish councils to county councils

c)   There are several websites from which walk descriptions together with GPX files can be downloaded. Some are free but others require a subscription. They can be accessed by entering your area of interest followed by footpath guides e.g. 'Shropshire footpath guides' into your search engine.

Chapter 14   Rights of way and access law in England and Wales

1   This chapter is not intended to be an authoritative treatise on rights of way legislation; it is no more than an attempt to give a general overview of the most important aspects of rights of way law. It is believed to be accurate as far as it goes but, in one brief chapter, it is impossible to mention all the exceptions to the information supplied.

2   The standard work on the subject is *Rights of Way; a Guide to Law and Practice* by John Riddall and John Trevelyan which runs to nearly 900 pages and is known among rights of way officers as the 'Blue Book' (see bibliography at the end of the chapter). This book should be consulted before taking any action with legal implications.

3   There are approximately 225,000 kilometres of public paths in England and Wales forming a dense network that covers the two countries. The path network is a priceless historical and recreational heritage as well as an important economic resource that must be safeguarded for the benefit of future generations.

4   Paths were established in prehistoric times before the Romans built our first road system. They were used for trading and linked centres where the essentials of life were to be found such as salt, flint, pottery etc. They often followed high-level routes where travelling was easier because the low-lying land had not yet been drained. The long-distance Ridgeway Path follows a prehistoric trading route for part of its length between Avebury in Wiltshire and Ivinghoe in Buckinghamshire. During the Middle Ages, the land was drained and reclaimed from the forest which, to a large extent, covered the country and then paths were used as a means of getting about the countryside by the shortest route.

5   The rise of the Romantic Movement in the eighteenth century encouraged a new attitude towards the countryside and walking for recreation became a popular pastime. The novels of Jane Austen and Thomas Hardy contain many references to walks being taken for pleasure on public paths. During those dreadful years between the two world wars, thousands of the unemployed left the industrial cities of the north each weekend to forget their unhappy lot for a while by walking the hills of Yorkshire, Derbyshire and Northumbria. Many of the battles to gain access to the moors were won at this time by walkers being prepared to trespass rather than be excluded from the fells.

Definition of terms

6   Most of the terms used in rights of way legislation have been defined by statute
   or the common law:

   a)   A *bridleway (BW)* is a highway over which members of the public have a
       right of way on foot, on horseback or leading a horse, and sometimes with a
       right to drive animals. There is also a right to ride bicycles providing that
       the rider gives way to equestrians and pedestrians. The local authority can
       make by-laws prohibiting the riding of bicycles on any particular highway .

   b)   A *byway open to all traffic (BOAT)* is a highway over which the public have
       a right of way for vehicular and all other kinds of traffic, but is used mainly
       by the public for the purpose for which footpaths and bridleways are used.

   c)   A *carriageway* is any way where the public have a right of way on foot, on
       horseback and in a motor vehicle.

   d)   A *footpath* is a highway over which the public have the right of way on foot
       only, other than such a highway at the side of the road (i.e. a footway or
       pavement).

   e)   A *footway* is a way, forming part of a carriageway, that is set aside for the
       use of pedestrians.

   f)   A *green lane* is a term that has no statutory or common law definition but is
       used to describe a broad, often unsurfaced track, usually running between
       hedges. A green lane may or may not be a right of way.

   g)   A *greenway* is a term that has no statutory or common law definition but is
       used to describe a network of largely vehicle-free routes connecting people
       to facilities and open spaces mostly in and around towns, cities and the
       countryside. They are often for shared use by people of all abilities on foot,
       bicycle or horseback, for commuting, play or leisure.

   h)   A *highway* is any way over which the public have the right of passage. It
       includes all such ways from footpaths to motorways.

   i)   A *highway authority* is the body responsible for the upkeep and mainte-
       nance of public highways. Other statutory bodies, e.g. national parks, may
       have limited rights of way powers but these do not relieve the highway
       authority of ultimate responsibility. The following authorities have a statu-
       tory duty to assert and protect the rights of those who use public paths:

       In England
           • London borough councils
           • county councils (including those that are unitary authorities)

• district councils that are unitary authorities

So me district councils have entered into an agreement with the county council to assume rights of way responsibilities.

In Wales

• county councils

• county borough councils

j) A *landholder* is the person or body legally responsible for the land. This may be

• an individual, a partnership, a company, or an organization. If it is a company then the directors are individually responsible

• the tenant if the land is leased

k) A *path* is the generic, non-legal term covering all routes that are not available to motorized vehicles. Paths may be

• public

• permissive

• private and not available to the general public

l) A *permissive path* is a path that is not a right of way but which the landholder allows the public to use, either under sufferance or by formal agreement, but for which there is no intention of permanent dedication. Sometimes a permissive path may be closed on one day every year to demonstrate that there is no intention to dedicate. Permissive paths are shown on *Explorer* and *Landranger* maps when the Ordnance Survey is notified of their existence.

l) A *public path* is an alternative term for a public right of way.

m) A *public right of way* is any way over which the public have a right of passage ranging from a footpath to a motorway. But when used colloquially it is understood to refer to

• footpaths

• bridleways

• byways open to all traffic

• restricted byways

• roads used as public paths

n) A *restricted byway* is a highway over which the public have the right of way on foot, on a horse or leading a horse, and in or on a non-motorized vehicle.

o) A *road* includes every type of highway from footpaths to carriageways and includes highways which the public may use only with the permission of the landholder.

p) A *road used as a public path (RUPP)* is a highway, other than a public path, used by the public mainly for the purpose for which footpaths and bridle-ways are so used. Under the Countryside and Rights of Way Act 2000 every RUPP must be reclassified as a restricted byway.

q) A *street* is a term that is synonymous with road.

Definitive Maps

7   In the immediate post-war years, it was decided to tidy the jungle of case law which largely governed the use of paths. The National Parks and Access to the Countryside Act 1949 laid upon county councils a duty to compile and publish Definitive Maps showing all public paths on a scale not less than 1:25,000. The county council normally invited each parish council to survey the paths in its parish and from this information the 'draft map' was compiled and published.

8   At this stage, it was possible to assert that a path shown on the draft map was not a right of way and had only been used with the permission of the landholder. In some cases, the exact line of the right of way was disputed. It was possible, also, to get paths not shown on the draft map included as rights of way, for the person who had supplied the information about paths in the parish may have been unaware that this path had been used by the public as a right of way.

9   The evidence was then sifted and negotiations took place between the interested parties on any points in dispute. If it was not possible to resolve any dispute by negotiation, a public inquiry was held by an inspector appointed by the Minister of Town and Country Planning. The inspector submitted the results of his inquiry to the minister, who made a decision in the light of the evidence. The 'provisional map' was then published incorporating all the revisions.

10 After the publication of the provisional map, a period of twenty-eight days was allowed for landholders to object to the inclusion on the map of paths which crossed their land. Any objections were heard at the Quarter Sessions with the highway authority defending the case. After any objections had been determined the county council then published their Definitive Map.

11 The Definitive Map is important because it provides conclusive evidence in law of the existence of a right of way *at the time that the map was made*. A path that appears on the Definitive Map is always a right of way, even if it was included by mistake, unless an extinguishment or diversion is granted, which can only be done by due legal process. Even though a path may be overgrown with vegetation, obstructed by barbed wire, have houses built across it and be ploughed up, there is still a right to use it, and the local authority, which has a statutory duty *'to assert and protect the rights of the public to the use and enjoyment of all*

highways and to prevent, as far as possible, the stopping-up or obstruction of those highways', can use its powers to have the path opened for public use.

12   The Definitive Map can usually be examined at the highway authority's offices. The local public library may have a copy and in any case will be able to tell you where it may be seen. Many highway authorities have published their Definitive Map on-line. Some highway authorities use the 1:25,000 map, others prefer the 1:10,000 scale. Rights of way are drawn on the map and allocated an identifying number. The highway authority notifies the Ordnance Survey of any changes to the rights of way network. Rights of way are depicted on the following maps:

a) Ordnance Survey maps
   • 1:25,000 *Explorer* series
   • 1:50,000 *Landranger* series

b) Automobile Association maps
   • 1:25,000 *Walker* series
   • 1:50,000 *Leisure* series

c) Geographia *Adventure Atlases.*

d) Harvey maps.

Alterations to the rights of way network

13   It is necessary from time to time for paths to be diverted or extinguished to allow development to take place, or for the land to be used more efficiently. In order to maintain the path network it is essential that any attempt to divert or extinguish a path without authority should be vigorously opposed, otherwise the changes will not appear on maps and a great deal of ill-will and confusion caused. Public paths may only be diverted or extinguished on specific grounds and by due legal process. Once a highway authority has determined that it wants to divert or extinguish a right of way it has to issue an order to set the process in motion. It is only when the order is confirmed that the change takes place.

14   Once an order has been made to divert or extinguish a right of way certain procedures have to be followed including, depending on the particular order, some or all of the following:

a) Advertising the order in local newspapers and the *London Gazette.*

b) Posting the order at each end of the affected right of way.

c) Consulting specified interested bodies including
   • persons likely to be affected
   • local authorities
   • national parks

- Natural England
- Ramblers' Association
- Open Spaces Society
- Byways and Bridleways Trust
- British Horse Society
- Auto-Cycle Union
- Cyclists' Tourist Club

15   If objections to the order are received, the matter is reported to the Secretary of State for the Environment, Food and Rural Affairs who may appoint an inspector from the Planning Inspectorate and hold a public inquiry, or may deal with the matter in other ways.

Grounds for diverting paths

16   A local authority (including a national park) may make an order to divert a public path in the interests of the landholder. (Highways Act 1980 section 119.)

17   A planning authority has the power to divert a public path if it considers it necessary to enable authorized development to take place. (Town and Country Planning Act 1990 section 257.)

18   The Secretary of State for the Environment, Food and Rural Affairs may authorize the diversion of any highway that crosses or enters the route of the highway under construction. (Highways Act 1980 section 18 and Town and Country Planning Act 1990 section 248.)

19   The Secretary of State for the Environment, Food and Rural Affairs may divert any public right of way, and a local authority may divert a footpath or bridleway on land held by a local authority. The Secretary of State has to be satisfied that an alternative right of way has been, or will be, provided. (Town and Country Planning Act 1990 section 251.)

20   Highway authorities have the power, subject to certain restrictions, to make diversion orders for the purpose of preventing or reducing crime. (Highways Act 1980 sections 118B and 118C as amended by the Countryside and Rights of Way Act 2000.)

21   Highway authorities have the power, subject to certain conditions, to make diversion orders for the purpose of school security and safeguarding children. (Highways Act 1980 sections 119B and 119C as amended by the Countryside and Rights of Way Act 2000.)

Grounds for extinguishing rights of way

22   A local authority (including a national park) may make an order to extinguish a highway, other than a classified road, if it considers that it is no longer required.

23   A planning authority has the power to extinguish a public path if it considers it necessary to enable authorized development to take place. (Town and Country Planning Act 1990 section 257.)

24   Highway authorities have the power, subject to certain restrictions, to make special extinguishment orders for the purpose of:

    a)   School security. (Highways Act 1980 sections 119B and 119C as amended by the Countryside and Rights of Way Act 2000.)

    b)   Preventing or reducing crime. (Highways Act 1980 sections 118B and 118C as amended by the Countryside and Rights of Way Act 2000.)

Creation of paths

25   Although both England and Wales are blessed with a very dense network of public rights of way, it is sometimes necessary to create paths. The most usual cases are short stretches to link existing rights of way to form a long-distance path, or where the changing pattern of land use makes it desirable for a new path to be created, either by agreement or order, to link with existing paths and thus preserve the path network.

26   The authority making the creation agreement or order, which may be a county council, district council or a national park, must bear the following considerations in mind:

    a)   The extent to which the path would add to the convenience or enjoyment of a substantial section of the public, or to the convenience of local residents.

    b)   The effect the path will have on the rights of persons interested in the land.

    c)   As far as possible new paths are created by agreement and the number of creation orders is small.

27   If a path is created by order, the procedure for advertising and objecting is similar to that for extinguishing and diverting paths (see 14:22-4). (Highways Act 1980 section 25.)

Duties, responsibilities, and problems on rights of way

28   Highway authorities have a duty to protect and assert the rights of the public to the use and enjoyment of highways. (Highways Act 1980 section 130 [1].)

29   Landholders have statutory duties and responsibilities for those rights of way that cross their property. If they receive grants under the Single Farm Payment Scheme, they are required to sign a declaration that all rights of way are in good condition. Failure to comply with the regulations may result in payments being withheld. (Common Agricultural Policy Single Payment and Support Schemes (Cross-compliance) (England) Regulations 2004 SI 2004 No 3196, Schedule, para 26-29.) Note that there is no such requirement in Wales.

Obstructions

30   There is no statutory definition of an obstruction but there are two useful judicial definitions:

  a) In *Seekings v Clarke 1961* Lord Chief Justice Parker remarked *'It is perfectly clear that anything which substantially prevents the public from having free access over the whole of the highway which is not purely temporary in nature is an unlawful obstruction.'*

  b) Mr Justice Byles in *R v Matthias 1861* stated *'A nuisance to a way is that which prevents the convenient use of the way by passengers'.*

31   Highway authorities have a statutory duty to prevent obstructions. They are required to:

  a) Prevent the stopping up or obstruction of those highways. (Highway Act 1980 section 130 (3).)

  b) Enforce the law through the courts or, after serving notice and getting no response, they may do what is necessary themselves and recover the cost from the landholder. (Highway Act 1980 section 143 (3).)

32   In certain circumstances, walkers may remove obstacles from the line of the path providing that

  • they remove no more than is actually necessary

  • that they did not undertake the journey with the specific intention of dealing with the obstruction

Walkers are advised to use this right with circumspection. If stock strays or becomes infected from neighbouring animals, it may result in causing thousands of pounds' worth of damage.

Ploughing and other surface disturbances

33   A landholder may, in the interests of good husbandry, plough or otherwise disturb the surface of footpaths and bridleways (except headland paths and paths with vehicular rights over them).

34   In some circumstances there may be a common law right to plough headland paths, but if this is not recorded in the statement accompanying the Definitive Map, then the onus of proof lies with the landholder.

35   If a right of way has been ploughed, or its surface disturbed, it must be restored to its minimum width and the line of the path must be made clear within 14 days (Highways Act 1980). The normal minimum width is defined as the legal width of the path, if known, or, failing that

- 1 metre for a cross-field footpath
- 1·5 metres for a headland footpath
- 2 metres for a cross-field bridleway
- 3 metres for a headland bridleway
- 3 metres for any carriageway

36   If the surface of a right of way is disturbed for a second time after ploughing (e.g. by harrowing), the surface and the line of the path must be restored within 24 hours. (Highways Act 1980.)

37   Highway authorities and non-unitary district councils have the right to prosecute landholders who fail to restore the surface of the path after ploughing or other disturbance. Alternatively, they may, after serving notice on the landholder, restore the surface of the path themselves and charge the cost to the offender. (Highways Act 1980.)

Crops

38   It is an offence for landholders to allow crops, other than grass, to obstruct the line of a right of way. (Highways Act 1980 section 137A.)

Gates and stiles

39   Landholders have a legal duty to maintain in good condition all gates and stiles crossed by public paths:

   a)   The highway authority is, in some cases, under an obligation to contribute at least 25 per cent of the approved cost of any repair work.

b) If the work is not done, the highway authority can do what is necessary and charge the cost to the landholder.

c) All gates on bridleways must be capable of being opened by a rider without dismounting.

d) Stiles must not obstruct bridleways. (Highways Act 1980 section 146.)

Bulls

40   Beef breed bulls, providing that are accompanied by cows or heifers, may be pastured in fields crossed by public paths. It is illegal to pasture bulls of recognized dairy breeds that are more than ten months old in fields crossed by public paths. (Wildlife and Countryside Act 1981 section 59.) Dairy breeds include

- Ayrshire
- British Friesian
- British Holstein
- Dairy Shorthorn
- Guernsey
- Jersey
- Kerry

Dangerous animals

41   It is illegal to have an animal known to be dangerous (including beef breed bulls) in fields crossed by public paths. (Animals Act 1971 section 59, Health and Safety at Work Act 1974 section 3.)

Waymarking and signposting

42   Waymarking may be defined as marking the course of the route at points along it. Waymarking is complementary to signposting, which is normally reserved for the points where a path makes a junction with a road. Signposts advertise a path and its initial direction; waymarks enable users to follow the path accurately at points where they might otherwise have difficulty.

43   The highway authority has a duty to erect and maintain a signpost where a public path leaves a metalled road and must indicate the classification of the right of way. (Countryside Act 1968 section 27.)

44   The highway authority has a duty to erect signposts and waymarks along the route of a path after it leaves a road if it thinks them necessary. Before doing so, it must consult with the landholders although their consent is not required.

(Countryside Act 1968 section 27.) Natural England has issued recommendations on the design of waymarks that have been widely adopted.

45   Volunteers wishing to undertake waymarking must first obtain the permission of the landholder and the highway authority because it is an offence to inscribe, paint or affix without lawful authority any picture, letter, sign or other mark upon the surface of a highway or upon any tree, structure or works in the highway. (Highways Act 1980 section 132.)

46   The National Trust sometimes uses the officially recommended signs to waymark its permissive routes but with the legend 'NT' superimposed on the arrow. This can cause confusion to map-readers especially where the network of both official and permissive routes is dense.

Footbridges

47   The highway authority has a general duty to maintain most bridges (Highways Act 1980 section 328 (2).) but if another authority, such as Network Rail or British Waterways, is responsible for the bridge then the duty of maintaining it falls on them.

Misleading notices

48   It is an offence to display a notice containing a misleading statement likely to deter the public from using a public path. Thus, it is an offence to erect a notice warning *'Beware of the bull'* if there is never a bull in that field. (National Parks and Access to the Countryside Act 1949 section 57.)

49   Notices such as *'Trespassers will be prosecuted'* and *'Private road'* are more difficult to deal with. The walker who strays from a public path *is* trespassing, except on access land (see 14:59-64), and the road *may* be private but have a right of way on foot over it. The solution in the latter case is for the highway authority to erect a footpath sign near the notice.

Trespass

50   Trespass may be defined as entering or remaining on land without lawful authority. In most cases, trespass is a civil matter and becomes a crime only in special circumstances which are unlikely to involve walkers seeking recreation in the countryside. The only remedies that the landholder has against trespassers who have no criminal intent are to

- require them to leave and to use just sufficient force to compel them to
- seek a court injunction prohibiting future trespass
- sue the trespasser for damages

Enforcing the law

51   As can be seen from the above outline, much of the law relating to public paths is fairly easily comprehended, but the mere existence of legislation does not guarantee compliance. For nearly fifty years after the passing of the National Parks and Access to the Countryside Act 1949, there were many areas of the country where public paths were in a neglected and shameful state. In recent years, the situation has improved markedly and, although there are still black spots, it is now possible to follow a walk on the map and be reasonably confident of finding the paths usable.

52   The three most serious problems likely to be encountered by walkers on public paths are obstructions that prevent free passage such as

- fences and hedges without gates or stiles to allow convenient passage
- buildings, farm machinery, piles of manure etc.
- non-restoration after ploughing or other disturbance of the surface
- obstructions by crops and overhanging vegetation

53   The following remedies are available should a problem be encountered:

a) Walkers who encounter problems within their own locality can approach the landholder direct. A tactful letter or telephone call may well result in the problem being resolved.

b) Many parish councils are jealous of their local paths and can sometimes get results quickly. The name of the parish clerk can be obtained from the public library or the chief executive of the district council.

c) Complain to your local councillor.

d) Ask the local rambling club or footpath society to take up the matter.

e) report it on-line to the Ramblers' Association (www.ramblers.org.uk).

Notifying the highway authority

54   The primary responsibility for enforcing the law lies with the highway authorities that have a statutory duty *'To assert and protect the rights of the public to the use and enjoyment of, and to prevent as far as possible the obstruction or stopping-up, the highways for which they are the authority.'* (Highways Act 1980 section 130 (1).)

55   If you decide to complain to the highway authority, go to the authority's website to see whether they have an on-line rights of way complaint form. If not, send a letter or email outlining the problem and giving a full grid reference.

56 The rights of way section of the highway authority is often under-staffed and it may be some time before one of its officers can take action. Occasionally, when a seemingly straightforward case of obstruction becomes complicated, it may remain at the back of the queue for action.

57 Should the highway authority prove dilatory there are two courses of action:

a) Complain to the Local Government Ombudsman
- in England: www.lgo.org.uk
- in Wales: www.ombudsman-wales.org.uk

The Local Government Ombudsman has the power to investigate and adjudicate on matters of maladministration. There is no power to enforce the decisions of the Ombudsman but they can exert a powerful influence.

b) Serve notice on the highway authority requesting that an obstruction be removed. If the authority fails to act the complainant can apply to the magistrates' court which has the power to require the highway authority to act within a specified time. (Highways Act 1980 sections 130A-C as amended by the Countryside and Rights of Way Act 2000 section 63.)

Private prosecutions

58 An individual or organization can prosecute in the magistrates' court anyone responsible for obstructing a highway without lawful authority for:

a) Wilful obstruction of the free passage along the path. (Highways Act 1980 section 137.)

b) Failure to make good the surface of a path after ploughing or other disturbance of the surface. (Highways Act 1980 section 134.)

c) Failure to prevent crops, other than grass, from obstructing the path. (Highways Act 1980 section 137A.)

d) Detailed information on how to proceed with a private prosecution will be found in *Rights of Way; a Guide to Law and Practice* (see 14:73).

Access

59 Access may be defined as a right to walk anywhere in an area that has been designated as access land. The walker is not restricted to following rights of way and has the right, subject to certain restrictions, to wander at will.

60 There has long been a limited amount of access land including
- common land (for definition see Glossary)
- where permission has been granted by a landowner (which could be revoked at any time)

• where access agreements have been negotiated by national parks and local authorities

61 Under the provisions of the Countryside and Rights of Way Act 2000, the right of access was greatly extended and put on a proper legal basis. Provision was also made for areas of access to be publicized. Under the terms of the Act access applies only to walkers; no rights are conferred on equestrians and cyclists.

62 Access land includes
- mountain
- moor
- heath
- down
- registered common land
- land that is more than 600 metres above sea level
- land that is expressly dedicated as access land

63 Within the boundaries of access land there may be small pockets, known as 'excepted land' to which the public will not have access. These include
- gardens
- cultivated land
- railways
- buildings
- quarries
- golf courses
- aerodromes
- racecourses
- land occupied by statutory undertakings such as water companies

Statutory restrictions on access

64 In certain circumstances access can be restricted:

a) Landowners are entitled to restrict access for up to 28 days in one calendar year. However, such restrictions do not apply on
- Christmas Day
- bank holidays
- more than four Saturdays or Sundays in a calendar year
- any Saturday between 1st June and 11th August
- any Sunday between 1st June and 30th September

Restrictions do not affect the use of rights of way.

b) Local authorities and national parks have the power to impose additional restrictions on access for
  • management of the land (such as heather burning)
  • prevention of fires or other dangers
  • conservation reasons
  • defence or national security

Contraventions of the law governing access

65   Persons contravening the regulations governing the use of access land lose their rights to be on the land or any other land with the same landowner. They must leave the property and are forbidden to return within 72 hours.

66   Needless to say, few walkers would fall foul of the regulations but it is worth remembering that the only right conferred on the public on access land is the right to walk. Camping is specifically excluded under the law.

Landowner's liability

67   The Occupiers' Liability Act 1984 was amended so that occupiers of access land owe no duty of care to the public except by reckless behaviour. Thus walkers would not normally be able to claim against the occupier should they be injured.

Maps and location of access land

68   Access land is depicted on *Explorer* maps covering England and Wales. Boundaries are coloured light orange and the area is given a light yellow tint. Information can also be obtained from the following websites
  • Natural England www.naturalengland.org.uk
  • Countryside Council for Wales www.ccw.gov.uk

Select bibliography

69   Agate, Elizabeth, *Footpaths; Practical Handbook.* British Trust for Conservation Volunteers, 2001.

70   Bonyhady, Tim, *The Law of the Countryside; the Rights of the Public.* Professional Books, 1987.

71   Jones, Brian and others, *Countryside Law* 4th ed. Shaw & Sons, 2004.

72   Radford, Andy, *Building Countryside Paths and Tracks.* Crowood Press, 2006.

73   Riddall, John, and Trevelyan, John, *Rights of Way; a Guide to Law and Practice* 4th ed. Published jointly by the Open Spaces Society and the Ramblers' Association, 2007. Note that a website *Blue Book Extra* (www.ramblers.org.uk/rightsofwaybook) has been created from which additions and amendments can be downloaded.

Chapter 15 Walking in Scotland

1 Most walkers would probably agree that some of the finest mountain scenery in the British Isles is to be found in the Highlands and Islands of Scotland. The combination of mountains and lochs makes for an unrivalled, ever-changing panorama, but it is a demanding terrain that even the most seasoned hill-walker has to treat with respect. The Lowlands of Scotland, lying south of the Glasgow-Edinburgh industrial belt, also has some splendid, if less rugged, walking. And one of the greatest joys of walking in Scotland is that, with a few exceptions, you can walk virtually anywhere you want.

2 In enclosed countryside, there are few paths across farmland. You can walk around the margins of fields, across pasture, and cross field boundaries, providing that you commit no damage, but it is only local people who have the time to explore who can enjoy this freedom. Gates and stiles are not marked on Ordnance Survey maps so it is difficult for strangers to work out purposeful routes.

3 Walkers should be aware that the Highlands of Scotland are plagued by clouds of minute midges during the summer months. They are harmless to humans but their bites are unpleasant and cause itching. Midges emerge in April and May, become most active in late May and early June and again in late July and early August before disappearing in October. Midge attacks are less frequent
- in conditions of low humidity
- at heights above 700 metres
- in wind speeds above 6 mph

The risk of midge bites can be reduced by:

a) Applying an insect repellent. It seems that there is no one brand that is universally effective and what works for one person will not necessarily be effective on another.

b) Wearing dark clothing fitting tightly at the wrists and ankles. There are also specially-designed hats with veils that cover the face and fit closely around the neck, and midge jackets made from nylon netting.

Legal aspects

4   Scotland is renowned for its liberal access law that allows the public to walk, with a few exceptions, over most of the countryside. In addition to the general right of access there are also public paths including

- rights of way
- core paths

Access

5   Under the Land Reform (Scotland) Act 2003, there is a statutory right of non-motorized (except for the disabled using a vehicle adapted for their use) public access over most land and inland water. The Act places new responsibilities on local authorities and national park authorities to uphold access rights.

6   The main points include:

a)   A statutory right of access over most land and inland water for recreational, educational and some commercial purposes, and for crossing land or water.

b)   Land managers and walkers must behave responsibly. Access should be taken in ways which are compatible with land management needs.

c)   Those enjoying the right of access as well as land managers must respect the environment, wildlife, and historic features.

7   Detailed guidance on responsible behaviour for the public and land managers is contained in the Scottish Outdoor Access Code which received parliamentary approval in 2004. The Code runs to 133 pages which can be downloaded from www.outdooraccess-scotland.com and is summarized below:

a)   When you are in the outdoors
- take responsibility for your own actions and act safely
- respect people's privacy and peace of mind
- help land managers to work safely and effectively
- care for the environment and take your litter home
- keep your dog under proper control
- take extra care if organizing an event or a business

b)   If you're managing the outdoors
- respect access rights
- act reasonably when asking people to avoid land management operations
- work with your local authority and other bodies to help integrate access and land management
- respect rights of way and customary access

8   Access rights apply to:

   a) Fields (except grassland cultivated for hay or silage that is above ankle height).

   b) Field margins (headlands).

   c) Bare ground in arable fields such as the 'tramlines' made by tractor wheels.

   d) Lightweight, wild camping (the Mountaineering Council of Scotland recommends that groups should be small and to camp no more than three nights in one place). Local authorities have the power to pass by-laws restricting camping. (It is currently banned on the east shore of Loch Lomond from 1st March to 31st October.)

   e) Golf courses (but keep off the greens and avoid interfering with play).

9   Walkers should respect reasonable requests to minimize disturbance and avoid areas where certain activities are taking place including:

   a) Shooting of deer, grouse or pheasants. Information is promised to be available on a dedicated website by 2014. The main shooting seasons are
   - grouse: Aug 12 to Dec 10
   - pheasant: Oct 1 to Feb 1
   - red deer: Jul 1 to Oct 20

   Shooting does not normally take place on Sundays.

   b) Agricultural, forestry and environmental work involving spraying and tree felling.

10   Access rights do not apply to
   - private gardens
   - areas within the curtilage of buildings
   - properties where an entrance fee is charged

Public paths

11   There are two categories of public path
   - rights of way
   - core paths

Rights of way

12   A right of way is a route along which the public have a right of passage. To be a right of way, a route must meet certain conditions:

   a) It must have been used by the public for at least twenty years.

b) It must connect two public places or places where the public have the right to resort.

c) It must follow a more or less defined route.

13   The Act classifies rights of way into three categories:

a) *Vindicated routes* that have been declared to be rights of way by the courts, or through some other legal process.

b) *Asserted routes* that have been accepted as rights of way by the landowner, or where the local authority has indicated that it would take legal action to protect them should that become necessary.

c) *Claimed routes* that appear to meet the common law conditions necessary to be regarded as rights of way, but which have not been formally vindicated or asserted.

14   The Scottish Rights of Way and Access Society (Scotways) has compiled a *Catalogue of Rights of Way* (CROW) containing records over 7,500 routes of known rights of way. It comprises a computer database with information about each route, and digital maps at a scale of 1:50,000 but it is not available on-line. Information is available from the Society.

15   Rights of way are not depicted by a special symbol on Ordnance Survey maps. Designated long-distance routes have the same lozenge symbol as those in England and Wales. Other paths are depicted by means of black dashes. Virtually all paths, irrespective of status, that are shown on Ordnance Survey maps may be used by walkers.

Core paths

16   Local authorities have a duty to produce a core path plan. This can normally be downloaded from their websites and can give you an idea of paths that are likely to be well maintained. Many of them are short and some are on roads.

Where to walk

17   The provisions of the Land Reform Act outlined above gives walkers a great deal of freedom to explore the countryside which works especially well in upland areas.

National parks

18   It has been argued that Scotland has such a wealth of wonderful, unspoilt mountain scenery that it is invidious to designate only two areas worthy of the accolade of national park status. They are

- Loch Lomond and the Trossachs: situated to the north of Glasgow (www.lochlomond-trossachs.org)
- The Cairngorms: centred on Braemar, is the largest national park in the United Kingdom (www.cairngorms.co.uk)

Long distance paths

19   Scotland has a number of long distance paths. Those that are promoted nationally are known as 'Great Trails' (formerly called 'Long Distance Routes'). They are waymarked and are depicted on Ordnance Survey maps with a lozenge symbol. There are also a handful of other long distance routes which, as yet, do not receive any national support.

20   A number of on-line resources provide information about long distance routes including

- The Long Distance Walkers Association (www.ldwa.org.uk)
- Scotland's Great Trails; the Official Guide (www.scotlandsgreattrails.org.uk)
- WalkHighlands (www.walkhighlands.co.uk)

Some long distance paths have a dedicated website.

Great Trails

21   The following routes have been designated Great Trails

- Annandale Way: 55 miles following the river Annan from Bridgend near Moffat to Annan
- Arran Coastal Way: a 65-mile circular walk around the Isle of Arran
- Ayrshire Coastal Path: 100 miles from Glenapp near Stranraer to Skelmorlie between Largs and Greenock
- Berwickshire Coastal Path: 30 miles from Berwick-on-Tweed to Cockburnspath
- Borders Abbeys Way: a 65-mile circular route connecting the abbey towns of Melrose, Dryburgh, Kelso and Jedburgh
- Cateran Trail: a 60-mile circular route from Blairgowrie
- Clyde Walkway: 40 miles from Glasgow to New Lanark
- Cross Borders Drove Road: 52 miles from Harperrig to Hawick

- Dava Way: 24 miles from Forres to Grantown-on-Spey
- Fife Coastal Path: 94 miles from Culross to the Tay Bridge
- Formartine and Buchan Way: 53 miles from Aberdeen to Peterhead and Fraserburgh along an old railway line
- Forth & Clyde and Union Canals: 65 miles from Bowling, west of Glasgow, to Edinburgh
- Great Glen Way: 73 miles from Fort William to Inverness
- John Muir Way: 45 miles from Musselburgh to Cockburnspath
- Kintyre Way: 90 miles from Tarbet across the Kintyre Peninsula to Southend
- Moray Coast Trail: 50 miles from Findhorn to Cullen
- Mull of Galloway Trail: 24 miles from Mull to Stranraer
- River Ayr Way: 41 miles from Glenbuck to Ayr
- Rob Roy Way: 94 miles from Drymen to Pitlochry
- Romans and Reivers Route: 52 miles from the Ae Forest in Dumfries and Galloway to Hawick
- St Cuthbert's Way: 62 miles from Melrose to the island of Lindisfarne in Northumberland
- Southern Upland Way: 212 miles traversing the country from Portpatrick in the west to Cockburnspath in the east
- Speyside Way: 65 miles from Buckie on the Moray Coast to Aviemore
- Three Lochs Way: 32 miles from Balloch to Helensburgh
- West Highland Way: 95 miles from Milngavie, Glasgow to Fort William
- West Island Way: 29 miles across the Isle of Bute

Other long distance paths

- Cape Wrath Trail: 200 miles from Fort William to Cape Wrath
- Carrick Way: a 100-mile circular route around the hills of North and South Carrick in Ayrshire
- Clyde Coast Way: 50 miles from Ayr to Greenock
- Cowal Way: 57 miles from Portavadie to Ardgartan
- East Highland Way: 78 miles from Fort William to Aviemore
- Rob Roy Way: 93 miles from Drymen to Pitlochry
- Sir Walter Scott Way: 93 miles from Moffat to Cockburnspath
- Skye Trail: 77 miles from Rubha Hunish in the far north to Broadford in the south

Select bibliography

For sources of footpath guides in the British Isles see Chapter 13 (13:31).

Chapter 16   Walking in Ireland

1   The Republic of Ireland and Northern Ireland and are separate countries but they share a common heritage that is reflected in their provisions for walking. In neither country is there a local network of public paths such as exists in England and Wales. In fact, there are few paths that are legally protected.

2   Walking in Ireland is almost entirely dependent on the goodwill of farmers and landowners. If walkers behave irresponsibly that goodwill breaks down and notices forbidding entry start to appear.

3   Those who walk in lowland areas are often confined to the network of attractive country lanes that carry little traffic.

4   In upland areas beyond the limits of cultivation, there is no right of access but walkers who wander at will are unlikely to be challenged providing that they do not damage walls and fences.

5   The Irish Farmers' Association in conjunction with the Mountaineering Council of Ireland has drawn up a Farmland Code of Conduct of good practice that is relevant to walkers in both countries:

Respect farmland and the rural environment.

> *Do not interfere with livestock, crops, machinery or other property.*
>
> *Guard against all risks of fire, especially near forests.*
>
> *Leave all farm gates as you find them.*
>
> *Always keep children under close control and supervision.*
>
> *Avoid entering farmland containing livestock. Your presence can cause stress to the livestock and even endanger your own safety.*
>
> *Do not enter farmland if you have dogs with you, even if on a leash, unless with the permission of the landowner.*
>
> *Always use gates, stiles or other recognized access points and avoid damage to fences, hedges and walls.*
>
> *Take all your litter home.*
>
> *Take special care on country roads.*
>
> *Avoid making unnecessary noise.*
>
> *Protect wildlife, plants and trees.*
>
> *Take heed of warning signs - they are there for your protection.*

6   Walking is a popular pastime in both countries and there are numerous footpath guides that describe routes that have become generally accepted by the farmers and landowners over whose land the paths cross.

1:50,000 maps covering all Ireland

7   There is close cooperation between the Republic's mapping agency, the Ordnance Survey Ireland (OSi), and the Ordnance Survey of Northern Ireland (OSNI) resulting in the island being covered by a compatible series of 1:50,000 maps each covering an area measuring 40 kilometres x 30 kilometres.

8   75 sheets, the *Discovery Series* are published by the Ordnance Survey Ireland and 18 sheets, the *Discoverer Series,* by the Ordnance Survey of Northern Ireland. They are similar to Ordnance Survey *Landranger* maps.

9   Important features shown include
   • the Irish grid (see 4:25-7)
   • contours at 10-metre intervals
   • paths and tracks
   • waymarked walks
   • the national cycle network
   • woods
   • water features
   • important buildings
   • historical features
   • youth hostels
   • picnic areas
   • campsites

Republic of Ireland

10   Walking is popular in the Republic despite there being few rights of way or access agreements. Walking is dependent on the goodwill of farmers and landowners who can legally exclude walkers from their land. Notices forbidding entry should be respected.

Rights of way

11   A public right of way is a person's right of passage along a road or path. A private right of way is the right to enter onto private lands, but only for the purposes of gaining access to or exiting from another piece of land.

12   The Occupiers' Liability Act 1995, ensures that a landowner cannot be held responsible for the welfare of persons engaging in recreational activities.

13   The Roads Act 1993, requires local authorities to protect the public's right to access public rights of way.

14   The Planning and Development Act 2000, gives landowners the right to apply to their local authority to have a public right of way extinguished for the purposes of development.

15   Section 24 of the Housing (Miscellaneous Provisions) Act 2002 added new rules governing criminal trespass to the Criminal Justice (Public Order) Act 1994, making it an offence for anyone to enter, occupy or bring anything onto privately owned land or land owned by local authorities if that act is likely to be detrimental to the amenities.

Maps

16   Ordnance Survey Ireland (OSi) is the official mapping agency. It publishes two series of topographic maps that are of interest to walkers
- 1:50,000 *Discovery* series (see 16:7-9)
- 1:25,000 *Leisure* series (see 16:17)

Leisure series

17   The four maps in this series have a scale 1:25,000 and cover the
- *Brandon Mountains*
- *Macgillycuddy's Reeks*
- *Aran Islands*
- *Killarney National Park*

There are long-term plans to revise some of the maps in this series and to extend coverage to other popular tourist areas.

EastWest Mapping

18   EastWest Mapping is a commercial publisher which has issued four maps of particular interest to walkers. The scale is 1:30.000 and the contour interval is 20 metres
- *The Dublin & North Wicklow Mountains*
- *Wicklow East*
- *Wicklow Mountains West*
- *Lugnaquilla & Glendalough*

19   Features depicted include
  • unsurfaced roads
  • tracks
  • large paths
  • small paths
  • intermittent paths
  • boardwalks
  • waymarked walking routes
  • signposted walks
  • agreed access points
  • gates
  • hillwalking access points to traditional routes
  • field boundaries (selected)
  • national parks
  • Coillte forests
  • picnic sites
  • castles
  • car parks
  • public telephones
  • information centres
  • public houses
  • restaurants
  • public conveniences
  • accommodation
  • campsites

20   The company publishes, in conjunction, with the Dublin Mountain Partnership
  • *The Dublin Mountains* with a scale of 1:25,000
  • The Dublin & North Wicklow Mountains Satmap SD card for use with a Satmap10 satnav (not compatible with any other satnav)

Harvey Maps

21   This publisher has issued three satnav-compatible maps in the *Superwalker* series (see 5:38-9). The scale is 1:30.000 and the contour interval is 15 metres
  • *MacGillycuddy's Reeks* (covers the whole of the Killarney National Park)
  • *Connemara*
  • *Wicklow Mountains*

22   Features depicted include
- tarmac tracks
- tracks and forest roads
- old or eroded routes
- intermittent paths

National Parks

23   The National Parks & Wildlife Service has created the following national parks
- Ballycroy
- The Burren
- Connemara
- Glenveagh
- Killarney
- Wicklow Mountains

Descriptions and information about national parks can be found at www.npws.ie/nationalparks from where there are links to individual parks.

National Waymarked Trails

24   There is a network of 43 National Waymarked Trails. Walkers should be aware that many of them include a surprisingly high proportion of walking on quiet lanes. Not all of them have a published guidebook. More detailed information can be obtained from the National Waymarked Trails website at www.irishtrails.ie/National_Waymarked_Trails.

Coillte Recreational Forests

25   Coillte, the forest agency, operates 11 forest parks and 150 recreation sites, most of which provide basic facilities such as
- walking trails
- parking
- picnic sites

Slí na Sláinte (Path to Health)

26   Slí na Sláinte, meaning 'Path to Health', was developed by the Irish Heart Foundation to encourage people to walk for leisure and good health.

27   The Slí na Sláinte logo as been placed at one-kilometre intervals on 190 walking routes which allows walkers to calculate the distance they walk.

National Waymarked Ways

28   Waymarked Ways are routes that have been developed with the agreement and support of landowners. They are waymarked and signposted. There are 43 Way-marked Ways. It is possible to search and find information on all National Way-marked Ways on the irishtrails.ie website.

29   The National Trails Office (NTO), a department of the Irish Sports Council is responsible for the registering and regulation of all Waymarked Ways and other walking routes. It maintains a National Trails Register which lists some 800 routes at www.irishtrails.ie. Maps and guidebooks are available for all trails that are approved by the National Trails Office.

Walking organizations

30   Two national organizations serve the interests of Irish walkers
   • The Walkers Association of Ireland
   • Mountaineering Ireland

The Walkers Association of Ireland

31   The Walkers Association of Ireland (WAI) is a forum for Irish hill-walkers and ramblers with the following aims
   • to give a sense of identity and purpose to hill-walking and rambling in its own right as a national sport
   • to provide information on matters relevant to walkers such as holidays, challenge walks, and access
   • to coordinate a walker's view on topics of special interest, such as access, the environment and mapping
   • to provide a forum for specialist interests such as satnavs, photography, nature, etc.
   • to establish a link to walkers' forums abroad
   • to seek discounts for walkers in sporting shops, transport bodies, restaurants, etc.
For more information access the website at www.walkersassociation.ie

Mountaineering Ireland

32   Mountaineering Ireland (formerly The Mountaineering Council of Ireland) is the representative body for walkers and climbers in Ireland. It is recognized as the national governing body for mountaineering, hill-walking and rambling by both the Irish Sports Council and Sport Northern Ireland. (See Appendix 1:39.)

Northern Ireland

33   The opportunities for walking in the Province are similar to those pertaining in the Republic and are described in general terms in paragraphs 16:1-6.

Public rights of way

34   There are few rights of way in Northern Ireland but those that exist are supported by the following legal framework:

a)   They are used as of right and not by a privilege granted by the landowner.

b)   They may be created specifically by or through the public openly using a path over a period of time with the acquiescence of the landowner.

c)   Landowners must not obstruct rights of way or prevent or deter anyone from exercising their rights of passage.

d)   Landowners have a duty to maintain stiles and gates.

35   District councils are required to:

a)   Assert, protect and keep open any public right of way and to compile and preserve maps and other records of the rights of way in their area.

b)   Signpost paths where considered necessary.

c)   Contribute at least a quarter of the cost of maintaining stiles and gates.

36   In addition to their statutory duties, councils have a right to

• maintain any public right of way
• establish new rights of way by agreement
• divert, extinguish or create paths, and confirm unopposed orders
• authorize the erection of new stiles and gates

37   Landowners have a right to:

a)   Plough a right of way across agricultural land (but not along headlands) providing
• it is necessary
• the district council is notified within 7 days
• the surface is restored, normally within 14 days

b)   Apply to the district council for the temporary diversion or closure of a right of way for up to three months.

c) Pasture a bull (except those of recognized dairy breeds) in a field that is crossed by a public right of way. But a bull that is more than 11 months old must be with cows or heifers.

Permissive access

38   Some landowners have entered into a permissive path agreement that allows the public to access their land for walking, cycling or horse-riding. Permissive paths are not rights of way and are subject to the agreement's terms and conditions.

39   Access is often available on land belonging to the
  • Water Service
  • Forest Service
  • National Trust
  • Woodland Trust

Maps

40   There are three publishers of topographic maps that are used by walkers:

a) The 1:50,000 *Discoverer Series,* published by the Ordnance Survey of Northern Ireland, which cover the whole of the Province (see 16:8-9).

b) The 1:25,000 *Activity Series,* published by the Ordnance Survey of Northern Ireland, which cover selected areas (see 16:41).

c) A single sheet of the 1:25,000 Harvey *Superwalker Series* (see 5:38-9) that covers the Mourne Mountains.

Activity Series

41   These detailed maps cover
  • *Lough Erne*
  • *Strangford Lough*
  • *The Mournes*
  • *Sperrins*
  • *Glens of Antrim*
  • *Causeway Coast and Rathlin Island*

42   Features depicted include
  • contours with a 10-metre interval
  • Irish grid (see 4:25-7)
  • waymarked walks

• selected camping and caravan sites
• visitor centres
• pubs in rural areas
• public conveniences in rural areas

Where to walk

43   There is much attractive walking to be found in the countryside of Northern Ireland despite the lack of a local footpath network. There are no national parks but there are eight designated Areas of Outstanding Natural Beauty (AONBs)

• Antrim Coast and Glens
• Binevenagh
• Causeway Coast
• Lagan Valley
• Mourne
• Ring of Gullion
• Sperrin
• Strangford and Lecale

Long Distance Paths

44   There are a number of long distance paths including

• Antrim Hills Way 35km/22miles
• Causeway Coast Way 53km/33miles
• Lecale Way 64km/40miles
• Mourne Way 42km/26miles
• Newry Canal Way 32km/20miles
• Ring of Gullion Way 58km/36miles
• Ulster Way 661km/411miles (this route comprises sections on paths linked by long sections on roads some of which carry heavy traffic)

Quality Walks

45   Outdoor Recreation Northern Ireland identifies and promotes some excellent short, medium and long distance walking routes. These have been assessed independently by walkers using the following criteria

• the availability of car parking, toilets and information on the walk
• the quality of the signposting and waymarking
• the amount and type of off-road walking
• the amount and type of road walking

• the quality of the scenery

46   All Quality Walks are listed on the WalkNi website, www.walkni.com/useful-info/quality walks, classified by county and distance.

The Ulster Federation of Rambling Clubs

47   The Ulster Federation of Rambling Clubs (UFRC) is the governing body for rambling and hill-walking clubs in Northern Ireland. It provides a forum for more than 30 clubs and its 2000 individual members to

• encourage recreational walking
• appreciate and respect the countryside
• improve access

For more information access its website at www.ufrc-online.co.uk

Select bibliography

For sources of footpath guides in the British Isles see Chapter 13 (13:31).

Chapter 17   Walking in the Isle of Man and the Channel Islands

1   The Crown Dependencies of the Isle of Man, Guernsey, and Jersey are small islands that offer delightful walking opportunities. Each one has its own distinctive culture and way of life.

The Isle of Man

2   The Isle of Man is situated in the Irish sea midway between England and Ireland. It is 32 miles long and 14 miles wide. The scenery is remarkably varied ranging from coastal dunes, wooded glens, and miniature mountain landscapes. Snaefell, at 620 metres, is the highest point in the island.

3   There are flights from several airports in the British Isles, and there are ferries from Liverpool, Heysham, Belfast and Dublin.

4   The island has a dense network of field paths that are legally protected, as well as unmade roads
   - green roads open to walkers, cyclists, equestrians and motor-cyclists
   - greenways which are not open to motor vehicles

and long distance trails including
   - Millennium Way: 28 miles from near Ramsey to Castletown
   - Raad Ny Foillan (Way of the Gull) also known as the Isle of Man Coast Path: 95 miles

For more information go to www.visitisleofman.com.

Maps

5   There are two maps that are suitable for walkers:

   a) The Ordnance Survey *Landranger* sheet 95 covers the whole of the island.

   b) The Isle of Man *Rights of Way and Outdoor Leisure Map* published by the Cartographic Section of the Isle of Man Government's Department of Local Government in two sheets at a scale of 1:25,000. It is a topographic map, similar in style to an Ordnance Survey *Explorer*.

Channel Islands

6   The Channel Islands are a group of small islands off the Normandy coast of France. There are eight permanently inhabited islands of which Guernsey and Jersey are the largest and offer the most significant walking opportunities. They both have magnificent coastal walks and charming villages and there is a dense network of rights of way. There are regular ferry services from the south coast of England, and flights from London Heathrow and some regional airports.

7   The Channel Islands Way is a 115-mile long distance path that follows the coasts of

- Jersey (48 miles)
- Guernsey (38 miles)
- Alderney (14 miles),
- Sark (9 miles)
- Herm (6 miles)

Maps

8   Guernsey and Jersey are responsible for their own mapping and have published topographic maps in the style of Ordnance Survey *Explorer* maps. They show field boundaries and public paths.

9   The map of Guernsey is on a single double-sided sheet with Guernsey on one side at a scale of 1:15,000. Maps of the islands of Alderney, Herm, Jethou and Sark are on the obverse at a scale of 1:10,000. The map employs three grids

- the unique Guernsey grid
- latitude and longitude
- Universal Transverse Mercator (UTM) grid

10   The map of Jersey has a scale of 1:25,000 and is on one sheet. It uses latitude and longitude.

11   Handheld satnavs can be used on the islands providing that they are tuned to the correct grid.

Select bibliography

For sources of footpath guides in the British Isles see Chapter 13 (13:31).

Chapter 18   Walking holidays

Please note: The information in this chapter applies to the whole of the British Isles but some of the examples, such as those about maps, apply specifically to Great Britain. Readers requiring information about other countries should substitute the local alternative.

1   Walkers who have gained some experience and pleasure in exploring local paths, and have become proficient in the use of map and compass, may wish to venture on a walking holiday. There are several kinds of walking holidays and some of them are suitable for families. Children are tough little creatures, and providing that they have been used to walking from an early age they should get a great deal of enjoyment from a walking holiday, especially if some days are set aside for a visit to the beach and places of interest.

2   Certain terms, which may be unfamiliar to some walkers, are used in this chapter:

a) A **wayfarer** is someone who walks a multi-day linear route such as a long-distance path.

b) **Wayfaring** is the activity of walking a long-distance route.

c) An **outfitter** is an organization that provides services connected with walking and other outdoor activities. It's a useful term used in the United States.

Types of holiday

3   Walking holidays may be either
- centre-based where you stay at one location
- wayfaring where you follow a linear route

4   Factors to take into account when planning any kind of overnight walking trip include:

a) The need to tailor the trip to your walking experience. However alluring it may seem, it would be unwise to attempt to backpack the Pennine Way, or undertake a strenuous itinerary in the Scottish Highlands, if you have never tackled anything more demanding than short walks in the Chilterns.

b) On the other hand, a centre-based holiday in the Lake District or Snowdonia could offer a mixture of pleasant valley walking and easy mountain paths that should prove enjoyable and extend your walking experience.

c) The cumulative effect of walking for several consecutive days can put a strain on your muscles and joints because your body has only a few hours to recover before you start out on another day. Also, you are more likely to suffer from blisters on a multi-day trip.

5   Some walkers like to buy a package from an outfitter (see 18:10-17) whilst others prefer to plan and organize their own trips (see 18:18-22).

Centre-based holidays

6   This type of trip is probably the most flexible, especially for families with children, because:

a) There is no obligation to walk every day. If the weather is wet alternative trips to places of interest can be arranged.

b) There are no restrictions on the amount of luggage that can be taken.

c) Clothes can be laundered and dried.

d) In self-catering accommodation, it is possible to provide for special needs and particular diets.

7   Accommodation that is suitable for centre-based trips include
   • hotels
   • bed & breakfast
   • campsites
   • hostels
   • holiday cottages

8   Some organizations like HF (formerly Holiday Fellowship) and Ramblers Worldwide Holidays own or lease the premises used for some of their trips. They are often similar to country hotels and as they can accommodate a large number of people, there is a wide range of activities and a choice of walks of varying degrees of difficulty. Thus it is possible to start the holiday with easy walks and gradually progress to more difficult routes.

9   There are organizations and businesses that offer courses on hill-walking, survival and related subjects and as these are usually located in upland areas it is possible, not only to have an enjoyable holiday, but also to extend your experience and improve your skills (see 23:10-16).

Wayfaring

10 Factors that should be taken into consideration when contemplating a wayfaring trip include:

   a) The need, unless backpacking, to move on every so often, sometimes every day, to new accommodation. If it has been reserved in advance, the wayfarer has little choice but to continue which makes it difficult to take an unplanned rest day.

   b) The amount of luggage taken is likely to be restricted. Even on a trip organized by an outfitter, or when using a luggage transfer service (see 18:16-17), you are likely to be allowed only one bag limited in size and weight.

Outfitters

11 A good outfitter will take care of all the necessary arrangements including

   • booking accommodation
   • luggage transfer

12 You have only to decide which trip you want, book it and follow the instructions on how to join the party. You should have like-minded, friendly people as companions (this appeals particularly to single persons).

13 Some outfitters offer guided trips, but others advertise 'self-guided tours'. This means that you are less likely to be part of a group, and you will have to find your own way by following a personalized walk description.

How to choose an outfitter

14 Some outfitters have been in business for a long time and have an established reputation, but others are small concerns and may be run as part-time ventures. There are laws and regulations for establishments catering for young people, but none for adults, so it is easy to run an outfitting business from home. All that is required is some knowledge of the outdoor world, a computer and a website. The only significant outlay is the cost of brochures and advertising.

15 The brochure and website of the outfitter should give essential information about the length and degree of difficulty of each day's walk. This, together with the description of the trip, should give you a clear idea as to whether it matches your requirements.

16 Some questions that should be asked before signing up with an outfitter include:

   a) How long has it been business? If it is only for a short period ask to see copies of letters from satisfied clients.

b) What is the experience and qualifications of the guides that are employed (see 23:10-17), and are they suitably insured?

c) What kind and quality of accommodation is used?

d) If transport is provided, ask whether the drivers have the requisite driving licence. Not all small outfitters are aware of the European Union regulations governing drivers of minibuses. Anyone who drives a minibus with more than eight passenger seats for hire and reward (i.e. is either paid or receives a tangible benefit) is normally required to possess a Passenger Carrying Vehicle (PCV) licence. (There are some exceptions for organizations such as educational establishments, but they are not likely to apply to the general run of outfitters.) If a driver of a minibus with more than eight passenger seats does not possess a PCV licence, then the insurance policy will be invalid.

e) Is the outfitter a member of the British Activity Providers Association? (See Appendix 1.) This organization has a code of practice that has been approved by the Office of Fair Trading and is particularly applicable to outfitters catering for young people.

17 Sources of information about outfitters and luggage transfer services can be found
- in the advertising pages of the walking magazines listed in Appendix 2.
- in the travel pages of the quality weekend newspapers
- by using a search engine to access the internet. Information can be obtained by entering 'Guided walks (plus the area of interest)' and 'Luggage transfers'

Planning your own trip

18 Planning your own trip can be rewarding and be tailored precisely to your own requirements. But it can be time-consuming because it involves consulting
- maps
- guidebooks
- timetables
- accommodation directories

19 An important factor to take into consideration in order to make a multi-day trip enjoyable, is a realistic daily schedule based on
- weight carried
- the terrain
- the weather

a) Experienced walkers are likely to know their physical limits but, if you are new to wayfaring, bear in mind that the extra weight carried, especially if camping, is likely to reduce the number of miles that can comfortably be completed in a day.

b) The nature of the terrain is also a consideration. A wayfarer who can manage fifteen miles in the Cotswolds might be over-extended covering a similar distance in the Scottish Highlands.

c) Adverse weather conditions could play havoc with an over-ambitious schedule.

20   Bearing in mind all the factors mentioned above, consider whether it is better to divide the length of the route by the number of days available to complete it, or to decide on a realistic daily mileage and complete part of the route, deferring the remainder for another occasion.

21   For example, Wainwright's popular Coast to Coast Walk is 190 miles long. If you can spare only fourteen days to complete it, including travel from and to home, you are left with twelve full days for walking. This means that you have to average sixteen miles per day which, for many, is an unrealistic schedule on a route that includes rough mountain tracks and extensive bogs.

22   A more agreeable solution might be to take ten days (eight days of walking) to cover the 82 miles from St Bees to Kirkby Stephen, and leave the rest of the route for another expedition.

Maps and guidebooks

23   Harvey publishes a *Long Distance Path Chart* of all the long-distance routes in the United Kingdom and the Isle of Man. It uses the same numbering system as *The Long Distance Walker's Handbook* (the on-line version can be accessed at www.ldwa.org.uk) where much basic information is available including

- start and finishing points
- general descriptions
- route profiles
- maps
- GPX files of routes
- guidebooks
- websites
- whether waymarked
- outfitters (described as 'walking support providers')
- badges and certificates for completers

24 Both maps and guidebooks are useful when planning a walk on a long-distance path. Their use when walking the route is a matter of personal preference but consider the following:

a) If the route is not shown on topographic maps with a special symbol, you will need the guidebook so that you can mark the route on your map.

b) A guidebook is likely to
   - describe the difficulty of the route
   - indicate facilities such as pubs, cafés, accommodation, shops etc. (but check that they are still available)
   - give information about interesting things to be seen on the route

c) A map is invaluable if a detour has to be made by circumstances such as
   - foul weather
   - injury
   - an obstruction
   - a missing footbridge

How to devise your own long-distance route

25 To devise and plan your own route you will need to:

a) Decide on the approximate distance that you are prepared to walk bearing in mind the factors covered in 18:17-21.

b) Establish the starting and finishing points and whether they can be accessed by public transport. There are several websites that will provide this information but those that covers all forms of transport are
   - for Great Britain: www.thetraveline.com
   - for the whole of Ireland: www.transportforireland.ie

The alternative is to arrange to be dropped off and collected by car.

26 The most difficult and time-consuming part of the process is working out the route to be followed. It is likely to be awkward to plan a long-distance route using mapping software because there are so many tiles to consult. In Great Britain paper *Landrangers* are usually easier to use. They can be consulted at one of the many public reference libraries that have a complete set. The following suggestions may be helpful:

a) Draw a line between your starting and finishing points on the appropriate Ordnance Survey 1:100,000 *Travel Map*. Then consult either a paper edition of the *Ordnance Survey Leisure Map Catalogue* available from map retailers, or the on-line version available from www.ordnancesurvey.co.uk. From these sources you will be able to establish which *Landrangers* are likely to cover your proposed route.

b) Compile a list of significant place names and/or make a rough tracing of the route which you can then finalize on *Explorer* maps or mapping software.

c) Establish that suitable accommodation is available at the finish of each day's walk.

d) Many towns and villages have websites which are useful for checking that there are food shops at strategic points along the route. Backpackers should note that it is possible to mail non-perishable food (but not fuel) to post offices to await collection. To take advantage of this service use this address

> Your name
>
> Poste Restante
>
> Name and address of post office
>
> (This can be obtained for the United Kingdom, together with opening hours, from www.postoffice.co.uk/branch-finder.)

Chapter 19 Backpacking

1 Backpacking may be defined as the craft of carrying the essentials necessary to
support life on a multi-day walking trip. Technically, it includes walking trips
using camping barns, bothies, hostels, hotels and bed & breakfast accommodation, but it is generally understood to refer to camping with a portable shelter.
Information about other types of walking holidays will be found in Chapter 18.

2 Some of the delights of backpacking include:

   a) The freedom to plan walking trips without the constraints of seeking accommodation or keeping to a schedule.

   b) The joy of waking early in the morning and sniffing the dawn air as you sup
the first hot drink of the day.

   c) The peculiar satisfaction of erecting your shelter in driving rain at the end
of a wet day and retiring dry and contented into your sleeping bag.

   d) The gratifying feeling of achievement at the end of a satisfying trip.

3 Some of the drawbacks of backpacking include:

   a) The weight of the kit and equipment that has to be carried. As a rule-of-
thumb guide, the lighter a particular item of gear is, the more expensive it is
likely to be. Thus, a down sleeping bag is both lighter and more expensive
than a synthetic bag with the same thermal rating. These considerations are
particularly important for solo backpackers because two people require only
one tent, stove and cooking utensils so the weight can be shared between
them. Many solo backpackers like to reduce weight as much as possible
consistent with comfort and safety.

   b) The camp chores of pitching your shelter and cooking your meals, especially in foul weather.

   c) The inevitable lowering of your normal standard of personal daintiness.

   d) The capital cost of the equipment.

4 Backpacking has few rules other than those required by common sense and
safety. Nowadays, there is much emphasis on reducing weight to a minimum on
the grounds that you can walk farther and with less fatigue, but if you like comfort and luxury, and don't mind the extra weight, then indulge yourself; it's your
choice.

5   There are several kinds of backpacking. The two extremes are described below but there are many gradations in between. Backpacking is essentially a personal pastime and there are no hard and fast rules other than those dictated by common sense and safety:

   a)   The laid-back approach where backpacking is treated as a means of exploring the countryside. If the weather turns foul, or the need for a bath and to catch up on laundry becomes urgent, the backpacker will, if necessary, seek a bothy, bunkhouse, camping barn, bed & breakfast, hostel or hotel accommodation. Advantage will also be taken of pubs, restaurants and shops.

   b)   The minimalist approach where, to some extent, backpacking is treated as a philosophy. Much of the attraction is self-sufficiency and employing skills to cope with every eventuality using the lightest equipment available.

6   This chapter is designed to give those new to backpacking a description of some of the basic techniques employed by the majority of backpackers. They are no more than a guide to good practice and once you have gained some experience you will start to do things your way; that is the essence of backpacking.

7   Backpacking kit is described in Chapter 20 and the planning of backpacking trips is covered in Chapter 18.

How to enjoy backpacking

8   There are skills that can make the difference between a backpacking trip that is a miserable slog and one that is an enjoyable experience even in adverse conditions. The most important of these are described below.

Weight

9   An important recipe for enjoying backpacking is to reduce the weight carried as much as possible consistent with safety and the level of comfort you require. Bear in mind that

     • a heavy pack is tiring and could even result in stress injuries
     • a light pack is less fatiguing and you can walk farther

10   The factors that affect the total weight on your feet are:

   a)   Your body weight mass index (BMI). If overweight, consider slimming.

   b)   The clothes that you wear. It is pointless to go to extreme lengths to save weight in your pack if your clothes and boots are unnecessarily heavy.

   c)   The weight of your pack and its contents.

11 When discussing backpacking weights it is usual to distinguish between *base-weight* and *total weight:*

    a) *Baseweight* is the weight of all your gear *excluding* food and water. The baseweight of your gear is likely to remain approximately the same throughout the course of a trip.

    b) *Total weight* includes the baseweight *plus* food and water. The weight of food and water carried can be considerable (a litre of water weighs one kilogram) and may vary during a trip depending on the amount that has to be carried before replenishing supplies.

How to reduce your baseweight

12 Although it is generally desirable to reduce weight as much as possible, the cost, together with the importance that you place on saving weight, should be considered. Super-lightweight items such as backpacks, tents and sleeping bags are usually considerably more expensive than the standard offerings as these examples demonstrate (2014 prices):

    a) A lightweight 50-litre backpack weighing 500 grams costs £110 whereas a standard 60-litre backpack can weigh upwards of 2000 grams and cost between £60 and £70.

    b) A down sleeping bag weighing 700 grams costs £300 but a comparable synthetic bag will weigh at least 2000 grams and cost £50.

    c) An ultra-lightweight one-person tent can weigh 900 grams and cost more than £300 whereas a standard one-person tent will weigh at least 1800 grams and cost £150.

13 Train yourself constantly to consider how weight can be saved. Before buying gear that will satisfy your comfort level and budget, ask yourself these questions and then consider the consequences. Here are some examples of this approach:

    a) A couple, or a group of friends, can usually carry lighter packs than solo backpackers by sharing the weight of some items such as

- tent
- cooking gear
- maps
- handheld satnav
- camera
- binoculars
- soap
- toothpaste
- toilet tissue

b) Pack small items (scourer, pot-holder miniature can-opener etc.) inside larger items such as a mug or cooking pot. This saves space and therefore weight by making it possible to use a smaller and lighter backpack.

c) Food is often sold in lightweight plastic containers which, when empty, can be used to pack small items such as tea bags. Plastic bags are also useful.

d) A titanium mug can double as a saucepan. Hot food can be eaten direct from the mug thus saving the weight and expense of cooking pots, plates and bowls. Some extreme backpackers dispense with cooking equipment entirely and rely on cold food and water.

e) Do you need a hydration system? A 2-litre plastic bottle that once contained drinks is lighter, costs nothing and serves just as well.

f) A spork comprises a spoon, fork and rudimentary knife and weighs less than traditional camp cutlery.

g) Instead of taking both trousers and shorts, wear trousers with zip-off legs. Alternatively, take shorts and when cold, wear nylon tights and/or your waterproof overtrousers. If you are still not warm enough you can pitch your tent and retire into your sleeping bag.

h) Wear your spare pair of socks as a substitute for gloves.

i) Antiseptic wipes sold in small packets can be used instead of toilet tissue. They are stronger, do not disintegrate when wet, and are also useful for cleaning and disinfecting

j) Consider whether you need a first aid kit. Blisters and minor cuts are the injuries most likely to be suffered and six Compeeds and a roll of surgical tape can cope with these. Even quite serious cuts can be dealt with by covering the injury with antiseptic wipes wrapped in an item of clothing, and then bound tightly with the length of duct tape that you wound round your water bottle for emergency repairs.

k) The weight of maps, guidebooks etc. can be reduced by
  • making photocopies of your intended route (but be aware of copyright implications)
  • printing extracts from mapping software
  • using the strip maps of those long-distance paths published by Harvey (see 5:37)
  • using a freezer bag for a map case

14   On your first backpacking trip, you are likely to carry more items of gear than you actually need because they have been chosen on the principle that they *might* be useful. At the end of the trip, divide your gear into three groups

- items that you used
- essential items, such as waterproofs, that you may not have used but could not do without
- items that you did not use and which you will not take on your next trip

Food

15   Water, and food purchased from shops, could easily be the most bulky and heaviest items in your backpack so the weight has to be reduced. This can be done as follows:

a) Lightweight meals in sealed packets are widely available from outdoor shops. They are
  - convenient and require little preparation apart from heating
  - the taste often leaves something to be desired
  - the packaging has to be disposed of in a litter bin
  - expensive

b) The shelves of a well-stocked supermarket are worth exploring for such items with short cooking times as
  - instant noodles
  - instant pasta
  - instant rice
  - dehydrated potatoes, other vegetables, and fruits
  - porridge

c) Many backpackers dehydrate their own food because it is usually lighter, tastier and cheaper than commercial backpacking food.

Dehydrating food

16   A dehydrator comprises a series of stacked trays containing air holes. Warm air is blown by a fan through the trays for several hours which dries the food and reduces the weight and bulk.

17   The trick is to cook an extra portion of complete meals such as casseroles, curries and shepherd's pies as part of your regular cooking and then to freeze them. Select foods that are low in fat to avoid the risk of rancidity. When you have as many meals as you have trays, thaw the food and record the weight of each individual meal. Number each tray and put a corresponding number on a small re-sealable plastic bag.

18   Spread each meal evenly on the bottom of a tray and switch on the dehydrator. After several hours, when the food is thoroughly dry, weigh each meal and subtract the figure from the weight of the meal before dehydration. The result indicates the amount of water to add for rehydration (1 gram = 1 millilitre).

19   When on the trail, add the requisite amount of water to the re-sealable bag containing your meal a couple of hours before you dine, then heat and enjoy.

20   Dehydrators can be purchased on-line and from some high street stores. The capital cost can be recovered from the considerable savings made on the raw materials.

Camping

21   There are two types of pitches used by backpackers
   • campsites
   • wild camping

Campsites

22   Campsites in Great Britain that are open on more than forty-two consecutive days, or more than sixty days in any twelve consecutive months, require a licence from the local authority which may attach conditions covering such matters as sanitation and the minimum distance between tents.

23   The facilities available on campsites range from the most basic offering little more than water, toilets and showers, to the sophisticated aimed at family campers with laundry rooms, electric hookups, licensed bars and swimming pools. Most backpackers prefer small, quiet sites.

Wild camping

24   This is the term that describes the practice of pitching a tent other than at a regulated campsite. The only places in the British Isles where there is a specific right to camp without the permission of the landowner are
   • in Scotland (but not in enclosed fields or close to houses and roads)
   • on Dartmoor (except on farmland, on moorland enclosed by walls, within 100 metres of a road, on flood plains, or on archaeological sites)
However, the practice is not illegal in the United Kingdom and the only remedy that a landowner has is to insist that you move on. In many upland areas beyond the limits of cultivation, discreet wild camping by backpackers is tolerated.

25 A backpacker in lowland countryside may occasionally be forced, by injury, illness or fatigue, to camp wild. If it proves impossible to obtain permission to camp, the following procedures should ensure an undisturbed night:

a) Find a field that contains no animals and is well away from houses and public paths. When in woodland, avoid pitching under elderly trees that may shed their branches. Check for droppings that could indicate that birds perch in the tree and might contaminate your tent.

b) Avoid attracting attention by cooking some distance away from your chosen pitch before erecting your tent.

c) Wait until it is nearly dark before pitching your tent and leave before breakfasting, and as early as possible, the next morning.

d) In the unlikely event, that you are discovered and instructed to move on, do not argue but apologize and leave immediately.

How to choose a pitch

26 An ideal pitch should fulfil the following conditions. It should be

• on level ground preferably slightly raised a little above the surrounding area to obviate the risk of flooding if it rains

• near a watercourse

• sheltered from the prevailing wind

27 It is rare for all these conditions to be met so compromises may have to be made. Bear in mind the following:

a) The most important consideration for the novice backpacker is finding shelter from the prevailing wind in the lee of crags, walls and hedges.

b) Avoid camping in hollows because even shallow depressions can flood in heavy rain. In certain conditions, they can become frost pockets which are caused by cold air rolling down a hillside and becoming trapped in the hollow. This can lower the temperature by several degrees.

c) In upland areas, do not pitch your tent too close to a watercourse if rain is expected. Small mountain streams can quickly become raging torrents.

d) When you have to pitch on a slope, ensure that your head will be higher than your feet and you won't slide into the wall of the tent.

Techniques with a tent

28 There are many tent designs so it is not possible to give detailed information on how to erect a tent. The only advice is to follow the instructions that should come with every new tent.

29   Before taking your tent on its first trip, practise pitching and striking it several times in your garden or local park until you are so familiar with the routine that you can do it in the dark.

30   Keep your tent readily accessible in your pack so that it can be removed without unpacking the rest of your kit. When pitching a tent in the rain, devise a system that will keep both your gear and the inner tent dry. This is one such method:

   a)   Pitch the tent whilst wearing your waterproofs and boots.

   b)   When the tent is pitched
   - open the flysheet door
   - put your rucksack inside the porch
   - enter the porch backwards and sit on a sheet of plastic
   - remove your boots and waterproofs and place them neatly in the porch, or under the eaves of the flysheet
   - if your clothes are wet, rather than merely damp, change into something dry
   - now you can enter the inner tent without making the groundsheet wet
   - pull your rucksack close to the door of the inner tent and unpack it carefully arranging everything that is dry on the groundsheet
   - you are now ready to cook a meal

31   Backpackers should camp responsibly. The only evidence left behind should be the impression made in the grass by the footprint of your tent. Do not
   - disturb rocks but, if you absolutely have to, replace them in their original position
   - light fires
   - make a noise
   - foul watercourses (see 1:32-4)
   - bury rubbish; keep it in your rucksack for proper disposal

Hygiene & washing

32   Your level of personal daintiness is likely to decline when backpacking. You will be exercising hard, have little or no access to baths or showers, and you are likely to be wearing the same clothes for several days between laundering. But, with care, this should not make you offensive to others especially if you wear underclothes made from Merino wool (see 19:34).

33 Washing properly can help to avoid body odours and it also produces a sense of well-being. It can be done in the tent at the end of the day as follows:

  a) Close the tent door and move your sleeping bag in its stuff sack, clothes etc. into a corner of the tent. If you consider it necessary, heat a small quantity of water.

  b) Undress completely, dip a J-cloth into the water, wring out the excess water, add a little soap to the cloth, and carefully sponge yourself in the following order
    • face
    • trunk
    • arms
    • legs
    • armpits
    • groin
    • feet

  Rinse the soap from the J-cloth and repeat the process to remove soap from your skin, then towel yourself with a dry J-cloth.

  c) Dress in your sleepwear then carefully mop up any spilt water. Place your sleeping mat or airbed into its correct position and lay out your sleeping bag ready for bed.

  d) Instructions for the proper disposal of human waste in the countryside are described in 1:32-4.

  e) The following technique avoids the need to leave the tent at night in order to urinate
    • men can use a clearly labelled, self-sealing Pour & Store plastic bag, or a wide-mouthed plastic bottle with a screw cap
    • women can use the same method with the aid of a Shewee (see 3:111)
    • the container should be emptied and rinsed in the morning

Laundry

34 Many modern fabrics worn by backpackers, especially Merino wool, have properties that help to resist the build-up of body odours so, unless you sweat profusely, you should be able to wear your baselayers for several days between launderings.

35 There are several ways of dealing with your laundry:

  a) Small garments such as socks and underwear can be washed in a plastic bag. Add water and liquid soap and agitate the bag for a minute or two, then remove the clothes and rinse them with clean water to remove the soap. The dirty water should be disposed of at least ten metres from watercourses. (This method requires more water than can be carried in a water bottle so is more suited to upland areas where the water is likely to smell nicer.)

b) Seek a campsite or overnight accommodation and wash your clothes in the wash basin. Most bed & breakfast establishments will let you hang up laundry to dry overnight.

c) You may be able to launder your clothes in the wash basin of a public convenience. Wall-mounted units that dispense water, soap and hot air are not suitable but the hot water can be used to fill a plastic bag and the clothes washed by the method outlined in a) above.

d) Modern synthetic fabrics and Merino wool will dry quickly if hung on the outside of a backpack. They can be worn whilst damp and your body heat will soon dry them. Unlike cotton, these fabrics feel warm when worn next to the skin (see 3:51-3).

Backpacking in winter

36   Backpacking in winter is a much more serious undertaking than backpacking in the more temperate months of the year. Factors to take into consideration are:

a) Most campsites are closed during the winter months so wild camping may be the only realistic option.

b) The hours of daylight are short, especially in Scotland. On 21st December, the shortest day of the year, sunrise in Fort William is at 0856 and sunset is at 1541 giving a theoretical 6 hours and 45 minutes of daylight. In conditions of thick cloud and mist the useful hours of daylight are likely to be fewer.

c) Inclement weather conditions such as snow and low temperatures require warm and robust, and therefore heavier equipment, making the use of ultralight gear less suitable.

d) Gas canisters do not work well in freezing conditions. Butane/isobutane/propane mixtures are the best but even these can be slow in subzero temperatures. Methylated spirit and petrol stoves are unaffected by the cold.

e) Water bottles for use in subzero temperatures should be made of flexible materials. They should not be filled completely to allow for ice expansion. There are several ways of preventing them from freezing
   • store them upside-down so that any ice that forms will be at the bottom of the bottle, but in extreme conditions they may still freeze solid
   • wrap the bottle in spare clothing and place it inside your sleeping bag
   • snow is a good insulator so, in extreme conditions, bury the bottle in a deep bank of snow and mark the spot with a trekking pole or ice-axe

f) If you need to melt snow to obtain water, be aware that you will require approximately ten times the volume of snow to get the equivalent amount of water. Thus, in order to get 500 millilitres of water you will require about 5,000 cubic centimetres of snow. The best way to melt snow is to heat a small quantity of water in a pan and then add snow a little at a time keeping the burner at a moderate heat.

Select bibliography

37   Coustick, Dave, *The Backpacker's Cookbook; a Practical Guide to Dining Out.* The Inn Pin, 2004.

38   Dillon, Paddy, *The National Trails; the 19 National Trails of England, Scotland and Wales.* Cicerone Press, 2007.

39   Hostetter, Kristin, *Don't Forget the Duct Tape; Tips & Tricks for Repairing Outdoor Gear* 2nd ed. The Mountaineers, 2006.

40   Jardine, Ray, *Trail Life; Ray Jardine's Lightweight Backpacking.* Adventure Lore Press, 2009. This is the bible of American backpacking techniques.

41   Long Distance Walkers Association, *The UK Trailwalker's Handbook* 8th ed. Cicerone Press, 2011.

42   Shillington, Ben, *Winter Backpacking.* Heliconia Press, 2010.

43   Townsend, Chris, *The Backpacker's Handbook* 4th ed. Ragged Mountain Press, 2011. This book by the well-known British outdoor writer is written for an American audience and is distributed in the United Kingdom. It is probably the most comprehensive treatise on the subject but not all of it is relevant to backpacking in the British Isles.

44   Traynor, John, *Lightweight Camping.* Cicerone Press, 2011.

Chapter 20 Backpacking kit and equipment

Definition of terms

1 Certain backpacking terms have received general acceptance
- *baseweight* is the weight of your rucksack and its contents excluding food and water
- *ultra-lightweight backpacking* is where the baseweight is less than 5 kg
- *lightweight backpacking* is where the baseweight is between 5-10 kg
- *conventional backpacking* is where the baseweight is between 10-15 kg
- *heavy backpacking* is where the baseweight exceeds 15 kg

Essential items

2 Not every walker will enjoy backpacking but if you are tempted, it would probably be wise to take your first trip with an experienced friend and borrow the equipment that you need. In addition to your normal walking kit, you will require the following essential items of equipment including
- shelter (tent, tarp or basha, bivvy bag)
- sleeping bag
- sleeping mat or inflatable mattress
- stove and fuel
- cooking utensils
- containers for food and drink
- spare clothing and footwear
- rucksack (also known as a 'backpack')

The pros and cons of these items are discussed below.

Shelters

3 The unpredictable weather conditions of the British Isles require backpackers to carry a shelter that will protect them from the elements and keep them and their gear snug, warm, dry and protected from flying insects.

4   In order to stay dry inside a shelter, there has to be a way of keeping the condensation, caused by body heat, which collects on the inner surface of the shelter, from dripping onto the occupants. The problem can be exacerbated if a
groundsheet is not used.

Tents

5   The most popular form of shelter among British backpackers is the tent because
it provides the best level of protection from rain, snow and wind, as well as a
measure of privacy, but it is usually heavier and more expensive than a tarp or
bivvy bag.

6   Tents come in a bewildering range of designs. Forty years ago, many designs,
such as the ridge and sloping ridge supported by rigid poles, were triangular in
section because this is the most stable construction. Nowadays, with the development of strong, flexible aluminium, fibreglass and carbon-fibre poles, the two
most popular designs are
   • geodesic with interlocking poles that form a rigid structure
   • a semicircular hoop with no interlocking poles which tends to allow the
     tent to sway in the wind

7   Most tents comprise a flysheet made from an impermeable, waterproof material
and an inner tent permanently attached to the groundsheet. The inner tent is
made from a permeable lightweight fabric with a tight weave that allows the
vapour given off by the occupants to pass through and condense on the inner
surface of the flysheet. Most of this condensation will run down the flysheet to
the ground, but any that drips onto the inner tent should not reach the occupants.

8   These are some of the features that should be considered when choosing a tent:
   a) Can it be erected flysheet first? This is important when pitching in the rain
      to prevent the inner tent becoming soaked.

   b) Can the tent be pitched with the inner tent already attached to the flysheet?
      This makes for faster pitching.

   c) Is there sufficient horizontal room for sleeping, and headroom when the
      occupant(s) are sitting?

   d) Does it have a porch large enough to store all your gear and wet clothing?
      This feature allows you to keep the inner tent free for your sleeping bag and
      dry clothing.

   e) Is there adequate ventilation to help reduce the risk of condensation?

f) Does the inner tent have a pocket in which to keep small items such as spectacles, sunglasses, wallet and money?

g) If it is designed to sleep two persons, does it have two entrances and two porches? This makes for greater ease, comfort and accessibility.

Tarps and bashas

9   Tarps, a contraction of 'tarpaulin', also known as 'bashas' from a Malay word for a shelter that was adopted by the British army during the Malaysia campaign of 1957-66, are popular with ultra-lightweight backpackers in the United States but have found only limited acceptance in the British Isles. This is because the air in the British Isles is often humid allowing condensation to form when the night-time temperature drops. The problem is exacerbated by the body heat expelled by the occupants.

10   Tarps comprise a large piece of waterproof material with eyelets along each edge to which guylines can be attached. They are designed to be tied to trees, fences, trekking poles etc. and then pegged out to form a shelter.

11   They are lighter than tents but require a separate groundsheet or a bivvy bag (see 20:14) which adds to the stated weight of the tarp. They take some skill to erect satisfactorily and rely on air currents to reduce condensation. Tarps do not provide as much privacy as tents.

12   Unlike tents, the profile of a tarp can be altered to suit the weather conditions
    • in fine weather it can be pitched high to give plenty of headroom
    • in strong winds it can be pitched low

13   There are hybrid tarps that have rudimentary porches which are useful when cooking.

Bivvy bags

14   A bivvy bag, the term is derived from 'bivouac', is a waterproof, breathable sleeping bag cover. There are no facilities for cooking, and no storage space for gear so that wet waterproofs and boots have to be kept outside in a plastic bag. Bivvy bags are used mostly by those taking part in mountain marathons and similar events who want to reduce weight to the absolute minimum.

Care of shelters

15   Your shelter will last longer if it is cared for properly
- groundsheets are at risk from puncture from sharp objects. They can be repaired in the field with duct tape
- flysheets and tarps can be soiled by bird droppings which should be sponged off as soon as possible
- guylines can be tripped over and damaged
- poles and pegs can bend or break

16   At the end of every trip
- sponge off mud and other contaminants
- ensure that the shelter is thoroughly dry
- make any repairs and renew frayed guylines, tapes etc.
- check that the poles are in good condition and are thoroughly dry
- wash and dry the pegs
- repack the shelter in its bag and store in a dry location away from direct sunlight to prevent ultraviolet light degradation

Sleeping bags

17   The purpose of a sleeping bag is to keep you warm at night by trapping your body heat. This is achieved by
- the design of the bag
- the insulation, known as the 'fill', used which is normally either down or synthetic (see 20:21-5)

Design

18   The most efficient shape to retain the maximum amount of body heat is the mummy bag, named after Egyptian funerary practices, where the bag conforms as close to the body as possible and is widest at the shoulder and narrowest at the foot. Most bags incorporate a hood.

19   The fill, which is either down or synthetic, has to be kept in place by a construction that keeps it evenly distributed and prevents it moving which could allow cold spots to form. The cheapest bags use the 'sewn-through' technique which results in cold spots.

20   Desirable features include
- a box foot that gives extra space for the feet
- an adjustable hood that fits closely to the face
- a long side-zip that can be used to adjust the temperature inside the bag

Down filling

21   Down comes from the under-plumage of geese and ducks that traps air providing insulation. Compressed down, when released, will fill with air and greatly increase in volume, a characteristic known as 'loft' or 'fill power'. The greater the loft, the better the insulation.

22   Loft/fill power is measured in terms of the number of cubic inches occupied by an ounce of uncompressed down. Down used in sleeping bags is graded by quality expressed in terms of its fill power which is likely to be between 500 and 850. The higher the fill power, the better the quality of the down and therefore its insulation. Fill power is a measure of the efficiency of the insulation but can also be a useful indication of the expected warmth. Thus, a bag designed for summer use with a rating of 750 will use less down than a winter bag with the same rating.

23   Down has the following advantages over other fillings
- weight for weight it is the most efficient insulator
- it is the lightest
- the most durable
- the most compressible

24   The main disadvantages of down are that it
- loses most of its insulating properties when wet but this can be mitigated by applying with Nikwax Down Proof
- readily absorbs water and takes a long time to dry
- expensive

Synthetic fillings

25   Synthetic fillings are manufactured from plastic materials in the form of hollow tubes and filaments that provide insulation by trapping air. Note that:
- a) Considerable improvements have been made to synthetic fills in recent years which make both the weight to warmth ratio and compressibility better, but they still cannot match the insulating qualities of down.
- b) The bulk of synthetic bags can be reduced by using compression straps.

   c) The significant advantages that synthetic bags have over down are that they
- tend not to absorb much water
- will dry more quickly
- retain some warmth when wet
- are less expensive than down

   d) The disadvantages of synthetic bags when compared with down bags are that they are heavier and bulkier.

Temperature ratings

26   When purchasing a sleeping bag it is important to select one that is suitable for the temperatures in which you intend to use it. A winter-weight bag can be uncomfortably hot in summer, and you will be cold in winter inside a summer-weight bag. Until recently, virtually the only guidance available was provided by the bag's manufacturer which was sometimes optimistic.

27   *'EN 13537 Requirements for Sleeping Bags'* is the official European Standard for sleeping bags which defines how to test, measure and label them. It applies to all sleeping bags with the exception of those for military use and those with a comfort range below -25°C). The standard requires a thermal manikin test which produces four temperature results:

   a) The Upper Limit is based on the highest temperature at which a 'standard' adult male is deemed to be able to have a comfortable night's sleep without excess sweating.

   b) The Lower Limit is based on the lowest temperature at which as 'standard' adult male is deemed to be able to have a comfortable night's sleep.

   c) The Comfort Rating is based on a 'standard' woman having a comfortable night's sleep.

   d) The Extreme Rating is a survival-only rating for a 'standard' adult woman.

   e) Note that this is not a European Directive so it is not a mandatory test, but manufacturers that conform to it are entitled to display the CE symbol on their products. Some manufacturers and retailers still prefer to supply their own temperature ratings.

28   Standard tests are useful but backpackers should be aware of other factors that can affect temperature ratings. These include

- your personal metabolism; some people sleep hot; others sleep cold
- the warmth of any clothing worn in the bag
- the efficiency of the insulation from the ground
- the number of persons sleeping in the tent
- the amount of hot food and drink taken before sleeping

29   Some backpackers use a thin polycotton or silk liner in their sleeping bags to protect the inside from dirt, body oils and odours. Silk liners, in particular, will marginally increase the warmth of the bag but a pair of nylon tights and a thin top will serve almost as well.

Care of sleeping bags

30   Down sleeping bags are expensive and their life can be extended by proper care:

a) At the end of every trip, thoroughly dry and air the bag and either hang it in a closet or wardrobe or roll it loosely in a cotton bag.

b) A lightweight summer bag that has become soiled can be washed in the bath using Nikwax Down Wash. Follow the care instructions carefully. Down is prone to damage so after gently squeezing out as much water as possible, carry it from the bath in a large plastic bag and, to prevent tearing the baffles, ensure that it is properly supported as it drips dry.

c) There are a number of companies, which can be found on the internet, that specialize both in the cleaning and repair of sleeping bags. Do not use a High Street cleaner. Be aware that the fumes used in traditional cleaning fluids are toxic and take a long time to evaporate from a down bag.

31   Synthetic sleeping bags are easier to care for and can be washed either in the bath or a washing machine with Nikwax Tech Wash but agitate as little as possible to avoid damaging the fill.

Sleeping mats and mattresses

32   The main source of heat loss from sleeping bags is through the ground, because the bag's insulation is compressed by body weight, so it is important that some other form of insulation is used. There are three kinds

- open-cell self-inflating foam mattresses
- lightweight airbeds that require inflating
- closed-cell foam mats and pads

a) Open cell self-inflating mattresses are supposed to inflate as soon as the valve is opened but often need to be blown up a little to reach the required thickness. When compared with sleeping mats both self-inflating mattresses and airbeds they
- offer greater comfort
- are heavier and bulkier
- come in several fixed lengths
- are usually used inside the tent to avoid the risk of a puncture
- are considerably more expensive

b) Closed-cell sleeping mats come in various thicknesses and sizes. When compared with self-inflating mattresses and airbeds they
- can be cut to size
- are less comfortable
- are lighter and less bulky
- are usually slid under the groundsheet to protect it from sharp objects
- are virtually indestructible
- less expensive

Cooking stoves

33   Some ultra-lightweight backpackers dispense with stoves in order to save weight and subsist on cold drinks and food, but most will prefer to carry the extra weight in order to enjoy the comforts of hot food and drink.

34   Stoves may be classified by the fuel used
- petrol
- methylated spirits
- gas
- multi-fuel
- solid fuel

The pros and cons of each are discussed below.

35   You can save fuel and reduce cooking times by using a windshield which you can either purchase or make at home.

36   Cooking stoves especially gas canister stoves, can leak and give off poisonous fumes including the deadly carbon monoxide. **Stoves and fuel should always be left outside the tent at night** in a plastic bag to protect them from the elements.

Petrol stoves

37 Lightweight petrol stoves, except for multi-fuel stoves, seem to have largely disappeared from the market.

a) Petrol-burning stoves are very efficient, noisy, and the flame is readily adjustable. They usually require priming with methylated spirit or a solid fuel tablet, and tend to be heavier than other stoves.

b) They work best with highly-refined 'white gas', also known as Coleman Gas, which is not widely available although it is stocked by some outdoor shops. Alternative fuels are
   • Aspen 4T 4-stroke chain-saw fuel
   • Panel Wipe which is used in automobile body shops

c) Unleaded petrol sold in filling stations can be used but in the long-term may clog the jets. It is difficult to get a small quantity of fuel from a petrol pump which means that you may have to carry sufficient for the whole trip.

d) Petrol is highly volatile and has to be handled with great care. Spare fuel should always be carried in a specially-designed metal bottle.

Methylated spirit and alcohol stoves

38 Stoves that burn methylated spirit, also known as denatured alcohol, are very simple because they do not require the fuel to be delivered under pressure:

a) Methylated spirit is ethanol mixed with unpalatable additives to render it undrinkable. It is widely available in hardware stores and pharmacies and can be carried in a lightweight plastic bottle.

b) It burns cleanly with a pale blue, noiseless flame that, depending on the additives it contains, may blacken the underside of pans with a non-sooty deposit that does not have to be removed.

c) Methylated spirit does not produce as much heat as pressure stoves so cooking times are a little longer. There is little temperature control other than the basic method of blanking off some of the jets.

d) A major advantage of these stoves is that they are sturdy, have no moving parts so nothing can go wrong or wear out.

e) The Trangia dominates the British market although other makes can occasionally be found. Trangia models range from a minimalist unit comprising burner, windshield, saucepan, combined frying pan and lid, and a pot holder, to a complete cookset which includes a kettle.

f) Some enthusiasts make their own ultra-lightweight stoves from aluminium drinks cans. Information can be found on a number of websites.

Gas stoves

39   Gas stoves are probably the most popular stoves in general use among backpackers in the British Isles. The fuel is delivered under pressure from a metal canister with a self-sealing valve. Note that:

a)   The gas is a mixture of butane, propane and, in some cases, isobutane. For summer use the ratio of the gases is unimportant but you should be aware that most mixtures do not work efficiently in sub-freezing temperatures unless they are kept warm. There are liquid-feed stoves with a pre-heating device that allows them to be used in subzero temperatures.

b)   Gas is clean and is easy to handle because the stove is either screwed directly into the canister, or by a hose, so there is no risk of spillage or mess.

c)   Canisters come in several sizes ranging from notional weights of 100 to 500 grms. Several makes are available but, in the British Isles, they all employ a standard thread so can be used with any gas stove.

d)   The canisters sold in some European countries do not employ a screw fitting and require an adaptor which should be purchased before travelling.

e)   Stoves that screw into the top of a gas canister tend to be less stable than those which employ a hose. Stability can be improved by
 • a gadget that clips onto the canister to give a larger footprint
 • attaching two short lengths of webbing or nylon cord, on opposite sides of the canister with duct tape and securing them to the ground with short groundsheet pegs

Multi-fuel stoves

40   As their name implies, multi-fuel stoves are capable of burning petrol, methylated spirits, and paraffin (also known as kerosene). Some also have adaptors that allow them to use gas canisters.

41   They are particularly useful for backpackers visiting third world countries where paraffin (kerosene) and petrol are the most readily available fuels.

Solid fuel stoves

42   These tiny, ultra-lightweight fold-up stoves burn hexamine or trioxane tablets. They are, with some exceptions
 • inefficient
 • take a long time to reach boiling point
 • the heat cannot be controlled
 • only suitable for those who want the lightest gear

Cookware, cutlery etc.

43 In addition to a stove, you may need some of the following
- water bottle or hydration system
- water purifier
- saucepan(s) with lid(s)
- frying pan
- pot holder
- pot cosy to keep food hot
- bowl(s)
- knife, fork and spoon (or a spork which is a combination of all three)
- mug
- matches, lighter, or flint and steel that will work when wet
- pot scourer and washing-up liquid
- J-cloth for use as tea towel
- plastic bags and containers for food

Rucksacks for backpacking

44 The purpose of a rucksack designed for backpacking is to carry all your gear as comfortably as possible and to keep it dry whilst on the move.

45 There is a bewildering number of sizes and designs of rucksacks for backpacking on the market. New models appear every season but most have a number of features in common.

46 The basic design of a rucksack is a sack which is carried on the back by a harness comprising two padded adjustable straps worn over the shoulders and secured on the hips by a padded belt.

47 The harness should be adjusted so that most of the weight is carried on the hips with the shoulder straps tightened just sufficiently to hold the pack against the back and to prevent them slipping off the shoulders.

48 Rucksacks are rarely waterproof so they should either be lined with a plastic bag and/or have a rain cover that fits over the pack.

49 The capacity of rucksacks is measured in litres and includes the volume of the pockets as well as the main sack. Rucksacks for backpacking range in size from 50 litres, which is sufficiently large for ultra-lightweight gear, to 100 litres plus suitable for long expeditions and winter use. Most backpackers find that a 60-70 litre rucksack is large enough for three-season use.

50   The weight of an empty rucksack can range from
- 400 grms for ultra-lightweight backpacking
- 3 kg and more for a large, fully-featured pack

The two types are described below.

Ultra-lightweight rucksacks

51   A 50-litre rucksack that weighs 400 grms can only achieve this weight by means of a simple design and by employing the lightest materials available. Other weight-saving features include:

a)   Elasticated pockets for carrying a water bottle and other small items.

b)   An extended lightweight collar that is closed with a toggle and is then folded over replacing a conventional lid.

c)   The back of the pack is not normally padded. Instead, there may be a pocket into which a folded sleeping mattress or mat can be inserted as a substitute for padding. Alternatively, the mattress or mat can be loosely rolled and allowed to unwind inside the pack. This has the advantage of giving shape to the pack whilst still providing some padding for the back.

d)   There is normally no mechanism for adjusting the length of the back to accommodate backpackers of different sizes although some brands offer their products in several back lengths.

52   Ultra-lightweight rucksacks are normally not suitable for weights greater than eight kilograms. They lack the inherent toughness of conventional backpacks and must be treated with care. A rain cover will give some protection from abrasion. Note that when travelling, your pack
- with luck, may be treated on planes as carry-on luggage
- will probably fit on the overhead rack or between the seats of a train
- will be too large for the cabin of a coach so some backpackers protect their rucksacks in strong refuse sacks before putting them in the hold

Conventional rucksacks

53   A conventional rucksack suitable for backpacking has the same basic design as an ultra-lightweight pack but is likely to be larger and more robust and have many more compartments, pockets, zips and other features. Some conventional rucksacks lack side pockets which is a design favoured by climbers.

54   A backpacking rucksack is likely to have some or all of the following features:

a)   External zipped pockets on either side of the main pack and in or on the lid and the hip belt.

b) Internal pockets for
   - hydration system
   - maps and documents

c) A method of adjusting the length of the back. This may also incorporate an adjustment that allows air to flow between the pack and your back to reduce sweating and discomfort.

d) The main sack may be divided into two compartments for keeping separate such items as
   - sleeping bag
   - clean clothes
   - soiled clothes
   - cooking equipment

Note that separate compartments reduce packing flexibility and that plastic bags will usually serve just as well.

55 External straps, belts, fastenings and attachments include
   - a padded hip belt to support the weight of the pack
   - a sternum strap (also known as a chest strap) which prevents the shoulder straps sliding off the shoulders, and also aids stability
   - compression straps to reduce the volume of the sack when it is not full
   - attachments for crampons, ice-axes and trekking poles

56 When purchasing a rucksack it is a good plan to take all the gear that you are likely to use to the shop in a plastic bag and place it in the pack of you initial choice. Then walk around the shop and assess its comfort and stability before actually buying it.

Clothing and equipment list

57 The following list of kit for an ultra-lightweight outfit is likely be suitable for a week-long backpacking trip anywhere in the British Isles (except Scotland} from April to October inclusive. The same outfit would serve in Scotland from May to September inclusive with the addition of a midge jacket and by substituting trousers for shorts. For longer trips, consider adding another Merino wool short-sleeved top and a pair of Merino wool underpants. Food and water have not been included in the list.

58 It is not intended to be an authoritative guide but to demonstrate just how light a practical outfit can be. Brand names have been omitted because there are many alternative items of similar weight that would serve equally well.

ITEM	WEIGHT IN GRAMS
Rucksack, plastic bag liner & rain cover	480
Tent and polycryo groundsheet-protector in plastic bag	1150
1-metre long closed cell sleeping mat	120
Down sleeping bag in stuff sack & plastic bag	690
Gas stove, windshield (home-made) & fuel	505
Disposable lighter	20
Titanium mug (doubles as cooking pot)	55
Pot holder	20
Pot cosy (home-made)	20
Spork	10
Tin opener	10
Half a nylon scouring pad	10
J-cloth used as tea towel	10
Assorted plastic bags	50
Pour & Store plastic bag for use as an in-tent urinal	10
1·5-litre home-made hydration system	90
Headtorch	35
1 metre of duct tape for emergency repairs	5
Waterproof jacket	350
Waterproof overtrousers	290
Ankle gaiters	90
Merino wool long-sleeved top	170
1 pair of liner socks	35
Nylon tights for sleepwear	40
Comb, toothbrush, toothpaste in tiny tube, multi-purpose concentrated soap, nail file, roll of sticking plaster, Compeed, antiseptic wipes, 2 J-cloths for washing	220
Maps printed on waterproof paper from software	50
Miniature radio and earphones	55
Spare batteries	65
Weight of clothes & equipment carried in pack	**4570**

Items carried on the person

Trekking poles	410
Credit card wallet for bank & phone cards & cash	50
Coins in plastic bag	70
Handheld satnav	90
Compass	40
Pen	15
Lightweight knife	20
House keys	47

Make your own gear (MYOG)

59   Some enthusiasts like to make their own gear. There are several websites that give advice and designs which can be found by searching the internet for 'make your own backpacking gear'.

60   Two mail-order companies that supply a wide range of fabrics, webbing, buckles and accessories are

- Pennine Outdoor (www.pennineoutdoor.co.uk)
- PointNorth (www.pointnorth.co.uk)

Purchasing backpacking gear

61   A complete backpacking outfit involves considerable expenditure, so for your first trip it is a good plan to borrow as much as you can just in case you decide that backpacking is not for you. (See 3:113-18) for advice on the best and most economical methods of purchasing equipment.)

Select bibliography

See the list of titles in the bibliography for Chapter 19.

Chapter 21   Challenge walks, peak-bagging, and walking festivals

Challenge walks

1   A specialized form of walking which appeals to some walkers is the challenge walk. Challenges may be defined as a walk in which there is an element of competition, or the requirement to complete an objective such as
   - walking a particular route within a specified time
   - climbing a specific number or type of summit (known as 'peak-bagging')

2   Some challenges require a high level of fitness and stamina although they are not races. There are no winners or losers; only participants who complete the challenge and those who do not. (There are a number of race events but these are outside the scope of this book.)

3   Most challenges fall into two well-defined categories
   - organized events that take place at a specific location and date
   - anytime challenges

4   The best source of information about challenge walks in the United Kingdom is the Long Distance Walkers Association (LDWA). This organization, which has groups throughout the country, not only stages more challenge walks than any other body, but also lists other challenge walks at www.ldwa.org.uk.

Organized challenge walks

5   Organized challenge walks may be of a set length of, say 20, 25, 50 and 100 miles, or follow a particular route that has to be completed within a specified time. They are usually massed start events and have marshals at checkpoints along the route. Drinks and refreshments are usually supplied at strategic locations. Very often there is a badge and/or certificate for those who successfully complete the challenge.

6   Many charities organize challenge walks to raise funds. Every participant is expected, and sometimes required as a condition of participating, to raise a specific sum from sponsors. Some charities hand over the organization of the event to a professional fund-raising body which means that either there is a substantial

registration fee, or some of the sponsorship money goes to the fund-raiser. There are also businesses that, for a fee, will train aspiring challengers.

7   Some events organized by charities, especially the Three Peaks Challenge which involves climbing the highest mountain in England, Wales and Scotland (Scafell Pike, Snowdon and Ben Nevis) within twenty-four hours, have become so popular that they have been criticized for damaging the countryside. The residents of Wasdale and Rosthwaite, the two villages from which the ascent of Scafell Pike can commence, have complained for years about the noise in the middle of the night, the narrow lanes choked with vehicles, and the fouling of fields with excrement. The problems have become so acute, especially at weekends closest to the summer solstice, that the national parks, local authorities and the Institute of Fundraising Events (www.institute-of-fundraising.org.uk) has published a 25-page code of practice for this event.

8   The Long Distance Walkers Association gives advice on organizing challenges in its handbook *Guidelines for Events; How to Organise a Challenge Walk.*

Anytime challenges

9   An anytime challenge can be completed by an individual or group of walkers at a time of their own choosing. There are so many challenges that it is impossible to list them all but www.ldwa.org.uk is a good source of information. Some well-known examples include

   • Land's End to John o' Groats (also known as the End to End Walk, its acronym LeJog and, when done in the reverse direction, the Groats End Walk)
   • completing all the National Trails

Peak-bagging

10   Peak-bagging is usually an anytime challenge that involves climbing all the peaks or tops in a particular class of summit. Many of these challenges came into being before topographic maps went metric which is why the names and height of some of them are expressed in feet. The compilation and classification of ticklists for peak-bagging continues to expand and be subject to revision so that it becomes increasingly arcane. Note that the term 'relative height' is the vertical distance between the summit of a hill or mountain and the lowest contour line encircling it that does not encompass any other summit.

11   The entry under *Hill Lists in the British Isles* in *Wikipaedia* gives a good introduction, and there is a great deal of information on the internet that can be accessed by entering 'peak-bagging' into your search engine. Walkers should be aware that not all the summits, particularly some of the county tops in England

and Wales, are accessible without trespassing, so the permission of the land-owner should be sought. Examples of some of the more popular peak-bagging challenges include:

a) *Corbetts,* named after the compiler J. Rooke Corbett, are Scottish peaks that are between 2,500 (762 metres) and 3,000 feet (914.4 metres) high with a relative height of at least 500 feet (152.4 metres).

b) *County Tops of Great Britain* are the highest summit in every county
   - 48 in England
   - 14 in Wales
   - 35 in Scotland

c) *Donalds,* named after the compiler Percy Donald, are the 89 hills and 51 tops in the Scottish Lowlands that are over 2,000 feet (609.6 metres) high with a relative height of 30 metres (98 feet) but 15 metres (49 feet) if the hill is of sufficient topographical interest.

d) *English 3000s* (Scafell Pike, Scafell, Helvellyn, and Skiddaw).

e) *Furths* are the mountains in England, Wales and Ireland that are more than 3,000 feet (914.4 metres) high. The name is derived from an obscure Scottish word meaning 'outwith'. It refers in this case to the 3000-feet mountains of the British Isles located outside Scotland. Furths are also known, colloquially, as 'the Irish munros'.

f) *Grahams,* named in memory of Fiona Graham, are the 224 Scottish mountains between 2,000 (609.6 metres) and 2,499 feet (762 metres) in height and with a relative height of at least 500 feet (152.4 metres) on all sides.

g) *Hewitts,* from the acronym **H**ills in **E**ngland, **W**ales and **I**reland that are **T**wo **T**housand, which refers to hills in these three countries that are at least 2,000 feet (609.6 metres) high and with a relative height of at least 30 metres.

h) *Marilyns,* a punning reference linking Marilyn Monroe to Sir Hector Munro, are mountains and hills in the United Kingdom, the Isle of Man, and the Republic of Ireland that have a relative height of at least 150 metres (492 feet) irrespective of the height of the summit.

i) *Munros,* named after the compiler Sir Hector Munro, are the 283 Scottish mountains more than 3,000 feet (914.4 metres) in height. A 'Munro top' is a summit that exceeds 3,000 feet but is not a separate mountain.

j) *Nuttalls,* named after the compilers John and Anne Nuttall, are hills in England and Wales that are at least 2,000 feet (610 metres) high.

k) *Wainwrights* are the fells described and mapped by A. Wainwright in his *Pictorial Guide to the Lakeland Fells.*

l)   *Welsh 3000s* comprise Snowdon, Tryfan, Glyder Fawr, Y Garn, Elidir Fawr, Carnedd Dafydd, Carnedd Llewelyn and Foel-fras.

m) *Yorkshire Three Peaks* are Pen-y-Ghent, Whernside and Ingleborough.

12   Some walkers devise personal challenges such as visiting every prehistoric hill-fort in England or walking every canal towpath.

Walking festivals

13   A walking festival is an event organized by a town or club to promote walking and green tourism whilst bringing economic benefits to the community. They vary in character from comparatively modest affairs held over a single weekend, to elaborate multi-day festivals that attract commercial sponsorship, attendance by celebrities, and provide evening entertainment. Some, such as the Isle of Wight Walking Festival that lasts for two weeks, and the Castlebar International Four Days' Walks, held annually in County Mayo since 1967, attract walkers from overseas.

14   The Ramblers' Association organizes two nation-wide events, the Summer Walking Festival and the Winter Walking Festival. Local Ramblers' Groups offer a series of guided walks that are free and open to the general public.

15   Walking festivals are listed and advertised in outdoor magazines. Enter 'Walking festivals' into your search engine and you will discover a number of sites that claim to have the most complete listing of these events.

Select bibliography

16   Bearhop, Derek A., Editor, *Munro's Tables and other Tables of Lesser Heights.* 4th ed. Scottish Mountaineering Trust, 1997.

17   Dawson, Alan, *The Relative Hills of Britain; Mountains, Munros and Marilyns.* Cicerone Press, 2013.

18   Dillon, Paddy, *The Mountains of Ireland; a Guide to Walking the Summits.* Cicerone Press, 2013.

19 Dillon, Paddy, *The National Trails; the 19 National Trails of England, Scotland and Wales.* Cicerone Press, 2007.

20 Johnson, Brian, *Walking the Corbetts; Vol 1 South of the Great Glen.* Cicerone Press, 2012.

21 Kew, Steve, *Walking the Munros; Vol 1 Southern, Central and Western Highlands* 2nd ed. Cicerone Press, 2012.

22 Kew, Steve, *Walking the Munros; Vol 2 Northern Highlands and the Cairngorms.* Cicerone Press, 2010.

23 Long Distance Walker's Association, *The UK Trailwalker's Handbook* 8th ed. Cicerone Press, 2011.

24 McCloy, Andrew, *The Land's End to John o' Groats Walk; a Guide to Planning the Ultimate Footpath Walking Adventure.* Cordee, 2002.

25 McNeish, Cameron, *The Munro Almanack* 3rd ed. Cicerone Press, 1998.

26 Muir, Jonny, *The UK's County Tops; 82 Walks to Reach the Top of 91 Historic Counties.* Cicerone Press, 2011.

27 Nuttall, John and Anne, *The Mountains of England and Wales: Vol 1 Wales* 3rd ed. Cicerone Press, 2009.

28 Nuttall, John and Anne, *The Mountains of England and Wales: Vol 2 England* 3rd ed. Cicerone Press, 2008.

29 Robinson, Andy, *The End to End Trail; Land's End to John O'Groats on Foot.* Cicerone Press, 2007.

30 Turnbull, Ronald, *Three Peaks, Ten Tors; Long Distance and Challenge Walks in the UK: Tools and Techniques, Routes and Reminiscences.* Cicerone Press, 2007.

Chapter 22 Clubs, walking with children, letterboxing & geocaching

Walking clubs

1   Many people enjoy walking with a group and there is much to commend it because:

   a) All the planning is done for you. The club's programme will tell you the length of each walk and the nature of the terrain so that you will be able to judge whether the walk is suitable for your circumstances.

   b) You should have a leader and be spared the problems of route-finding.

   c) You will enjoy the company of like-minded people who will be pleased to advise and share their knowledge and expertise with you.

   d) Some clubs run classes in map-reading skills which can be invaluable for the novice walker.

   e) Most clubs normally permit visitors to attend a couple of walks to establish that they are to their liking before expecting them to join.

2   Information about clubs in your area can usually be obtained from your local public library or from the appropriate national association

      • in Great Britain from the Ramblers' Association (see Appendix 4)
      • in Northern Ireland from the Ulster Federation of Rambling Clubs (see 16:47)
      • in the Republic of Ireland from the Walkers Association of Ireland (see 16:31)

3   Choose a club that matches your walking profile. For example, if you have small children, a club that specializes in 20-mile walks is not for you.

4   Many clubs have walks of different lengths to suit all abilities, and some organize short midweek walks that appeal to those with pre-school children and the retired. It is a good plan to telephone the secretary of the club and discuss your needs before committing yourself.

5   Every summer the Ramblers' Association organizes a nation-wide Family Rambling Day in Great Britain when members of the public are invited to sample walking with a local Ramblers' Group.

Special interest walking clubs

6   There are a number of nation-wide clubs in the United Kingdom that cater for walkers with particular interests.

Christian Rambling Club

7   The Christian Rambling Club (www.crc.org.uk) is a non-denominational club that offers Christian fellowship as well as walks.

The Gay Outdoor Club

8   The Gay Outdoor Club (www.goc.org.uk) operates throughout Great Britain through 30 local groups. It provides a wide range of outdoor and indoor sports and recreational activities, including walking, for gay, lesbian, bisexual and transgender men and women.

The Long Distance Walkers' Association

9   The LDWA (www.ldwa.org.uk) is a club for people who enjoy walking long distances. The Association:

   a) Has groups throughout England, Wales and southern Scotland which organize
     • long day-walks of around 20 miles
     • challenge walks ranging from 20 to 100 miles which usually have to be completed within a specified time

   b) Publishes *The Long Distance Walkers' Handbook* which is a directory of basic facts about more than 1300 long distance paths. This information is also available on-line from the LDWA website. The *Long Distance Path Chart,* published by Harvey in association with the LDWA, shows all long distance paths on a 1:625,000 map.

   c) Publishes *Strider,* its house magazine, three times a year, containing articles, news and information about forthcoming events.

Red Rope

10   Red Rope is a national walking and climbing club organized on socialist and green ethical principles. It has branches throughout the country.

Walking for Health

11   Walking for Health is a government-sponsored scheme organized by the Ramblers' Association in partnership with Macmillan Cancer Support with the aims of:

    a) Encouraging more people to become physically active in their local communities.

    b) Supporting 600 local schemes of health walk schemes across England which offer regular short walks over easy terrain with trained walk leaders.

Walking for the blind and partially sighted

12   Most blind people are able to move around towns but find it difficult to negotiate paths and stiles. They often find walking uphill easier than going downhill.

13   Some routes suitable for the blind have been developed but most of them are short and less suited to the fit and healthy.

14   A number of rambling clubs arrange walks specifically for the blind. Sighted walkers accompany the blind and give a commentary on conditions underfoot as well as advice and assistance in climbing stiles. Guide dogs are often unfamiliar with the countryside and need to be kept under close control to prevent them worrying stock (1:21-5).

Walking for the disabled

15   Some local authorities and organizations such as national parks and the National Trust have developed walks that are accessible by wheelchairs and mobility scooters. A number of highway authorities are replacing stiles with kissing gates to make walking easier for the elderly and those with limited mobility.

16   The Disabled Ramblers (www.disabledramblers.co.uk) exist to serve the interests of the severely disabled to explore the countryside. Able-bodied volunteers support members and help with loading scooters etc. A toilet for the disabled is carried on an off-road mobility scooter.

Walking with children

17   Walking with small children can be an enjoyable and inexpensive family activity if thoughtfully planned. Small babies are best carried in a front sling available from High Street shops that specialize in children's needs.

18   Once the child can support its head, it is ready for a child carrier, also known as a papoose, that is carried on the back like a rucksack. Small children enjoy child carriers because they see the world from a different perspective, and the warmth and proximity of their parent's body makes them feel loved and secure.

19   Look for the following features when choosing a child carrier:

   a)   Ensure that the child can fall asleep in the carrier safely without its head jerking to the rhythm of your step. This requires adequate padding of the interior of the carrier and some form of gentle head restraint in addition to the straps that prevent the child from falling out.

   b)   The carrier should have an adjustable frame that will allow the child to be lifted into it when it is standing on the ground, and there should be pockets to stow nappies, extra clothing, food and other essentials. More sophisticated models will come with a built-in waterproof cover and hood.

   c)   The child carriers best suited for walkers are to be found in outdoor shops because the cheaper models sold in High Street chain stores are usually designed for short-distance urban use and may lack some of the desirable features described above.

20   It is impossible to turn your head sufficiently far to see what your child is doing when in its carrier, so it is advisable to keep a small pocket-mirror handy so that you are able to check.

21   An oversize umbrella will provide useful protection in the event of a heavy shower and can be strapped to the frame of the child carrier when not in use.

22   Walk only in settled conditions when fair weather is promised, and choose sensible routes that do not involve difficult terrain or excessively steep hills because a small child can be badly frightened, and even hurt, should you stumble and fall.

23   From the age of about three, many children will not sit in a child carrier for long and will want to do at least some walking. As a rule-of-thumb guide, once children reach this age and are physically capable of walking, they should be able to manage one mile for every year of their age without becoming overtired.

24   A three-year old will, from time to time, seek a rest on the shoulders of an adult but with a little gentle encouragement will soon be happy to trot along unaided.

25   The trick is to make the walk interesting so that children do not notice how far they are walking. Canal towpaths and river walks are ideal because there is

always something going on and a new vista around every bend. Canals have boats to wave to, and locks are an endless source of fascination. Larger rivers also have boats but even smaller streams are interesting to children who love to throw stones into pools and to paddle in the shallows. Other features of interest to children are windmills, castles, grand houses, lakes, viewpoints etc.

26   Collecting feathers, acorns and conkers (but not wild flowers) add interest to a walk. Small rewards such as the promise of an ice cream from a village shop, or a ploughman's lunch taken in the garden of a rural public house help to encourage children. And finally, if they get fractious, there are the old favourites to entertain them like 'I spy' and the singing of nursery rhymes.

27   Apart from a child carrier, there is no need to purchase special walking clothing for small children even though it is now widely available. An ordinary plastic mac and sou'wester will cope adequately with showers, and trainers in dry weather and wellingtons in wet are perfectly satisfactory. It is advisable to carry a spare set of clothing for small children in case of 'accidents'.

28   Children from the age of twelve should be able to walk as far as an adult and will want (although not necessarily need) proper boots and waterproofs. It should be possible to get two seasons' use from jackets and overtrousers but footwear will probably have to be replaced every season.

Letterboxing and geocaching

29   Letterboxing and geocaching are activities that combine walking and navigation skills to discover hidden weatherproof containers.

Letterboxing

30   Letterboxing was started on Dartmoor 150 years ago by a guide who left a box and notebook at Cranmere Pool in which walkers and tourists could record their visit. This developed into a popular Dartmoor pastime which has spread, to a limited extent, to other parts of the country. The letterboxer purchases a logbook which describes the location of letterboxes which then have to be discovered. Inside every letterbox will be found a notebook in which to record the visit, and a rubber stamp and inkpad that is used to stamp the logbook.

Geocaching

31   Geocaching, now a world-wide sport, has a number of similarities with letterboxing. Geocachers hide a small waterproof box containing a few items of

small value, a logbook, and a pen or pencil. The geocacher records the grid reference of their cache on a satnav and logs its location on a dedicated website.

32   Other geocachers who access the website will record the location and search for the cache with the aid of their satnavs. They make an entry in the logbook, re-move one of the items in the box, replace it with something of their own, and record their find on the website.

33   The governing body of the sport in this country is the Geocaching Association of Great Britain. Further information, including the code of conduct for geo-cachers, can be found on the Association's website at http://gagb.co.uk.

Select bibliography

34   Camerone, Layne, *The Geocaching Handbook.* Falcon Press, 2006.

35   Marsh, Terry, *Geocaching in the UK.* Cicerone Press, 2011.

36   Youngman, Angela, *Walking with Kids; Games and Activities to Make Walking Fun.* Sigma Leisure, 2011.

Chapter 23 Leading and guiding walks & walking tours

1 The information in this chapter is aimed at experienced walkers who require information on how to lead day-walks and multi-day walking tours.

2 For the purposes of this book it is convenient to divide walks leaders into three categories
- informal: where several friends decide to take a walk and one of them agrees to work out a route
- formal: an unpaid volunteer who leads walks for a club or organization, subsequently referred to as a 'leader'
- professional: a guide who leads walks for financial reward, subsequently referred to as a 'guide'

This chapter will concentrate on formal leading and professional guiding but some of the information may be of interest to informal leaders. Members of the groups that are being led or guided are described as 'clients'.

Qualities required of guides and leaders

3 Anyone who takes on the task of leading walks must have the requisite experience of the terrain in which the walk will take place. If your experience, however long, is restricted to lowland walking, it would be unwise to lead walks in upland areas where conditions can be entirely different.

4 Leaders and guides need to be paragons of all the virtues and should have
- a pleasant personality
- a sense of humour
- tact
- sensitivity to clients' needs
- group management skills
- the ability to demonstrate unobtrusive yet firm leadership

They should never adopt a superior attitude towards their clients and keep in mind that reaching the summit of Great Gable in the Lake District, or even Leith Hill in Surrey, could be a personal Everest for some of their clients.

5   Guides and leaders must always be straightforward and honest with their clients. Even with meticulous planning the unexpected can happen such as

- losing a map
- becoming disorientated in mist
- taking the wrong path
- injury or death (it does happen!)
- missing footbridge, major obstruction, or path closure for repair which occurred after the reconnaissance of the route
- missing a bus or train

6   Should a serious emergency arise, guides and leaders should immediately take control of the situation and exert their authority. If possible, move the group away from the location of the problem and put someone in charge of the clients with strict instructions to sit them down and keep them calm. Always be upfront and explain what the problem is and the steps you are taking to resolve it. If you dissemble you run the risk of being found out and compromising your management of the group.

Safety

7   Leaders and guides have an obligation to keep their clients safe. The first safety consideration is the size of the group. In the temperate months of the year, one experienced guide, plus a volunteer backmarker, should be able to handle

- up to twenty adult clients on a lowland walk
- up to twelve adult clients in upland areas

8   Members of groups often seem to lose all sense of individual responsibility and need to be reminded from time to time of safety issues. This is particularly important when crossing or following roads. Some clients seem oblivious of the danger from traffic and although instructed to walk in single file close to the verge facing oncoming traffic may start to stray towards the centre of road. Leaders and guides should normally hold up the traffic when crossing roads, except on busy main roads when it may be safer to line up the clients on the verge and cross together when there is a gap in the traffic. It is wise to ensure that clients cross to the left-hand side of the road in good time when approaching right-hand bends.

9   Leaders and guides should be properly dressed and equipped for the type of walk or tour they are leading. Essential items include

- map
- compass
- first aid kit

- mobile phone
- whistle

Depending on the type of walk they should consider carrying

- satnav
- extra bottle of water
- small quantity of high-energy food
- emergency shelter(s) large enough for the whole group
- insulating blanket
- head torch
- walking poles
- poncho, hat and gloves for emergency use
- telephone numbers of local taxi firms, doctors, hospitals and dentists

Emergency items can be shared and carried by members of the group.

Professional qualifications

10   There is no legal obligation for those leading and guiding walks in the United Kingdom to obtain professional qualifications, but many organizations, especially those involving children and vulnerable adults, will require them as well as a Criminal Records Bureau (CRB) check. Information about the latter can be obtained from www.homeoffice.gov.uk/agencies-public-bodies/crb. The two most relevant qualifications for walks leaders are the

- Walking Group Leader Award (WGL)
- Mountain Leader Award (ML)

11   Both awards are conferred by Mountain Leader Training UK (MLT) which is the coordinating body for

- Mountain Leader Training England (MLTE)
- Mountain Leader Training Wales (MLTW)
- Mountain Leader Training Scotland (MLTS)
- Mountain Leader Training Northern Ireland (MLTNI)

Training facilities for these awards are provided by a number of organizations and individuals approved by the MLT. Details can be accessed from the MLT website www.mountain-training.org.

The Walking Group Leader Award

12   The WGL award is designed for those who wish to lead groups of hill-walkers in non-mountainous upland terrain comprising moor, bog, hill, fell or down. Such areas are often subject to extreme weather conditions and require an element of self-sufficiency. To join a course you must first be able to demonstrate

your experience walking in the hills and mountains in the form of a walking log containing at least twenty quality mountain or hill-walking days.

13   The course includes instruction and assessment of the following skills
   • group management
   • navigation
   • emergency procedures
   • access
   • conservation
   • remote supervision

Mountain Leader Award

14   This qualification is for those who want to lead groups in the mountains of the United Kingdom and Ireland in summer conditions. It includes
   • navigation
   • group management
   • mountain hazards
   • river crossings
   • emergency ropework

The WGL award is not a pre-condition for acceptance for training but is often the route that is followed.

Winter Mountain Leader Award

15   This award is administered by Mountain Training Scotland and is valid throughout the United Kingdom and Ireland. It trains people in the skills required to lead groups on hill-walking expeditions in winter conditions.

Other training courses and qualifications

16   A number of organizations conduct training sessions for their staff and some are open to the general public. Most of them, are aimed at those who lead walks in lowland countryside. Training courses are organized by, among others
   • the Ramblers
   • education authorities
   • youth groups

Insurance

17   This is a litigious age and it is wise to be insured against civil liability claims. There are three main providers of insurance:

a)   Organizations of which you are a member, such as the Ramblers, the British Mountaineering Council, and the Long Distance Walkers' Association, may provide cover *but it is likely to be restricted to events that are conducted in their name.* Thus, if you are a member of the Ramblers and are asked to lead a walk for a Ramblers group, you will automatically be insured. But when leading for the Mothers' Union, you would not be covered by the Ramblers' policy.

  b)   Many clubs and organizations have their own insurance that will cover non-members who have been invited to organize an event. Leaders and guides should check the insurance cover before agreeing to lead a walk.

  c)   Guides and leaders who organize walks for the general public should consider making their own arrangements for insurance. Perkins Slade Ltd (www.perkins-slade.com) are brokers which specialize in this kind of insurance and can usually arrange £5 million of civil liability cover.

Planning a guided walk

18   The secret of good guiding and leading is meticulous planning and leaving nothing to chance. Leaders and guides who have been contracted to conduct a walk should consult with the clients' representatives on their requirements. Sometimes it will be left to the leader or guide to decide on a suitable route. Considerations that should be borne in mind when deciding on a suitable walk include the age, fitness and number of clients. Most members of an Over-60 club would probably not be happy on a twelve-mile walk, nor would a group of Venture Scouts be excited by the prospect of a three-mile stroll.

19   Other matters that have to be agreed are
  • refreshment stops (pub lunch, café or picnic)
  • method of travel to the start of the walk (public transport, coach or car)
  • whether dogs and children are allowed

20   Once these matters have been agreed the detailed planning can commence. Leaders and guides should reconnoitre the route (colloquially known as a 'recce') to familiarize themselves with it and note any physical problems such as ploughed fields, missing stiles etc. and how they can be circumvented.

21   Leaders and guides may be required to complete a 'risk assessment' form. This can be a headache but there is a formula that will make the assessment relatively easy. On a scale of 1-5 where 1 is low and 5 is high:

   a)   Assess the likelihood of an incident (e.g. 2).

   b)   Assess the severity of the consequences of an incident (e.g. 3).

   c)   Multiply the two figures (2 x 3 = 6) to obtain the risk factor.

   d)   This should be compared against a scale of 1-25. Thus, in this example the risk factor is low.

   e)   Depending on the risk factor, decide on
        • how best to reduce the risk
        • the best way of dealing with an incident

22   Notes should be made of the location of
        • pubs and cafés
        • toilet facilities (including areas of cover on the route suitable for emergency stops)
        • escape routes (especially important in upland areas)
        • items of interest (castles, churches, prehistoric sites etc.) that can be briefly described during the walk

23   The details of the walk should be circulated which can best be illustrated by the example below which is based on using public transport:

   a)   It is wise to list the time of the return train sometime later than the group's estimated time of arrival at the station to take into account
        • slow walkers
        • untoward delays
        • emergencies

   b)   If travelling to the start of the walk by car, details of the parking arrangements should be substituted. It is usually more satisfactory for cars to be parked at the *finish* of a linear walk and to use public transport to get to the start. This method ensures that everyone will get home should the last bus of the day be cancelled.

A circular walk around Sevenoaks and Knole, Kent

Date: Saturday 29th January

Description: After walking through Sevenoaks, we enter the deer park of Knole which is one of the grandest of Elizabethan mansions. We then climb onto the North Downs and follow a ridge that gives extensive views over the Weald of Kent to the South Downs. Our route then descends to Ightham (pronounced eyetam) Mote which is a wonderfully preserved moated manor house dating from 1340. After lunch we pass through orchards and hop fields to cross Knole Park and return to the station.

Distance: 10.27 miles/16.71 kilometres

Total ascent: 1001 feet/346 metres in a series of short hills

Lunch: at a pleasant pub after 6 miles

Toilet facilities: on the train, at the station and at the pub

Map: Ordnance Survey *Explorer* 147

Meet: 0900 near the ticket office of Charing Cross Station

Depart: 0930

Arrive: Sevenoaks 1005

Depart: Sevenoaks 1629

Arrive: Charing Cross 1703

Closing date for applications: Saturday 22nd January

Notes, terms and conditions

Parties are limited to twenty walkers on a first-come first-served basis after which a waiting list will apply.

The cost of the walk is £... excluding fares and lunches.

Please reserve your place by mailing a cheque made out to ...

Rail tickets are purchased on the day of travel so if you have to cancel at the last moment please telephone me on my mobile.

Refunds will be given if you can find someone to take your place, or the walk has to be cancelled.

Bring suitable footwear (preferably boots), waterproofs, a spare sweater, trail snacks, and water.

Lunch will be eaten in a pub.

Muddy boots should be removed, or covered in supermarket bags, before entering pubs.

Toilet facilities are limited. They are usually available on the train, at the railway station and at the pub. Please inform the guide if you need some privacy on the trail so that the group can stroll on and wait for you.

Sorry, no dogs.

The guide is familiar with all the routes advertised and carries a first aid kit, map, compass and a satnav.

The routes are not inherently dangerous but stiles and path surfaces can be slippery, and great care must be exercised when walking on roads.

Members of the group must accept full and sole responsibility for their own safety.

24   After the closing date for applications, the pub should be telephoned to make a reservation for lunch. If the group is large, it's a good plan to ask for a menu to

be emailed to the guide who can edit it to list the alternatives (e.g. salad or vegetables, brown or white bread) from which the clients can make their selection (see example below). The order can be telephoned to the pub which should ensure that the meals will be served promptly on arrival.

LUNCH MENU

Please indicate your choice by putting your initials in a circle against the item. If you make an error, please completely obliterate your initials. The order will be telephoned to the pub from the train.

	£
STARTERS	
Vegetable soup with a crusty roll	4.50
Smoked mackerel on a bed of salad	6.50
Prawns in a Marie Rose sauce with garnish	5.50

	£
MAIN MEALS	
Shepherd's pie served with brussel sprouts	9.50
Beef casserole	10.50
Pan fried calves liver with chips and peas	11.00
Vegetarian lasagna served with a side salad	8.50

SANDWICHES all served with a salad garnish   **5.50**

Ham on brown bread
Ham on white bread
Cheese on brown bread
Cheese on white bread

DESSERTS   **4.00**

Fruit salad
Vanilla ice cream
Sticky toffee pudding

On the day

25 Guides and leaders should arrive at the meeting point early to be ready to greet the clients:

a) When the group has assembled, the guides should introduce themselves and go over the plans for the day as well as mentioning the need to have waterproofs, water etc. At the same time guides and leaders should run their eyes over the group to ensure that everyone is suitably dressed.

b) Ask the clients not to walk ahead of the leader. Remind them that the path network is dense and they could easily take the wrong path and get lost.

c) Mention that they should not stray from the line of the path, even when walking through pasture, and to walk in single file where necessary.

d) If the group is large and there is only one guide, it is a good plan to ask for a volunteer to be the backmarker and gate-shutter.

e) Mention the need to report any problem that a client may have to the guide. Remind them of the importance of dressing a hot spot on their feet before it develops into blister.

f) The guide should assess the fitness of the group during the first mile and to set a suitable pace. In practice, the average speed of the group is *always* set by the slowest walker.

g) At the conclusion of the walk, guides and leaders should express the hope that everyone has enjoyed themselves, and thank them for attending.

Walking tours

26 Some tour companies at the lower end of the market recruit guides with the offer of a 'free holiday'. Guides should enjoy the experience of conducting a walking tour but if they do their job properly if is far from being a holiday.

27 It is important that guides contracted to lead a walking tour deliver exactly what is promised in the brochure published by the holiday company. Failure to do so could result in the firm being in breach of contract. The only exception to this fundamental principle, apart from factors beyond the guide's control, are on the grounds of safety such as unsuitable weather conditions.

28 Most reputable tour companies take care to describe the degree of difficulty and the level of fitness required to participate in the trip accurately. Clients who have chosen a trip that is too strenuous for their level of fitness have only them-selves to blame, and the enjoyment of those who have chosen properly should not be compromised. If there is only one person in the group capable of com-pleting the trip then the needs of that person must be satisfied first. Guides should do their best to accommodate the others in the group but not at the ex-pense of the person who has made the correct choice.

29 Guides should keep careful records of their expenses and monies spent on be-half of the holiday company so that they can submit accurate accounts at the end of the trip.

30 Most of the advice given in the section 'Planning a guided walk' (see 23:18-24) applies equally to guides of walking tours. But there are matters, such as a clash of personalities, within the group that the guide should quickly defuse.

31 Walkers tend to be nice people and most clients are pleasant and likeable but occasionally a client may exhibit unreasonable or disruptive behaviour. A tactful word, in private, is usually all that is required but in extreme cases of offensive behaviour, it may be necessary to contact the tour company and request permission to expel the client from the trip.

32 Responsible guides avoid relationships with their clients that go beyond the merely friendly. Clients like to respect their guides and expect to get equal attention from them. Once the group is aware that 'something is going on' they are likely to become mildly resentful, to gossip, and to start looking for other faults in their guide. The situation is aggravated if either party is known to be married.

33 Romances between clients are not the concern of the guide providing that the attraction is mutual. However, if one of the parties does not welcome the attention, then the guide may have to deal with an awkward situation discreetly. It may be possible to arrange for a married couple to 'protect' the woman by inviting her to sit with them at meals and generally to keep an eye on her welfare so that she is not left alone. Or it may fall to the guide to gently suggest that the ardour of the lovelorn should be cooled.

And finally

34 Leading and guiding walks and tours can, and should be, satisfying and rewarding experiences. The look of joy, wonder and delight on the faces of your clients as they gaze down on Wasdale from the summit of Great Gable, marvel at the magnificent sweep of the Cornish coast from Nare Head, or just savour the delectable harmony of the vernacular architecture and intimacy of the Cotswold countryside, makes it so worthwhile.

35 Every walk that you lead should be treated as a learning experience. Reflect critically on the events of each day and consider whether you have made any mistakes or could have made it even more enjoyable for your clients.

Select bibliography

36 Langmuir, Eric, *Mountaincraft and Leadership* 4th ed., Mountain Leader Training Board, 2013.

37   Long, Steve and others, *Hillwalking; the Official Handbook of the Mountain Leader a Walking Group Leader Schemes.* Mountain Leader Training UK, 2003.

38   Saunders, Colin, *Navigation and Leadership; a Manual for Walkers* 2nd ed revised by Julian Tippett. Ramblers' Association, 1994. This teaching text is out of print but it ca▮ downloaded from www.ramblers.org.uk.

Appendix 1 Useful organizations in the United Kingdom & Ireland

1   Adventure and Environmental Awareness Group
    www.aea-uk.org
    Aims: To encourage awareness, understanding and concern for the natural environment amongst those involved with education and recreation.

2   Association for the Protection of Rural Scotland
    www.ruralscotland.btik.com
    Aims: To protect and enhance Scotland's rural landscapes for future generations; promote effective planning and landscape protection systems; encourage genuinely sustainable development; raise awareness of the importance of Scotland's landscapes to its people and economy; promote the activity of land managers who care for Scotland's landscapes.

3   Association of Heads of Outdoor Education Centres
    www.ahoec.org
    Aims: To provide quality in outdoor learning, inspirational experiences, challenging activities, excitement and fun, all with a lifelong positive impact.

4   Association of Lowland Search and Rescue
    www.alsar.org.uk
    Aims: ALSAR is the body that coordinates the work of lowland rescue teams who search for, and bring to safety, anyone who is in need of help in the lowland areas of England and Northern Ireland.

5   Backpackers' Club
    www.backpackersclub.co.uk
    Aims: To promote and encourage backpacking for the benefit of its members.

6   Black Environment Network
    www.ben-network.org.uk
    Aims: Promotes full ethnic participation in the built and natural environment.

7   British Activity Providers' Association
www.thebapa.org.uk

Aims: The trade association for private sector providers of activity holidays and courses in the UK. Promotes high standards within the industry.

8   British Association of Mountain Guides
www.bmg.org.uk

Aims: Trains and assesses mountain guides in climbing, mountaineering and ski mountaineering. Sets professional standards for services offered by BMG members. Promotes safety, enjoyment, and good practice in climbing and mountaineering.

9   British Mountaineering Council
www.thebmc.co.uk

Aims: To foster and promote the interests of British mountaineers and mountaineering in the United Kingdom and overseas; jointly with the Mountaineering Council of Scotland, it is the representative body of British mountaineers.

10   British Textile Technology Group
www.bttg.co.uk

Aims: To provide research, consultancy and testing for the textile industry.

11   British Trust for Conservation Volunteers
www.btcv.org.uk

Aims: To involve people of all ages in practical conservation work including footpath improvement, bridge-building, and the repair of stone walls.

12   Byways and Bridleway Trust
www.bbtrust.org.uk

Aims: To keep byways and bridleways open for everyone.

13   Camping and Caravanning Club
www.campingandcaravanningclub.co.uk

Aims: The promotion of knowledge, love and care of the countryside through camping and kindred activities.

14   Campaign for National Parks
www.cnp.org.uk

Aims: To protect and promote the national parks of England and Wales.

15   Christian Rambling Club
www.crc-net.org.uk

Aims: To provide opportunities to enjoy walking at the weekend whilst still having Christian fellowship.
There are groups throughout England and South Wales.

16   Council for the Protection of Rural England
www.cpre.org.uk

Aims: Works to protect, promote and enhance our towns and countryside to make them better places to live, work and enjoy, and to ensure the countryside is protected for now and future generations.

17   Council for the Protection of Rural Wales
www.cprw.org.uk

Aims: To secure the protection and enhancement of the diverse landscapes and environment of Wales.

18   Country Land and Business Association
www.cla.org.uk

Aims: To speak for a living and working countryside.

19   Countryside Alliance
www.countryside-alliance.org.uk

Aims: To promote the interests of field sports and rural people.

20   Countryside Management Association (formerly the Association of Countryside Rangers)
www.countrysidemanagement.org.uk

Aims: To further the interests of countryside staff working in England and Wales.

21   Disabled Ramblers' Association
www.disabledramblers.co.uk

Aims: To encourage the disabled to explore the countryside and to liaise with local authorities to provide suitable routes.

22   Discover Ireland
www.discoverireland.ie

Aims: To provide comprehensive information and listings for accommodation; activities; events; and tourist attractions.

23   Forestry Commission of Great Britain
www.forestry.gov.uk

Aims: *To protect and expand Britain's forests and woodlands.*
The responsibility for forests is split between the:
Forestry Commission England (www.forestry.gov.uk/england)
Forestry Commission for Scotland (www.forestry.gov.uk/scotland)
Forestry Commission for Wales (www.forestry.gov.uk/wales)

24   Forest Service for Northern Ireland
www.forestserviceni.gov.uk

Aims: The Forest Service of the Department of Agriculture and Rural Development is the authority responsible for state forestry and is required to manage existing woods and forests; to promote economic and environmental benefits; provide recreational opportunities for the people of Northern Ireland; secure an expansion of tree cover to increase these benefits and opportunities.

25   Friends of the Earth (England, Wales and Northern Ireland)
www.foe.co.uk

Aims: Campaigns for a healthy environment.

26   Friends of the Earth (Scotland)
www.foe-scotland.org.uk

Aims: Campaigns for a world where everyone can enjoy a healthy environment and a fair share of the Earth's resources.

27   Friends of the Lake District
www.fld.org.uk

Aims: To promote an energetic and consistent application of unified planning policy for the Lake District; to organize concerted action for protecting the landscape and natural beauty of the Lake District and the county of Cumbria.

28   Gay Outdoor Club
www.goc.org.uk

Aims: To provide a wide range of outdoor recreational activities for gay, lesbian, bisexual and transgender men and women. There are groups throughout Great Britain.

29   Hostelling International Northern Ireland (formerly the Youth Hostels Association of Northern Ireland)
www.hini.org.uk
Aims: To help all, especially young people of limited means, to a greater knowledge, love and care of the countryside.

30   Institute for Outdoor Learning
www.outdoor-learning.org
Aims: To encourage the provision of outdoor learning by developing quality, safety and the opportunity to experience outdoor activity.

31   Institute of Public Rights of Way and Access Management
www.iprow.co.uk
Aims: To represent individuals involved in the management of public rights of way and other access in England, Wales, Scotland and Northern Ireland, principally as local government officers.

32   John Muir Trust
www.jmt.org
Aims: To conserve wild land and wild places.

33   Leave No Trace Ireland
www.leavenotraceireland.org
Aims: To promote responsible recreational use of the outdoors with a proper respect for the environment throughout the island of Ireland.

34   Long Distance Walkers Association
www.ldwa.org.uk
Aims: To further the interests of those who enjoy long-distance walking; to promote organized challenge walks, new walking routes, and to publish information on all aspects of non-competitive walking.

35   Mountain Bothies' Association
www.mountainbothies.org.uk
Aims: To maintain simple unlocked shelters in mountain country for the use of walkers, climbers and other outdoor enthusiasts.

36   Mountain Leader Training Scotland
www.educationscotland.gov.uk
Administers the Mountain Leader Award, the Walking Group Leader Award and the Winter Mountain Leader Award in Scotland.

37   Mountain Rescue England and Wales
www.mountain.rescue.org.uk

Aims: To organize and co-ordinate the mountain rescue activities of England and Wales.

38   Mountain Rescue Committee of Scotland
www.mountainrescuescotland.org

Aims: To co-ordinate the work of mountain rescue organizations in Scotland.

39   Mountaineering Council of Scotland
www.mcofs.org.uk

Aims: To promote the interests of mountaineers, climbers and hill-walkers in Scotland.

40   Mountaineering Ireland
www.mountaineering.ie

Aims: The governing body for walkers and climbers in the island of Ireland; represents the interests of walkers and climbers; improves access to the Irish hills and crags; promotes mountain training programmes and qualifications; encourages responsible and sustainable use of the mountain environment.

41   National Trails Office
www.irishtrails.ie

Aims: To co-ordinate and drive the implementation of an Irish Trails Strategy and to promote the use of recreational trails in Ireland.

42   National Trust
www.nationaltrust.org.uk

Aims: To give people access to the countryside and to acquire land and buildings in England, Wales and Northern Ireland worthy of permanent preservation.

43   National Trust for Scotland
www.nts.org.uk

Aims: To promote the permanent preservation for the benefit of the nation beautiful landscapes, buildings, places and articles in Scotland of national architectural, artistic, antiquarian or historic interest.

44   Natural England
www.naturalengland.org.uk

Aims: To protect and improve the natural environment of England and encourage people to enjoy and get involved in their surroundings.

45   Northern Ireland Environment Agency
www.doeni.gov.uk

Aims: To protect, conserve and promote the natural environment and built heritage of Northern Ireland for present and future generations.

46   Northern Ireland Tourist Board
www.nitb.com

Aims: To develop tourism and market Northern Ireland as a tourist destination to visitors within Northern Ireland and from the Republic of Ireland.

47   Open Spaces Society
www.oss.org.uk
Aims: To protect the common land, village greens, open spaces and public paths of the United Kingdom.

48   Ordnance Survey
www.ordnancesurvey.co.uk

Aims: To survey and map England, Wales, Scotland and the Isle of Man.

49   Ordnance Survey Ireland
www.isi.ie

Aims: To survey and map the Republic of Ireland.

50   Ordnance Survey of Northern Ireland
www.nidirect.gov.uk

Aims: To survey and map Northern Ireland.

51   Outdoor Industries Association
www.outdoorindustriesassociation.co.uk

Aims: To look after the interests of manufacturers, distributors and retailers of outdoor equipment.

52   Outdoor Recreation Northern Ireland
www.outdoorrecreationni.com

Aims: To bring together all groups and bodies which have an interest in, or involvement with, outdoor recreation in Northern Ireland.

53   Outdoor Writers and Photographers' Guild
www.owpg.org.uk
Aims: To meet the professional needs of outdoor writers and photographers and others associated with the outdoor media.

54   Ramblers' Association
www.ramblersassociation.org.uk

Aims: The national organization that protects the interests of walkers in Great Britain (see Appendix 4).

55   Red Rope
www.redrope.org.uk

Aims: To promote access to the countryside for socialist walkers and climbers.

56   Scottish Christian Hillwalking Club
www.christianhillwalking.co.uk

Aims: To bring Christians together to enjoy hill-walking and fellowship.

57   Scottish Natural Heritage
www.snh.gov.uk

Aims: To promote care for and improve the natural heritage; help people enjoy it responsibly; enable greater understanding and awareness of it; promote its sustainable use now and for future generations.

58   Scottish Wild Land Group
www.swlg.org.uk

Aims: To protect and conserve wild land in Scotland.

59   Scottish Youth Hostels Association
www.syha.org.uk

Aims: To provide comfortable, value accommodation with a friendly welcome for people travelling round Scotland.

60   Scotways
www.scotways.com

Aims: To safeguard access to the Scottish countryside.

61   Sport Scotland Avalanche Information Service
www.sais.gov.uk
Aims: To provide information about avalanches and to give daily forecasts of weather, avalanches and conditions in Scottish mountains.

62   Ulster Federation of Rambling Clubs
www.ufrc-online.co.uk

Aims: Promotes walking and is the governing body for rambling and hill-walking clubs in Northern Ireland.

63   Ulster Society for the Preservation of the Countryside
www.uspc.org.uk
Aims: Campaigns to protect the beauty of the countryside of Northern Ireland.

64   VisitEngland (formerly the English Tourist Board)
www.visitengland.org
Aims: The national tourist board is required to foster tourism by working in partnership with the industry; to deliver inspirational marketing campaigns; to provide advocacy for the industry and our visitors.

65   VisitScotland
www.visitscotland.com (formerly the Scottish Tourist Board)
Aims: The national tourist board is required to market Scotland to all parts of the world in order to attract visitors.

66   VisitWales (formerly the Wales Tourist Board)
www.visitwales.co.uk
Aims: The country's national tourist board is required to market Wales to all parts of the world in order to attract visitors.

67   Walk Northern Ireland
www.walkni.com
Aims: To provide comprehensive information about all aspects of walking in Northern Ireland.

68   Walkers' Association of Ireland
www.walkersassociation.ie
Aims: To give a sense of identity and purpose to hill walking and rambling as a national sport in Ireland; provide information on matters relevant to walkers; provide a forum for specialist interests; establish a link to walkers abroad.

69   Walking for Health
www.walkingforhealth.org.uk
Aims: To encourage those with a sedentary life-style to take up walking as a gentle exercise to improve their health.

70   Youth Hostels Association
www.yha.org.uk
Aims: To inspire all, especially young people, to broaden their horizons gaining knowledge and independence through new experiences of adventure and discovery. Provides inexpensive hostels in England and Wales.

Appendix 2 Magazines about walking

1   The magazines listed here are, with the exception of *Walk,* commercial publications that are supported by income from subscriptions and advertising. They all publish articles and features on the same or similar subjects, so the choice for walkers interested in keeping up with the latest news and information lies more between style than content. Many of the bodies listed in *Appendix 1 Useful Organizations* publish magazines or journals.

2   *Country Walking*
www.livefortheoutdoors.com/countrywalking

A monthly publication that claims to be Britain's bestselling walking magazine. It seems to be aimed at those who enjoy lowland walking but also make the occasional foray into upland areas. It makes for easy reading with frequent references to celebrities and popular culture. Most issues contain an article on an essential walking skill. There are many pages of gear reviews, route descriptions illustrated with *Landranger* mapping, and some striking photographs.

3   *The Great Outdoors (tgo)*
www.tgomagazine.co.uk

This monthly publication could be described as the thinking walker's magazine. It concentrates on hill-walking, with a strong emphasis on Scotland, but also has the occasional piece about lowland walking. There is comprehensive coverage of news of interest to walkers, an interesting correspondence section, contributions from knowledgeable and thoughtful columnists, and articles on walking skills as well as gear reviews and route descriptions.

4   *Trail*

www.livefortheoutdoors.com/trail

A monthly publication that comes from the same publishers as *Country Walking* and claims to be Britain's best selling hill-walking magazine. It tends to be laddish in tone with 'magnificent', 'incredible', 'best', 'classic' being some of the favourite adjectives. Every issue contains gear reviews, walk descriptions and some excellent photos. *Trail* has occasionally published articles that have contained serious errors. The December 2003 issue could have led readers to believe that a winter crossing of the Lairig Ghru could be made *'without the faff of ice-axe and crampons'.*

5   *Walk*

www.walkmag.co.uk

The glossy, quarterly house magazine of the Ramblers' Association which is also sold to the general public. It contains a round-up of news of interest both to members of the Ramblers' Association and the general walking public. Many of the articles are bland and include subjects about nature and the environment that are of general interest to walkers. Walking skills are covered as are reviews of gear and books.

6   *Walking World Ireland*

www.walkingworldireland.com

A monthly magazine aimed at all Irish walkers. It publishes articles on hill-walking, the environment and wildlife, and has sections devoted to walking routes and gear reviews.

Appendix 3   The literature of walking

1   This is not a comprehensive bibliography but a list of some of the books that the author has enjoyed. Many, alas, are out of print but it should be possible to track them down via the internet or borrow them from a public library. Note that date given after the title is the date of the original publication; some titles have been reprinted.

2   Belloc, Hilaire
    The Four Men. 1911.
    The Old Road. 1904.
    The Path to Rome. 1902.
Three charming books about the author's walking exploits in which he reflects on European culture and history.

3   Borrow, George
    Wild Wales. 1864.
The fascinating story, and literary classic, of the author's walk around Wales.

4   Brown, Hamish
    Hamish's Mountain Walk; the First Traverse of All the Scottish Munros in One Journey. 1978.
    Hamish's Groat's End Walk; One Man and His Dog on a Hill Route through Britain and Ireland. 1981.
Two delightful books describing long walking trips.

5   Bryson, Bill
    A Walk in the Woods; Rediscovering America on the Appalachian Trail. 1998.
A well-written and amusing account of a walk along the Appalachian Trail.

6   Davies, W. H.
    The Autobiography of a Super-Tramp. 1908.
An account of the poet's walking and hopping railroad freight cars adventure around the United States in 1893.

7   Fermor, Patrick Leigh
    A Time of Gifts. 1977.
    Between Woods and Water. 1986.
Classics of travel writing that describe a walk from the Hook of Holland to the Danube taken by the author in 1933.

8   Fletcher, Colin
   The Man who Walked through Time. 1967.
   An account of his walk through the Grand Canyon by the first person known to have completed this feat.

9   Graham, Stephen
   A Tramp's Sketches. 1918.
   A Vagabond in the Caucasus. 1911.
   Graham walked thousands of miles in many parts of the world. These are two of his best books.

10   Hillaby, John
   Journey to the Jade Sea. 1964.
   Journey through Britain. 1968.
   Journey through Europe. 1972.
   Journey through Love. 1976.
   Journey Home. 1983.
   Some of the most literate writings about walking that have become classics.

11   Hudson, W. H.
   Afoot in England. 1909
   A fascinating account of the author's walks through the countryside of early twentieth century England.

12   Kilvert, Francis
   Diary. 3 vols 1938-40 with an abridged edition in 1944.
   An account of the life of a country clergyman in the Welsh Marches. It contains many delightful descriptions of his walks taken in the years 1870-9.

13   Macfarlane, Robert
   The Old Ways; A Journey on Foot. 2012.
   A fascinating exploration of the relationship between paths, walking and the imagination.

14   Newby, Eric
   A Short Walk in the Hindu Kush. 1958.
   Love and War in the Appenines. 1971.
   Classics of walking and travel-writing.

15   Snow, Sebastian
   The Rucksack Man. 1976.
   An engaging account of the author's unsuccessful attempt to walk from the extreme tip of South America to Alaska.

16   Starkie, Walter
   Raggle-taggle. 1933.
   Spanish Raggle-taggle. 1934.
   Don Gypsy. 1936.
   The Waveless Plain. 1938.
   The Road to Santiago, 1957.
   Scholars and Gypsies. 1963.
   Starkie was interested in Romany culture and walked extensively through Europe studying its traditions.

17   Stevenson, Robert Louis
   Travels with a Donkey. 1879.
   A literary classic relating Stevenson's journey on foot with Modestine, his donkey, across the Cevennes in central France.
   He also wrote a number of essays about walks and walking.

18   Taplin. Kim
   The English Path. 2000.
   The history of paths illustrated from the writings of poets and novelists.

19   Theroux, Paul
   The Kingdom by the Sea: a Journey Round the Coast of Great Britain. 1983.
   An American novelist's thoughts, impressions and musings during a journey on foot and by train and bus around our coast.

20   Wallington, Mark
   500-mile Walkies; One Man and His Dog Versus the South West Peninsula Path. 1986.
   This entertaining book is a genuinely amusing account of a long walk.

21   Wordsworth, Dorothy
   The Journals of Dorothy Wordsworth. 2 vols. 1941.
   The sister of William, the great poet, records their life together and includes descriptions of many of their walks.

Appendix 4   The Ramblers' Association

1   The Ramblers' Association, colloquially known as 'the Ramblers', is unques-
    tionably the most important organization for walkers in Great Britain. It was
    founded as the National Council of Ramblers' Federation in 1931 and changed
    its name to the Ramblers' Association in 1934.

2   There are countless walkers in the UK (one estimate puts it at six million) yet a
    mere 120,000 are members of the Ramblers' Association. Nevertheless, the
    influence and importance of the organization is out of all proportion to its size,
    and it is a matter of regret that so few walkers have any idea of the debt that
    they owe to the Ramblers.

3   It was largely due to the indefatigable campaigning of the Ramblers' Associa-
    tion that we now have
        • a legally protected network of public rights of way in England and Wales
        • the depiction of English and Welsh public rights of way on Ordnance Survey
          Landranger and *Explorer* maps
        • public access to large areas of open countryside in England and Wales
        • the depiction of English and Welsh access areas on Ordnance Survey
          Explorer maps
        • public access to virtually the whole of the Scottish countryside
        • national trails
        •1:25,000 mapping which the Ordnance Survey had planned to discontinue

4   The Ramblers' Association also take on important legal cases to protect existing
    rights and to clarify anomalies in legislation. One case went to the House of Lords
    which resulted in a significant change to the law.

5   Other benefits of membership include
        • programmes of guided walks
        • *Walk,* the Ramblers' Association magazine
        • discounts on purchases from many outdoor shops
        • Ramblers' Association on-line shop
        • map-lending service

6   But there is an unfortunate downside to the Ramblers' Association. For many years it was a complacent organization that stifled constructive criticism from its members. The Association suffered a setback in 2008 when it teetered on the brink of insolvency. The rescue operation involved making staff redundant and reducing the salaries of those who were retained.

7   The newly-appointed Hon. Treasurer produced a critical report, commissioned by the Trustees, in which he pointed out that between December 2005 and September 2007 there had been
   • 7 Chief Executives either substantive, acting, interim or joint
   • 3 Directors of Finance & Resources, either substantive or interim, up to April 2008
   • 3 Directors of Campaigns & Policies
   N.B. The report contained no hint of fraud or improper behaviour and it is clear that the problems were caused solely by poor governance.

8   This crisis was a chastening experience for the Ramblers and has resulted in more openness and consultation with the members. Also, the internet has provided opportunities for members to discuss matters outwith control from Central Office.

9   Another matter of concern is the Ramblers' attitude to the statistics that bear on the condition of the rights of way network in England. The Association has a history of selective quotations from official documents that give a misleading picture of the state of public paths in England (see Appendix 5).

10   Despite these faults, most of which have been rectified, all who regularly walk in the countryside of Great Britain should consider whether they have a moral obligation to join the Ramblers' Association. After all, without its persistent lobbying and herculean efforts, there would be no paths on which to walk.

Appendix 5 Public rights of way in England; the condition of the network

1   There has been confusion and controversy about the usability of the public rights of way (PRoW) network in England so here is an examination of the available evidence.

2   It is universally accepted that, although rights of way had been legally protected in England since the passing of the National Parks and Access to the Countryside Act in 1949, the overall condition of the network was in a parlous condition for at least the next four decades.

3   In 1987, the Countryside Commission launched its Milestones Initiative with the stated aim of making all rights of way in England *'easy to find; easy to follow; easy to use'* by the end of the century.

4   The Countryside Agency (the successor to the Countryside Commission) authorized an independent review, *The Rights of Way Condition Survey 2000,* to establish whether the target had been achieved. This is the most detailed and comprehensive survey of the condition of rights of way in England, and is particularly valuable because it is the only survey that provides detailed statistical breakdown of the condition of

  • crossings (gates, stiles, bridges and steps)
  • signposts
  • waymarks
  • ploughing and cropping
  • surface and overhanging vegetation

5   The results of the survey showed that none of the targets had been met, nevertheless the final figures indicated a remarkable improvement in the state of public rights of way during the previous thirteen years. The most significant findings include

  • all users found three-quarters of the network to be usable
  • walkers found 89 per cent of the network usable with only four per cent impossible to use

6   Unfortunately, few walkers are aware of these findings because the Ramblers' Association never mention them, preferring to quote a passage that states *'...a walker is likely to encounter an obstruction or problem every 2 km/1·25 miles.'* This appears to contradict the other findings but this is because the Ramblers' Association ignore the qualifying statement *'In practice, however, problems on the legal line could often be avoided by making a minor detour. For this reason, although there might have been a number of problems present, the actual effect on a user could have been negligible if they were easily circumvented.'*

7   The only other source of official information about the condition of public rights of way in England is the Best Value Performance Indicators 178 (BVPI) published annually by the Audit Commission between 2001 and 2008. These were designed to measure both 'ease of use' and how well highway authorities were carrying out their statutory duties in respect of rights of way.

8   The statistics were compiled from the results of a random sample of 5 per cent of each highway authority's public rights of way. The sample was walked by inspectors who noted the overall condition of the path and 'failed' it if it was not legally compliant, or did not match the strict criteria laid down in the tests. They were instructed

   i)   *'...to assume ...that the route is being used by a user or users, consistent with the status of the path, who are suitably attired and equipped with a 1:25,000 map but without a compass.'*

   ii) *'... to have regard to all users on bridleways and byways and to consider whether the condition of the path is fit for purpose for all legitimate public users.'*

   iii) *'...to confine themselves to the legal line of the path and ignore any unofficial diversions...'*

9   The problem with drawing conclusions from the BVPI survey is that they are raw statistics that do not break down the faults encountered into meaningful categories.

10 It is obvious that those paths that passed all the tests are easy to use, but it does not follow that a path that failed one of the tests was necessarily difficult, let alone impossible, to use. For example, the following faults that would fail a path, would not make it impossible to use by walkers

   • deviations from the Definitive Map
   • missing signpost or waymark
   • mud in a gateway
   • up-growth around the base of a stile

- stile slightly out of repair
- gate that had dropped hinges and had to be lifted slightly
- gate that could not be opened from the saddle of a horse
- low branches that would obstruct an equestrian but not a walker

11 Highway authorities have long complained that the BVPI statistics give a misleading picture of the true condition of rights of way because one minor fault, such as a missing waymark, could fail a path that is in all other respects easy to use. The Countryside Agency recommended in 2005 that *'BVPI 178 should be designed to measure ease of use from a user's perspective...and should be given a new label such as "percentage of paths complying with legal requirements.'*

12 Suggestions from other organizations include grading the percentage of paths under headings such as 'easy to use', 'acceptable', 'difficult' and 'inaccessible'. The collection of BVPI statistics has been discontinued.

13 The Ramblers' Association has consistently misinterpreted the BVPI statistics. By assuming, incorrectly, that all paths that fail the test are difficult or impossible to use, they were able to state that *'35% of all public rights of way in England are officially difficult to use (Audit Commission 2004)'.* The Audit Commission made no such statement. All that the statistics show is that *at least* 65 per cent of paths were easy to use. Some of the remaining 35 per cent would be easy to use even though they had failed the strict tests.

13 In fact, the Ramblers' Association's CEO actually stated in an interview with John Humphreys on the *'Today'* programme in 2008, and repeated the claim in *'Walk'*, the Ramblers' Association's magazine, that *'... one third of paths in England are inaccessible'.* When used without a qualifying adjective 'inaccessible' means 'impossible to use by anyone'. When challenged at a Ramblers' Association meeting he stated *'that it was justified in the context in which it was made'.*

14 The Ramblers' Association spent several years defending their interpretation of the statistics and have never explicitly acknowledged that their use of them was misleading. But it is pleasing to note that these partial quotations have been removed from Ramblers' Association's publications and website.

15 What *is* the overall condition of the rights of way network in England? It varies between highway authorities but in my extensive experience of walking in parts of the country ranging from Cornwall to Cumbria the network is, overall, in a reasonable condition and walkers can expect to be able to pass through the countryside without encountering too many problems.

16   However, the future of rights of way is bleak. Government cuts will mean that many highway authorities will no longer be able to carry out much maintenance of the path network, so the condition of many rights of way is likely to deteriorate. Some of the effects could be ameliorated by walkers carrying a pair of secateurs and a stout stick as part of their regular walking gear in order to cut and beat back encroaching vegetation. Walking clubs could form working parties to carry out repairs and maintenance on path furniture, but should be aware of the insurance implications and the dreaded health and safety regulations.

Appendix 6   Some hoary old myths examined

1   There are a number of topics that have been repeated in books and magazines about walking for many years without challenge until they have been accepted as received wisdom. Three examples are examined below.

Tranter's Variations to Naismith's Rule

2   The classic definition of Naismith's Rule for calculating the time required to complete a walk in upland countryside is:
'Allow one hour for every five kilometres measured on the map, plus an additional half hour for every three hundred metres climbed..

3   The calculation assumes average fitness and conditions and does not take into account fatigue, foul weather, the terrain underfoot, the weight of the pack etc.

4   Philip Tranter devised a table to be used with Naismith's Rule to take some of these factors into account (see Fig. 44). In order to use the chart you have to establish your fitness level. This is done by calculating the time it takes you to climb, when fresh, a height of 300 metres in a distance of 800 metres.

Tranter's variations										
FITNESS LEVEL	60	120	180	240	300	360	420	480	540	600
15	30	60	90	120	165	210	270	330	405	465
20	40	75	135	195	270	330	390	465	525	600
25	50	90	180	255	330	420	510	600	690	795
30	60	120	210	300	405	510	630	750	870	
35	70	145	230	320	425	540	660			
40	80	165	255	345	450	570	690			
45	90	180	270	365	480					
50	100	195	285	390	510					

Figure 44   Tranter's variations

5   This begs a number of questions. Where can you find a hill that will satisfy these exacting requirements? Do you have to establish your fitness level before commencing every walk? Or do you do it once and then guess how fit you are in relation to your original calculation?

6   Having established your fitness level Tranter next tries to take into account other factors and suggest the following amendments:

For every 13 kilograms carried on your back drop one fitness line. (Most walkers will find that carrying only 5 kilograms will adversely affect their fitness level.)

For poor visibility or strong winds drop one fitness line. (If there is poor visibility accompanied by strong winds should the walker drop 2 fitness lines?)

For waterlogged or slippery conditions drop one fitness line.

For snow drop up to four fitness lines. (This is imprecise and needs more detailed guidance.)

7   There is little evidence to suggest that many walkers routinely rely on Tranter's Variations. Indeed, many walkers find that the classic definition of Naismith's Rule only works for the fit and experienced and that it requires amendment before it can be used. A more realistic formula for many walkers is:

Allow 15 minutes for every kilometre measured on the map plus 1.5 minutes for every 10-metre contour crossed when climbing (2.5 minutes for maps with a 15-metre contour interval).

8   Some walkers may argue that this is too slow, but it can be amended in the light of experience. In most cases, it is better to overestimate the time that it will take to complete a walk. Better to finish early rather than too late.

Do wild animals dig up human faeces?

9   It is often claimed that human waste should be buried at least 12 centimetres deep to prevent contamination and to avoid the risk that wild animals will dig it up. There seems to be little evidence to support this belief.

10   We humans are one of the few creatures that find their faeces repugnant. Faeces and toilet tissue that are covered with earth well away from watercourses pose a negligible risk to human or animal health. Anyone who has experimented with lightly covering excrement with soil in their garden will know that it decomposes within two or three weeks.

11 For decades, tons of human waste has been deposited from train lavatories on railway tracks and left for nature to take care of. There seems to be no evidence that it has contaminated water supplies or affected the health of workers maintaining the track.

The Kinder Scout Mass Trespass; an alternative view

12 In 2012 the walking world celebrated the eightieth anniversary of the mass trespass on Kinder Scout in the Peak District. We were told that a group of idealistic young men took on the might of the wicked grouse-shooting landowners who would not allow the general public access to their property, and went to prison for their pains. It has been claimed that their actions had the long-term effect of achieving, albeit decades later, the right of access to open country that we in Great Britain now enjoy.

13 It's not quite as simple as that. The first thing to note is that trespass in itself is not normally a criminal offence but a civil wrong ('tort' is the legal term). Landowners have a right to require a trespasser to leave their property and may use just sufficient force to eject anyone who refuses to leave.

14 In 1932, there were several paths across the Kinder plateau but very few were acknowledged rights of way. Ramblers from Manchester and Sheffield had tried for many years, without success, to get access to Kinder Scout and the adjacent moorlands.

15 The British Workers' Sports Federation (BWSF), a communist-front organization, of whom access campaigners had never heard, suddenly appeared on the scene. The leader was the late Bennie Rothman who, in the course of a long life, gave several conflicting accounts of the events surrounding the trespass.

16 Rothman organized and advertised the intention of the BSFW to hold a mass trespass on Kinder Scout on 24th April 1932. The National Council of Ramblers' Federations (the forerunner of the Ramblers' Association) expressed alarm and urged its members to have nothing to do with the event.

17 The demonstrators met in Hayfield and marched along the Snake Path, a recognized public path, to Ashop Head some two miles from the summit of Kinder Scout. A line of eight gamekeepers was stationed to one side of the path and were attacked by some forty of the trespassers. A fight ensued and a number of people were injured although none seriously. The outnumbered keepers withdrew and the demonstrators held a victory party.

18   The simple fact is that the demonstrators never got anywhere near the summit of Kinder Scout and managed to trespass for little more than a hundred metres.

19   On their return to Hayfield, the demonstrators were met by policemen, and several trespassers, including Rothman, were arrested. They were sent to trial charged with riotous assembly and assault and were sentenced to short terms of imprisonment.

20   It is doubtful whether the mass trespass achieved anything other than some short-lived publicity. Landowners were able to use the incident to demonstrate what was likely to happen if the public were granted access to the grouse moors. Indeed, some leading members of the Federation of Rambling Clubs believed that the cause of access had been set back by several years. The Second World War intervened and it was not until the passing of the National Parks and Access to the Countryside Act 1949 that rights of way in England and Wales were put on a proper legal footing.

21   The real heroes of the access movement were not Bennie Rothman and other johnnies-come-lately, but G.B.H. Ward, who had an injunction taken out against him forbidding him to trespass, Edwin Royce, Harold Wild, Stephen Morton, Fred Heardman and others who laboured and campaigned for years for access to the moors of the High Peak. Alas, their names are mostly forgotten.

22   A case can be made for regarding the Kinder Scout trespassers as little more than politically-inspired hooligans who had more interest in bashing the landed classes than in promoting access for the general public. It is a matter of regret that it took so long for landowners to open up the moors to the general public, but that does not excuse the use of violence against gamekeepers who were only doing their duty in keeping out trespassers. Those who celebrate the actions of the British Workers' Sports Federation should remember that property owners still have the right to use reasonable force to eject a trespasser who refuses to leave when asked.

GLOSSARY

Please check the index for definitions that do not appear in the Glossary.

Amble A short walk.

Anklets Short, ankle-length gaiters.

Arête A narrow, exposed mountain ridge.

Balaclava A hat that encloses the ears, mouth, chin and neck.

Bealach see *Pass.*

Beck A term used in the north of England for a minor watercourse.

Bench mark A mark made by surveyors on a permanent object such as a wall to indicate a known elevation above sea level.

Benighted The condition of being stranded after dark.

Bimble An aimless stroll following no particular route.

Bivouac bag (bivvy bag) A simple plastic or nylon bag carried for emergency use in upland areas.

Bog Marshy ground with stagnant pools found in areas of peat.

Bog-trotting Derisive term used to describe a tedious walk across boggy terrain.

Boreen A narrow, country lane in Ireland.

Bothy A primitive structure providing shelter in upland terrain. Bothies are located mostly in the remoter areas of the north of England and especially in Scotland. They normally lack facilities and merely provide protection from the elements.

Box quilting A method of constructing baffles in duvet clothing and sleeping bags that keeps the insulation in place.

Brew, brew-up A hot drink taken *al fresco.*

Brocken spectre A combination of atmospheric conditions which results in mountaineers seeing their own shadow cast on a wall of cloud or mist. So named after the Brocken in the Harz Mountains of Germany where the phenomenon is relatively common and where it was first described.

Bum bag A small bag secured to the body by a waist strap. Known in North America as a *fanny-pack.*

Bunkhouse Inexpensive, self-catering accommodation for groups and individuals. Bunks or beds are provided, and sometimes linen, but most walkers will bring their own sleeping bag.

Burn A stream, especially in Scotland and Northumberland.

Bwlch see *Pass.*

Cairn A pile of rocks to mark the summit of a mountain, or the route of a path.

Camping barn Sometimes known as a *stone tent,* a camping barn offers simple accommodation including washing, toilet, and kitchen facilities. There are sleeping platforms instead of beds, and the sexes normally share the facilities.

Cirque The technical term for a steep-sided rounded hollow in the side of a mountain usually formed by glaciation. There is often a lake in the cirque that feeds a watercourse. The Scottish name is *corrie* and the lake is a *lochan.* The Welsh name is *cwm* and the lake is a *llyn.* The English name is *combe* and the lake is a *tarn.*

Clag A colloquial expression for low cloud and/or mist that results in reduced visibility.

Clints see *limestone pavements.*

Clitters Mounds of shattered granite found especially on Dartmoor.

Clough A ravine or valley with steep sides. A term much used in the Peak District.

Col see *Pass.*

Combe A narrow valley in the south of England that has grassy slopes running into the side of a hill. Also used to describe a steep valley running in from the sea. *Coomb* and *coombe* are variant spellings. Note that in the Lake District the term coomb is sometimes used to describe a *cirque* (q.v.).

Common Designated land over which the general public have the right of fresh air and exercise. Certain categories of persons may also have other rights, e.g. grazing animals and the collection of wood for fuel.

Corrie see *cirque.*

Crag A steep and rugged rock.

Crag-fast The condition of being unable to move on a crag or cliff.

Cwm see *cirque.*

Dodd A rounded summit, found especially in the Lake District.

Doline see *shake hole.*

Drift road see *drove road.*

Drove road A route once used for driving cattle and sheep to market.

Edge A term used particularly in the Peak District and the Pennines to describe a rocky escarpment.

Edging A technique employed when contouring a steep slope. The soles of the boots are pressed sideways into the slope to provide a better grip.

Elitism, elitist Weasel words, sometimes applied disparagingly to those who prefer to walk alone, and to others who want to reserve the wild places from the effects of mass tourism.

Enclosure (1) A parcel of land bounded by walls, hedges or fences; a field. (2) The act of dividing open land with walls, hedges and fences.

Escarpment A steep slope or inland cliff particularly in chalk country. The steepest part is the *scarp* and the more gradual slope is the *dip*.

Exposure The cooling of the body temperature caused by climatic conditions. Also used to describe the sensation of apprehension when walking along an unprotected, narrow arête.

Fanny pack see *bum bag*.

Featherbed A bright green swamp of sphagnum moss found in boggy areas in the north of England.

Fell Often used in the Lake District and Pennines to describe a mountain. Also used to describe a moor or mountainside.

Fell-walking see hill-walking.

Fixed rope A rope or chain secured to rocks to assist walkers to negotiate a difficult or dangerous path.

Ghyll A pseudo-archaic form of *gill* (q.v.).

Gill A mountain stream or ravine, particularly in the Lake District and Pennines.

Glacier cream A cream used in snowy conditions to protect the exposed parts of the body from the harmful effects of ultraviolet radiation.

Glen A narrow valley, especially in Scotland and Ireland.

Glissading The technique of descending snow slopes by sliding on the feet.

Glory A phenomenon associated with *Brocken spectres* (q.v.) in which walkers see their greatly magnified shadows surrounded by a multi-coloured ring cast on a cloud or a bank of mist.

Gorge A narrow valley with almost perpendicular sides.

Greasy rock Stones and boulders covered with lichen, moss and grass which makes them slippery when wet.

Green lanes There is no statutory definition but they are usually unsurfaced public highways and are often classed as *byways* or *restricted byways*.

Grikes see *limestone pavements*.

Grough A peat bog, especially in the Peak District.

Gully A ravine made by the action of water.

Hachures A form of shading on maps to represent the shape of the land. Some maps use contours as well as hachures.

Hag A peat bog.

Hanging valley A valley in a mountainside above the main valley.

Hause see *Pass*.

Headland path A path that runs alongside a field boundary.

Helm Wind The name of the strong north-easterly wind that sometimes blows over Cross Fell (893 metres), the highest point in the Pennines.

Hill-walking A term used to describe serious walking in upland areas of the British Isles. Also known as *fell-walking.*

Hoolie A slang term used by walkers to describe gale-force winds often accompanied by rain.

Hoosier A crude, temporary gate made of barbed wire strung between a fixed post and one moveable stake.

Howff A Scottish term used to describe a natural shelter, such as a jumble of rocks or a rocky overhang, that can be used to escape the elements.

Hush The scar left by the method of exposing veins of lead by releasing water from a moorland dam.

Hut A shelter belonging to a climbing or walking club for the exclusive use of their members.

Intake Land in the upland areas of northern England that has been 'taken in' from moorland and improved for grazing. The wall that defines the boundary of intakes is known as the *intake wall.*

Kanter A non-competitive event in which the participants have to navigate along a set route and record their progress at checkpoints.

Kissing gate A small gate hung in a stock-proof U or V-shaped enclosure. Also known as a *wicket gate.*

Knott The term for the outcrops of rock found in the Lake District.

Lapse rate The rate of change in temperature caused by increased altitude. As a rule of thumb guide, temperature decreases by 2°C every 300 metres of elevation gained.

Limestone pavements Large flat areas of limestone, found especially in the Yorkshire Dales, containing fissures caused by erosion. The surfaces are *clints* and the fissures are *grikes*.

Llyn see *corrie.*

Metamorphism The change in the structure of snowflakes caused by atmospheric conditions. It is one of the main causes of *avalanches* (q.v.).

Moor, moorland High, uncultivated ground often covered in heather.

Mountain There is no universally accepted definition of a mountain. In the British Isles it is generally regarded as an eminence that is at least 300 metres higher than its foot.

Mountain rescue posts These are located in suitable places such as huts, hotels, police stations and farms. They usually, but not always, have a telephone and contain first aid equipment and a stretcher. Often marked on maps.

Mountain rescue teams Volunteers who undertake rescue work. They are usually members of the walking and climbing fraternity living locally who give their services free.

Munro One of the 282 Scottish mountains that exceed 3,000 feet (914.4 metres) in elevation.

Munro tables A list of Scottish mountains over 914.4 metres (3000 feet) compiled by Sir Hugh Munro and regularly revised.

Needle A tall sharp-pointed rock or crag found particularly in the Lake District.

Open country Countryside beyond the limits of *enclosure* (q.v.)

Outcrop A natural pile of rocks on a mountain or moor.

Pass Low ground between two mountains which provides easy access to the next valley. It is sometimes called a *col,* a *bealach* in Scotland, a *bwlch* in Wales, and a *hause* in the Lake District

Peak The summit of a mountain.

Pike The name given to some mountains and hills in the north of England that have a sharply defined peak.

Ravine A pronounced cleft in a mountainside.

Ridge A crest where the terrain falls steeply away on either side.

Saddle A broad dip between two areas of higher ground in mountainous terrain.

Scar A cliff or rock face of limestone formed by a geological fault.

Scarp see *escarpment.*

Scramble Easy climbing on rocks without using technical aids.

Scree Areas of small stones on steep mountainsides.

Scree-running The practice of running down a scree by digging the heels into the loose stone.

Shake hole also known as *sink hole* and *doline* is a funnel-shaped depression formed by the action of water dissolving the underlying rock. Examples can be found in limestone areas and many are depicted on *Explorer* maps.

Sike A term used to describe a ditch or streamlet especially in the north of England.

Sink hole see *shake hole.*

Snow-blindness Temporary blindness caused by ultraviolet rays reflected off snow.

Snow goggles Worn in the mountains to protect the eyes from snow glare, ultraviolet rays, snow, hail, rain, and wind.

Spot height Dots on topographical maps that indicate the elevation.

Spur Lower land that projects from a mountain or hill.

Stile A narrow structure giving walkers access through or over a field boundary.

Stone tent see *camping barn.*

Stone chute A natural channel down which rocks may fall from a mountainside.

Stonefall Small rocks that fall from mountainsides due to the effects of erosion, rain, snow, frost, the sun, and the careless actions of walkers and climbers.

Stoptous see *anklets.*

Strath Wide valley found in Scotland.

Swallow hole A shake hole (q,v,) that has been eroded by an underground stream. Often known as a pot hole.

Tarn see *corrie.*

Tog rating The unit that measures the thermal resistance of textiles, thus giving an indication of relative warmth. The higher the number the greater the thermal resistance and, therefore, the warmer the material.

Tor A granite hill or rocky peak, particularly on Dartmoor and in Cornwall.

Tramp, tramping Old-fashioned terms for walking.

Trek, trekking A long walk.

Triangulation pillar A stone or concrete pillar erected by the Ordnance Survey to mark an exact elevation.

Trig point see *triangulation pillar.*

Verglas A thin coating of ice on rocks.

Waymark A symbol indicating the direction of a path.

Wicket gate see *kissing gate.*

Index

The index refers first to the Chapter and then to the paragraph number e.g. 3:21 is Chapter 3 paragraph 21

Index

Animals Act 1971 1:24
bulls 1:9, 14:40
dangerous animals 14:41
diseases of 1:11–41
Farmland Code of Conduct 16:5
feminine hygiene
MoonCup 3:112
SheWee 3:111
fingerprints 4:46–7
fires 1:36
first aid
blisters 11:6–9
dehydration 11:32–5
hyperthermia 11:21–2
hypothermia 11:23–31
sprained ankles 11:17–18
sunburn 11:19
ticks 11:10–16
windburn 11:20
First Aid Manual 11:69
fleeces 3:58
flowers 1:31
foot and mouth disease 1:18
footbeds 3:78
footbridges 2:16, 14:47
Ordnance Survey conventions 5:19
footpath guides
general considerations 10:1–3
judging quality of 10:7–8
limitations of 10:9
useful features 10:4–6
writing and publishing 10:10–21
Footpaths, a Practical Handbook 14:69
footpaths, definition 14:6 *see also* rights of way
footways, definition 14:6
footwear
approach shoes 3:69–71
boots 3:72–90
general considerations 3:69–71
socks 3:91
fording rivers
general considerations 11:47–50
techniques 11:51–5
Forgey, William 11:70
Forte, Carlo 5:48
foul weather navigation 8:24–31
fowl pest 1:19
Freedom to Roam *see* access
frostnip 12:20
fruits 1:31
Fugawi 9:30
Furths 21:11
Fyffe, Allen 12:35

G

gaiters 3:43–5
GALILEO 9:2
Garmin 9:30
gates, responsibility for maintenance 14:39
Gay Outdoor Club 22:8
gear *see* equipment
geese 1:8
geocaching 22:31–3
Geocaching Association of Great Britain 22:33
Geocaching Handbook 22:34
Geocaching in the UK 22:35
Geographia maps for walkers 5:36
Get Fit Walking 2:17, 11:74
Getamap 9:36
Getting to Grips with GPS 9:51
Global Navigation Satellite System
definition of terms 9:2
description 9:3–7
Global Navigation System (Russian) 9:2–7
Global Positioning System (USA) 9:2–7
GLONASS *see* Global Navigation System (Russian)
gloves 3:95
Glyndwr's Way 13:24
GNSS *see* Global Navigation Satellite System
goats 1:8
goggles 12:31
Gore-Tex 3:27
Gormly, Peter 11:68
GoTo 9:24
GPS *see* Global Positioning System (USA)
GPS compasses *see* satnavs
GPS Exchange Format (GPX) files 9:28
GPS for Walkers 9:52
GPS receivers *see* satnavs
GPX files 9:28
Graham, Fiona 21:11
Grahams 21:11
grass 2:8
Great Outdoors, The 25:3
Great Trails 15:21
green lanes, definition 14:6
greenways, definition 14:6
grid references 4:15–24
grid systems
Alderney 4:28
Channel Islands 4:28
grid references 4:15–24
Guernsey 4:28
Ireland, Republic of 4:25–7
Jersey 4:28
National Grid (Great Britain and the Isle of Man) 4:11
Northern Ireland 4:25–7

338

Index